AF250989

EFFECT OF ELEMENTS ON PLANTS

ENV BOOKS SERIES

EFFECT OF ELEMENTS
ON
PLANTS

Editors

Dr. Prasann Kumar
Division of Research and Development
Lovely Professional University
Jalandhar - 144 411 (Punjab)
(India)

&

Dr. Pawan Kumar 'Bharti'
Society for Environment, Health Awareness of
Nutrition & Toxicology (SEHAT)
B-225/5D, Top Floor, Subhash Gali, Road No. 7, Block B
Ashok Nagar, Shahdara, Delhi - 110 093
(India)

DISCOVERY PUBLISHING HOUSE PVT. LTD.
INDIA

Published by:

Namit Wasan

DISCOVERY PUBLISHING HOUSE PVT. LTD.
4383/4B, Ansari Road, Darya Ganj
New Delhi-110 002 (India)
Phone : +91-11-23279245; 23253475; 43596065
E-mail : discoverybooksindia@gmail.com
           discoverypublishinghouse@gmail.com
           namitwasan9@gmail.com
web   : www.discoverypublishinggroup.com

First Edition: **2020**

ISBN: 978-93-88854-44-3

Effect of Elements on Plants

This book has been published in good faith that the material provided by authors/editors is original. Every effort is made to ensure accuracy of material, but the publisher and printer will not be held responsible for any inadvertent error(s). In case of any dispute, all legal matters are to be settled under Delhi jurisdiction only.

M.S. Swaminathan Research Foundation

M.S. Swaminathan
Founder Chairman
Ex-Member of Parliament (Rajya Sabha)

Foreword

I am very glad to know that a several books are being edited under the aegis of ENVBOOKS series, Delhi, India on various sub-themes of Agriculture and environment like:

'Cultivation Techniques for Agriculture Crops'

'Air Pollution and Control'

'Seed and Food Storage Technologies'

'Heavy Metals and Impacts on Plants'

'Climate Change and Agriculture Production'

'Scientific Writing and Research Methodology'

'Laboratory Management'

'Statistical Tools in Science'

'Advances in Chemistry and Chemical Sciences'

'Irrigation techniques in Crop management' 'Waste Management Practices'

'Vermitechnology, Farm and Fertilizers'

'Animal Science and Pest Control'

'Recent Research in Biochemistry and Molecular Biology'

'Water Management and Sustainability'

'Soil Quality and Agriculture'

I am very happy to learn that a number of editors and authors from different institutions and university of different nations are involved in editing these books. The books are the compendium of screened-in manuscripts received from different countries like UK, Canada, Egypt, Nigeria, Ghana, Ethiopia, China, South Africa, Japan, Guyana, PNG, Nepal, South America, and various parts of India. I am feeling delighted in writing forward to these books and congratulate to Dr. Pawan Kumar Bharti, Editor-in-Chief and founder of ENVBOOKS series and of course his team for their tenacity and hard work in compiling these valuable compendiums.

I hope these books will be beneficial for academician, researchers, industrialist, policy makers and students as study material and will work as reference for further research work.

M.S. Swaminathan

Preface

Trace elements in plants are of general concern because of their importance in both animal nutrition and plant growth. Consequently, these elements are the most extensively studied in plants and foodstuffs. Researchers surveyed those other elements which have been shown to have some beneficial effects on the growth of a few plant species only, and, although evidence for this essentiality continues to accumulate, their conclusive essentiality for higher plants still needs confirmation. Plants use these trace elements in small quantities, and these include the following: titanium, vanadium, cobalt, nickel, aluminium, silicon, arsenic, selenium, fluorine and iodine. Their effects on plant growth are evaluated by various researchers, and covered many aspects like absorption, transport and accumulation, biochemical functions, deficiency and toxicity.

Plant nutrition is the study of the chemical elements and compounds necessary for plant growth, plant metabolism and their external supply. In its absence the plant is unable to complete a normal life cycle, or that the element is part of some essential plant constituent or metabolite. This is in accordance with Justus von Liebig's law of the minimum. The total essential plant nutrients include seventeen different elements: carbon, oxygen and hydrogen which are absorbed from the air, whereas other nutrients including nitrogen are typically obtained from the soil.

Thanks are due to publisher and contributors from various institutions and universities.

The present book updates the subject content of micro-nutrients, plant morphology, Mitigation of Cadmium and Lead Toxicity in Legumes, Effect of Nitrogen and Phosphorus on Pearl Millet, Fluorine, Aluminium and heavy metal stress; Cadmium Induced Toxicity in Legumes; biochemical changes of fenugreek.

The book will be helpful for the researchers, academia working in the field of micro-nutrients, heavy metal stress, cadmium toxicity, plant morphology, biochemical changes in plants.

–Editors
(envbooks@gmail.com)

Contents

Effect of Elements on Plants

Edited by: Dr. Prasann Kumar and Dr. Pawan Kumar 'Bharti'

ISBN: 978-93-88854-44-3

Edition: **2020**

Published by: Discovery Publishing House Pvt. Ltd., New Delhi (India)

Plant Morphology
An Overview

Prasann Kumar[1,2*], Shipa Rani Dey[1]

GRAPHICAL ABSTRACT

Keywords: Agriculture, Biotic, Crop, Morphology, Overview, Plant

INTRODUCTION

Plant morphology "represents a study of the development, form, and structure of plants, and, by implication, an attempt to interpret these on

[1] Department of Agronomy, School of Agriculture, Lovely Professional University, Jalandhar - 144 411 Punjab, (India)

[2] Divison of Research and Development, Lovely Professional University, Jalandhar - 144 411 Punjab, (India)

the basis of similarity of plan and origin".When structures in different species are believed to exist and develop as a result of common, inherited genetic pathways, those structures are termed homologous. For example, the leaves of pine, oak, and cabbage all look very different, but share certain basic structures and arrangement of parts. The homology of leaves is an easy conclusion to make. There are four major areas of investigation in plant morphology, and each overlaps with another field of the biological sciences.The plant morphologist goes further, and discovers that the spines of cactus also share the same basic structure and development as leaves in other plants, and therefore cactus spines are homologous to leaves as well.First of all, morphology is comparative, meaning that the morphologist examines structures in many different plants of the same or different species, then draws comparisons and formulates ideas about similarities.

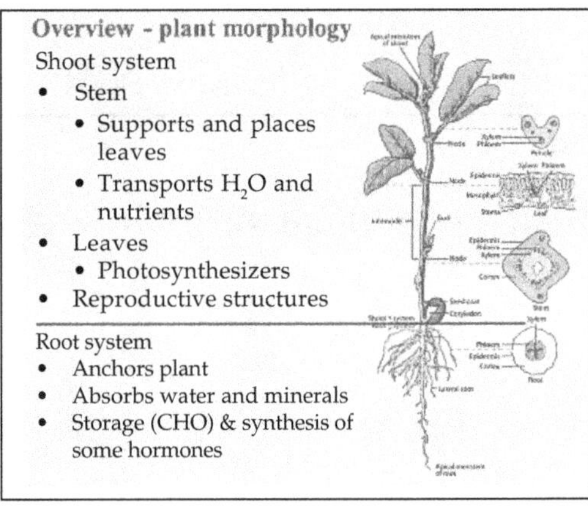

Fig. 1.1: Plant morphology: An overview

Source: based on review of literature

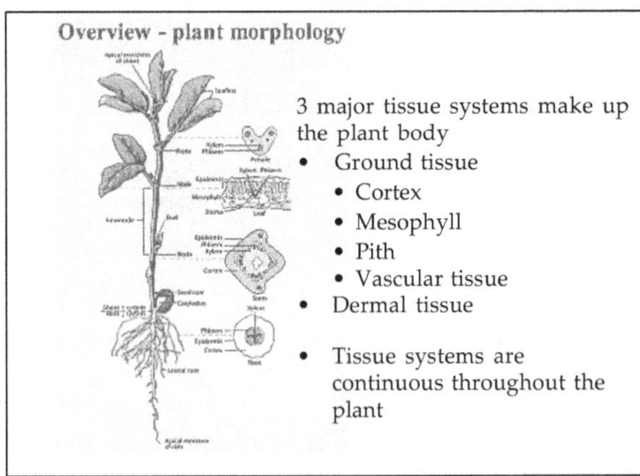

Fig. 1.2: Tissue systems make up of plants

Source: based on review of literature

Tissue Systems

- Ground tissue includes:
    - Parenchyma tissue
    - Collenchyma tissue
    - Sclerenchyma tissue
- Vascular tissue includes
    - Xylem tissue
    - Phloem tissue
    - Dermal tissue
    - Epidermis

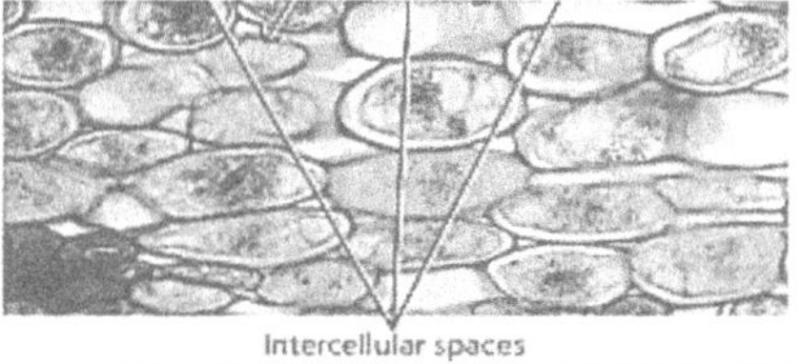

Fig. 1.3: Parenchyma tissue system of plants
Source: based on review of literature

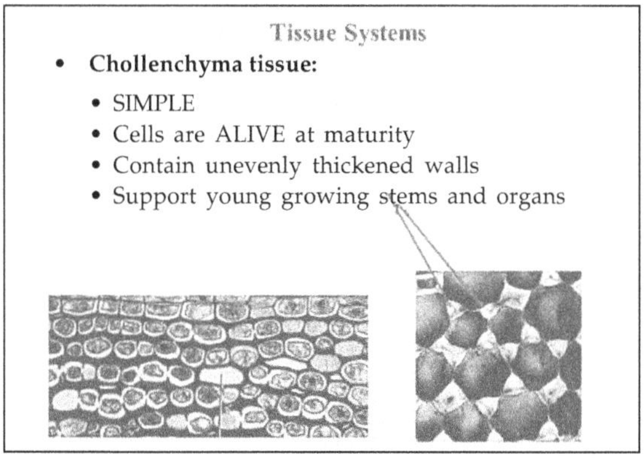

Fig. 1.4: Chollenchyma tissue system of plants
Source: based on review of literature

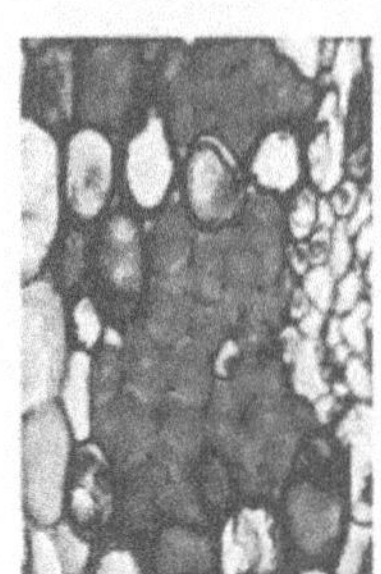

Tissue Systems

- **Sclerenchyma tissue**
  - SIMPLE
  - Cells are dead at maturity
  - Typically lack protoplasts
  - Posses secondary walls with lignin
    - Strong polymer
  - Support stems and organs that have stopped growing

fibres   sclereid

Economically important tissue!
e.g. Hemp fibres

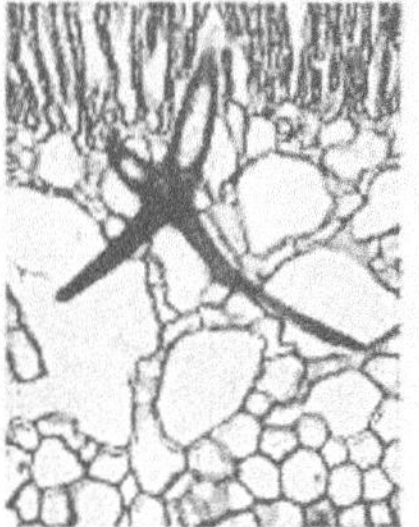

Fig. 1.5: Sclerenchyma tissue system of plant
Source: based on review of literature

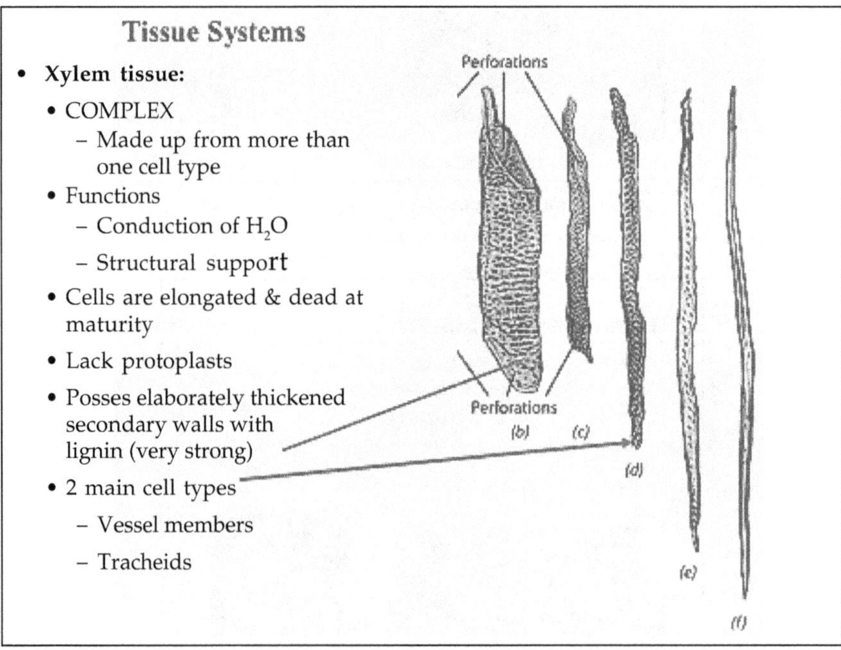

Tissue Systems

- **Xylem tissue:**
  - COMPLEX
    - Made up from more than one cell type
  - Functions
    - Conduction of H_2O
    - Structural support
  - Cells are elongated & dead at maturity
  - Lack protoplasts
  - Posses elaborately thickened secondary walls with lignin (very strong)
  - 2 main cell types
    - Vessel members
    - Tracheids

Fig. 1.6: Xylem tissue system
Source: based on review of literature

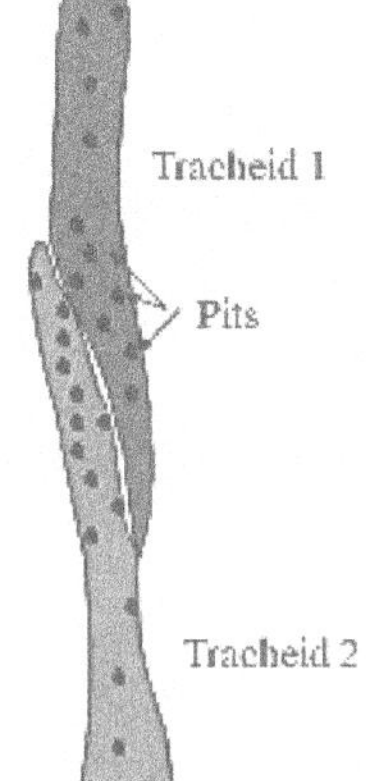
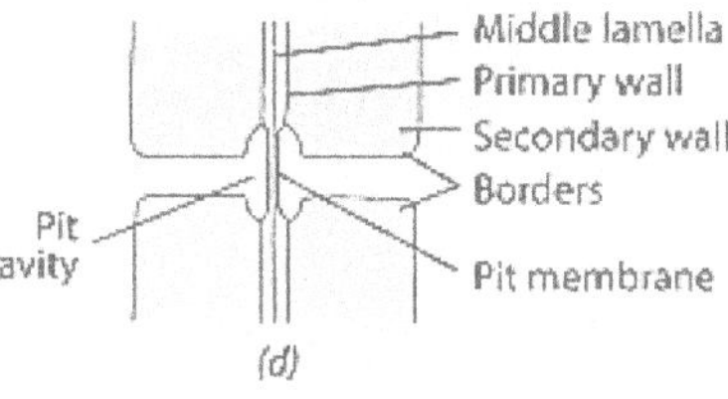

Tissue Systems

- **Tracheids (primitive)**
  - Trachieds "stack" longitudinally in the stem overlapping at tapered ends

How does H_2O pass from one tracheids to the next?
- Passes through aligned pits of neighbouring trachieds
- Pit membrane consists of $1°$ wall only

Fig. 1.7: Tracheids tissue system
Source: based on review of literature

Tissue Systems

- **Vessel members (advanced)**
  - Stack end to end to form a vessel (long)
  - Perforation plate at ea. end to a member permits easy water flow

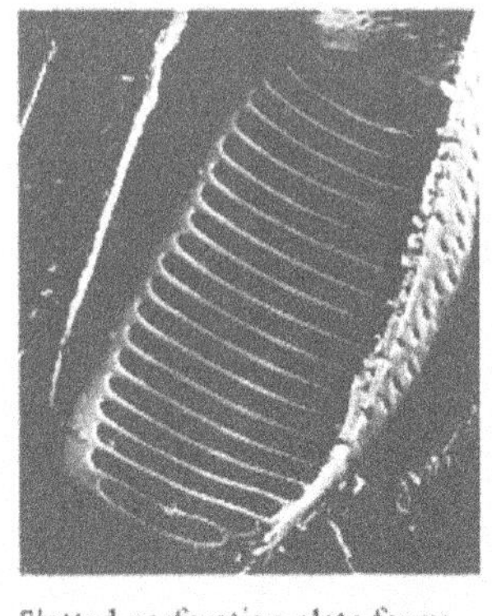

Fig. 1.8: Vessel member's tissue system
Source: based on review of literature

- Xylem is a complex tissue:
  - Also present
    - Parenchyma tissue (nutrient storage)
    - Fibres/sclereids
- Phloem tissue
  - Complex
  - Functions
    - Conduction of nutrients
  - Cells are alive at maturity but highly modified
    - Lack:
      - Nucleus
      - Definition between cytoplasm and vacuole
  - 2 main cell types
    - Sieve cells
    - Sieve tube members

Tissue Systems

- **Sieve tube members (advanced)**
  - Elongated cells
  - Sieve tube members stack end to end to form a sieve tube
  - End walls form sieve plates an contain pores that connect the cytoplasm of two sieve cells for solute transfer

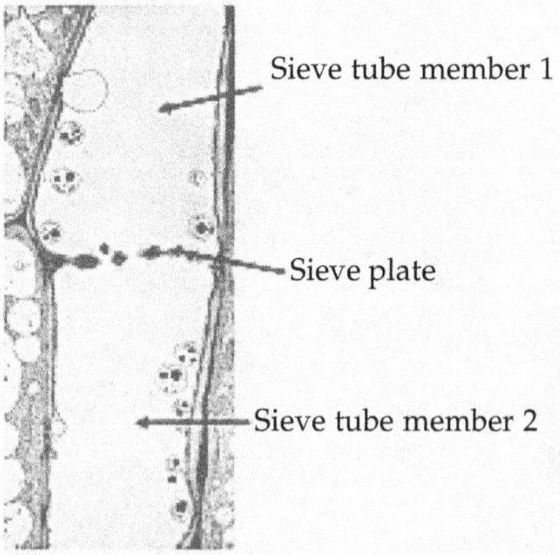

Fig. 1.9: Sieve tube member's tissue system

Source: based on review of literature

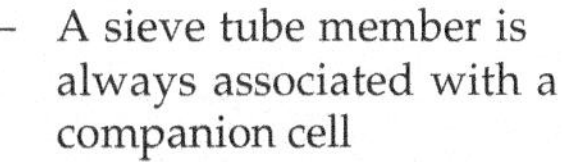

Tissue Systems

– **Sieve tube members and sieve cells are connected to specialized cells**

– A sieve tube member is always associated with a companion cell

- Connected via plasmodesmata
- Companion cell provides:
  - metabolic function
  - Loads sugars for transport

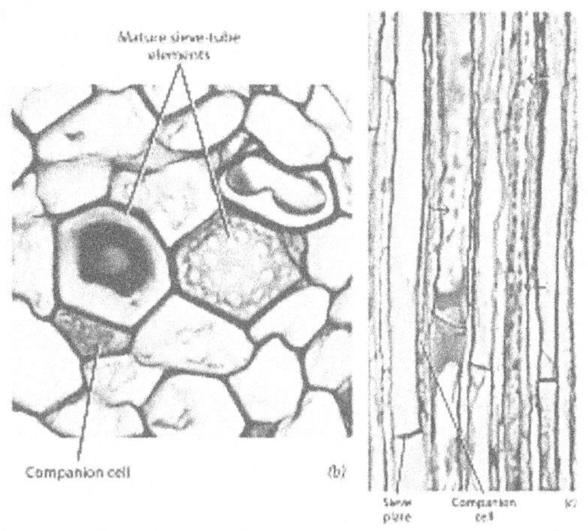

Fig. 1.10: Sieve tube members and sieve cells
Source: based on review of literature

Tissue Systems

- **Dermal tissue**
  - Functions
    - Mechanical protection
  - Made up of epidermal (parenchymal) cells
    - Cells overlaid with a wasy cuticle to minimize H2O loss

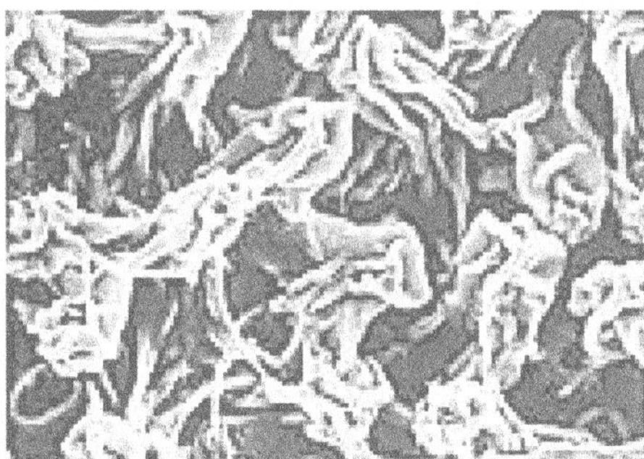

Fig. 1.11: Dermal tissue system
Source: based on review of literature

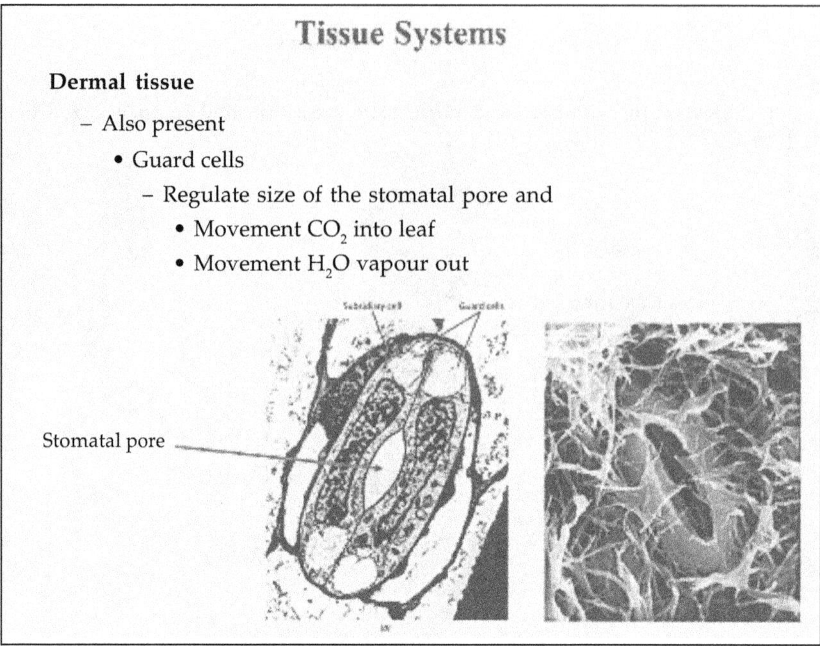

Fig. 1.12: Continuation of figure 1.11
Source: based on review of literature

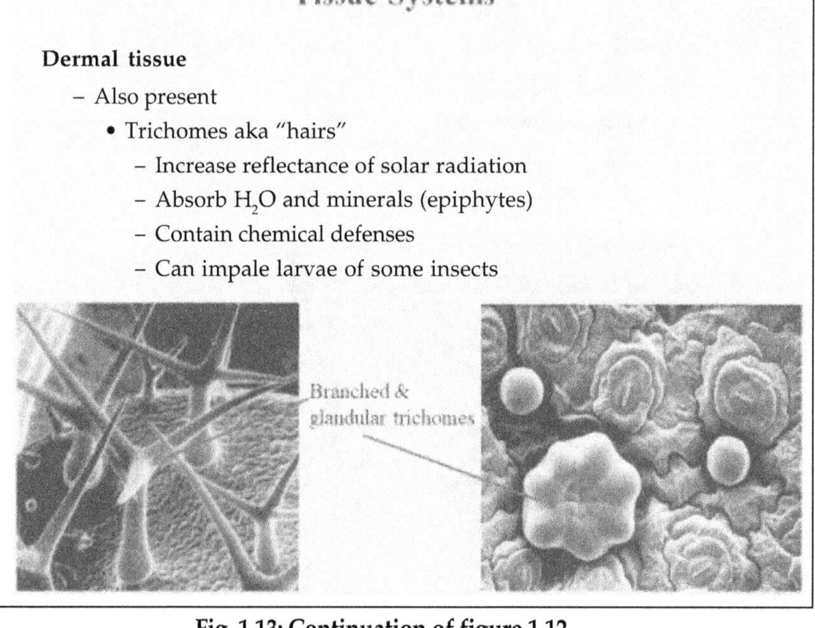

Fig. 1.13: Continuation of figure 1.12
Source: based on review of literature

Root anatomy

Root structure
- Simple
- Epidermis (outer layer of cells)
  - Protects root
  - Plays important role in water uptake
    - Facilitated by root hairs
    - Tubular extension from epidermal cell
      - Increase surface area for water uptake
    - Produced in zone of maturation
      - Short lived

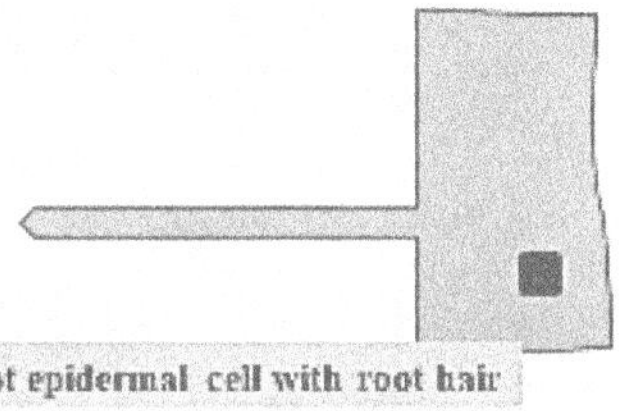

Fig. 1.14: Root anatomy
Source: based on review of literature

Root anatomy

Cortex
- Ground tissue that occupies most volume of root
- Cells often adapted for storage
  - Starch
  - Numerous air spaces exist
    - Roots need to respire!
  - Innermost boundary of cortex is the endodermis

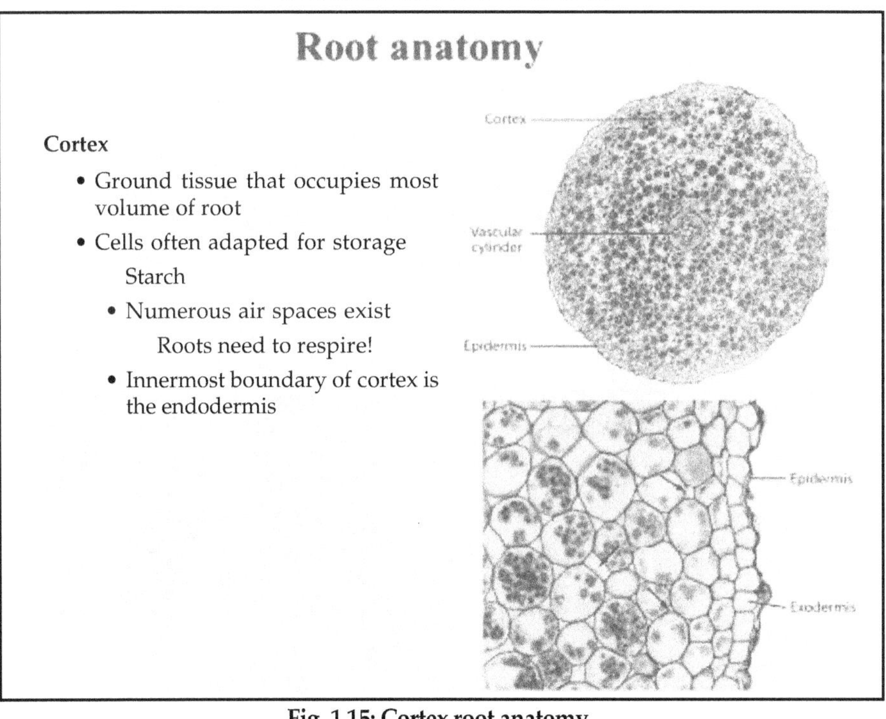

Fig. 1.15: Cortex root anatomy
Source: based on review of literature

Root anatomy

Vasculature in a eudicot root

- Protostele
  - Vascular tissue occupies the centre of root
  - Xylem arrangeed as a "star"
  - Phloem tissue is located between the arms of the xylem "star"
  - Pericycle tissue surrounds vascular tissue

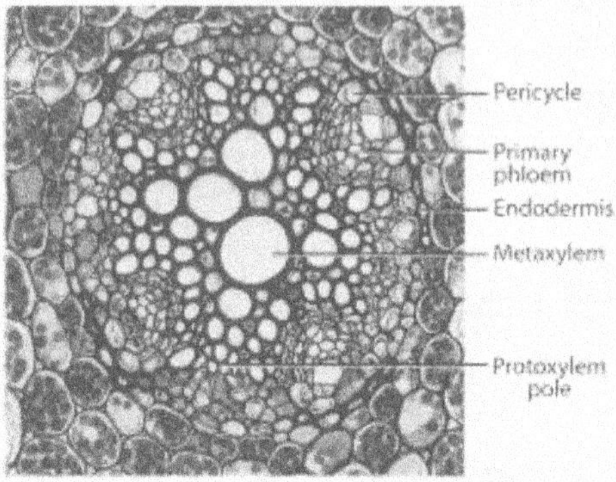

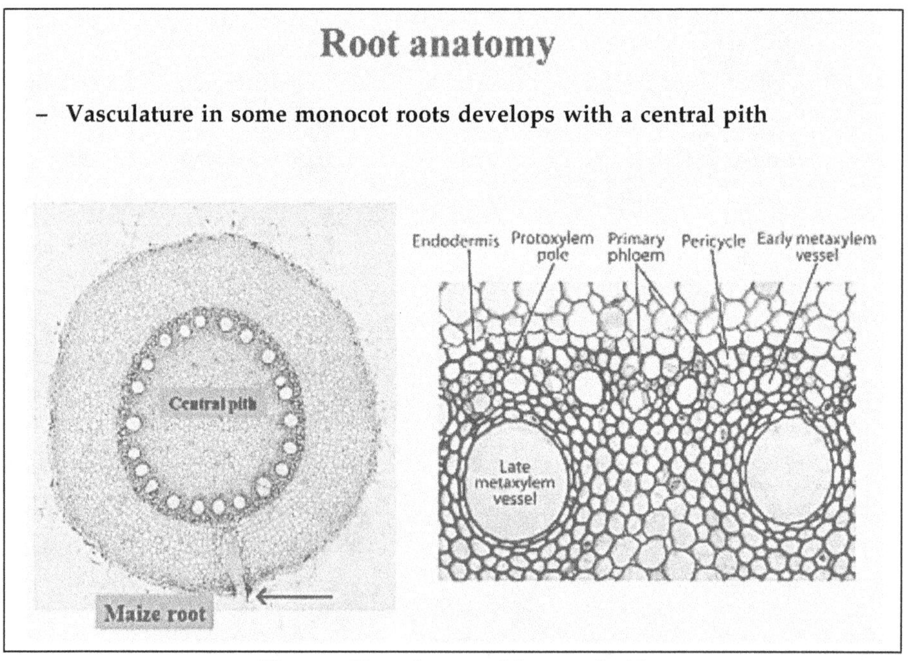

Fig. 1.16: Vasculature in a eudicot root
Source: based on review of literature

Root anatomy

– Vasculature in some monocot roots develops with a central pith

Fig. 1.17: Vasculature with central pith
Source: based on review of literature

Stem anatomy

- **Primary structure of a eudicot stem**
  - 1° vascular tissue are present as a cylinder of strands separated by ground tissue
    - Interfascicular rays or pith rays
  - 1° phloem is present at the outside of the bundle
  - 1° xylem is present on the inside of the bundle
  - Ground tissue in centre of stem is the pith
  - Ground tissue that lies outside the vascular bundle is the cortex
  - Outermost layer is the epidermis
    - Contains stomata and trichomes

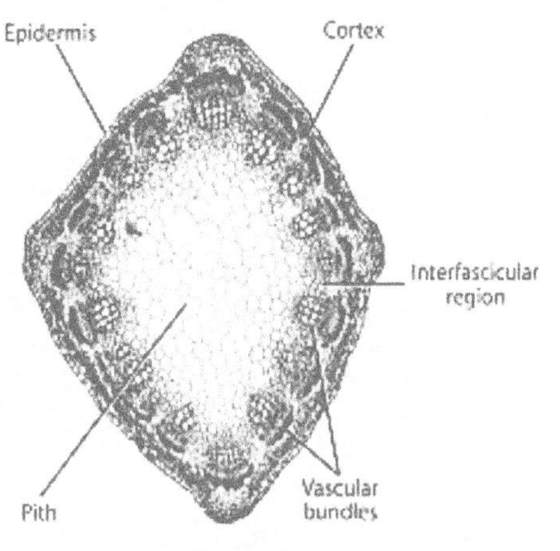

Fig. 1.18: Stem anatomy
Source: based on review of literature

Stem anatomy

- **Primary structure of a eudicot stem**
  - Single layer of cells between 1° phloem & 1° xylem remain meristematic
    - Become vascular cambium
      - Cylinderical meristem that is responsible for 2° growth
    - Remainder of cambium arises from interfascicular parenchyma
  - Note, not all eudicots undergo 2° growth
    - No cambium arises

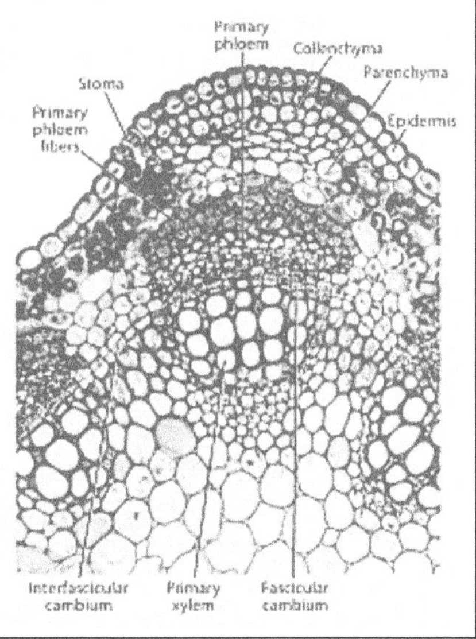

Fig. 1.19: Stem anatomy of eudicot stem
Source: based on review of literature

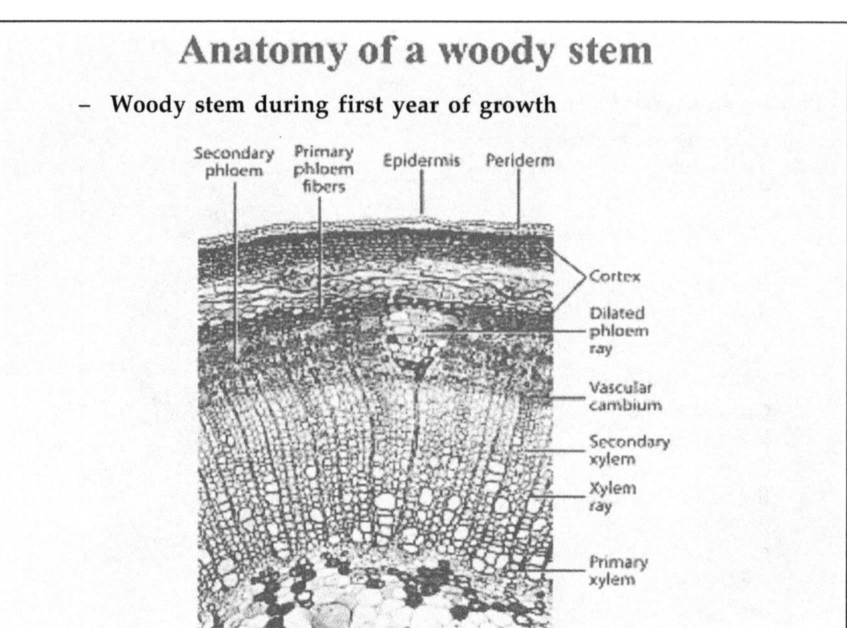

Fig. 1.20: Woody stem anatomy
Source: based on review of literature

Leaves

- **Evolved to photosynthesize**
  - **Divided into**
    - **Blade or lamina**
    - **Petiole or stalk**

  - **Leaf anatomy is influenced by the amount of available water:**
    - **Plants can be grouped according to their water requirements:**
    - **mesophyte**
      - **Plant with plentiful water supply**
    - **hydrophyte**
      - **Grows partially or completely submerged**
    - **xerophyte**
      - **Adapted to dry environment**

Fig. 1.21: Leaves anatomy
Source: based on review of literature

Leaf anatomy

- General features of mesophytic leaves (eudicot)
  - Stomata more numerous on lower surface
    - sheltered
      - Photosynthetic tissue (mesophyll) is differentiated into:
    - Upper palisade parenchyma
      - Upright cells with many cps
    - Lower spongy mesophyll
      - Permeated by air spaces
  - Vasculature is netted venation
    - Xylem towards upper surface
    - Phloem toward lower suface
    - Small veins collect P/S product
      - Surrounded by a bundle sheath
      - Controls entry/exist of material
    - Large veins transport P/S products from leaf

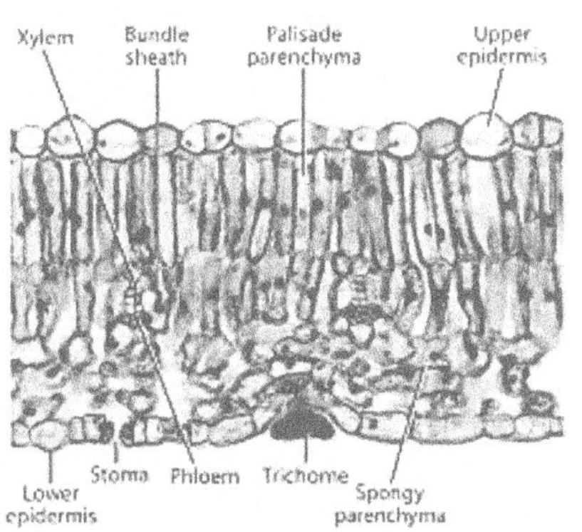

Fig. 1.22: Continuation of figure 2.21
Source: based on review of literature

Leaf anatomy

- Anatomical modifications in hydrophytes
  - Problem = obtaining enough CO_2 & O_2
    - Stomates not present or in upper epidermis (floating leaf)
    - Thin cuticle
    - Large amounts of air in spongy mesophyll
      - Gas exchange
      - buoyancy
    - Reduced vascular tissue
      - Partic xylem
    - Reduced amount of support tissue

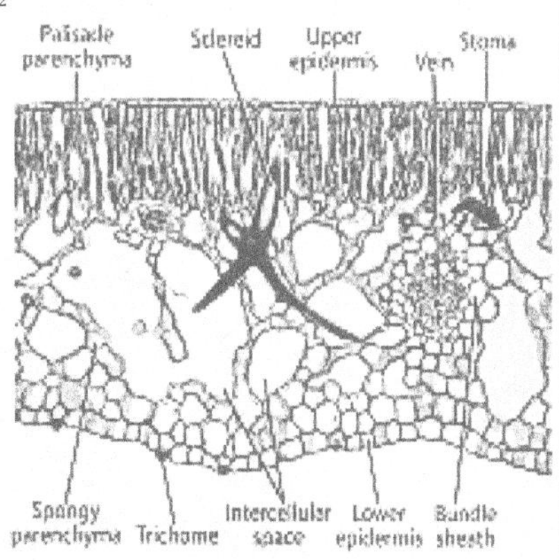

Fig. 1.23: Anatomical modifications in leaves
Source: based on review of literature

Leaf anatomy

- Modifications present in xerophytes
  - Problem = getting enough water
    - Many of these plants have reduced leaf size or no leaves
    - Large number of stomates
      - Optimize gas exchange when water is plentiful?
      - Remember stomates usually shut
    - Stomates generally sunk in depression in leaf surface
      - Assoc. with trichomes
      - Both increase depth of boundary layer & slow rate of water loss
    - Thick cuticle
    - Multiple epidermis
      - Modified to store water
    - More supporting tissue to compensate for reduced turgor

Fig. 1.24: Modification present in xerophytes
Source: based on review of literature

Leaf anatomy

- General features of monocot leaves
  - Parallelvenation system
  - Lack a defined palisade/spongy mesophyll layers
    - Leaves tend to be vertically oriented
  - Anatomy modified according to mode of P/S
- C4 photosynthesis
  - Carbon fixed to form a C4 acid in mesophyll cell
  - C4 acid is transported to bundle sheath cell & decarboxylated
  - Released CO_2 is reflexed by C3 P/S

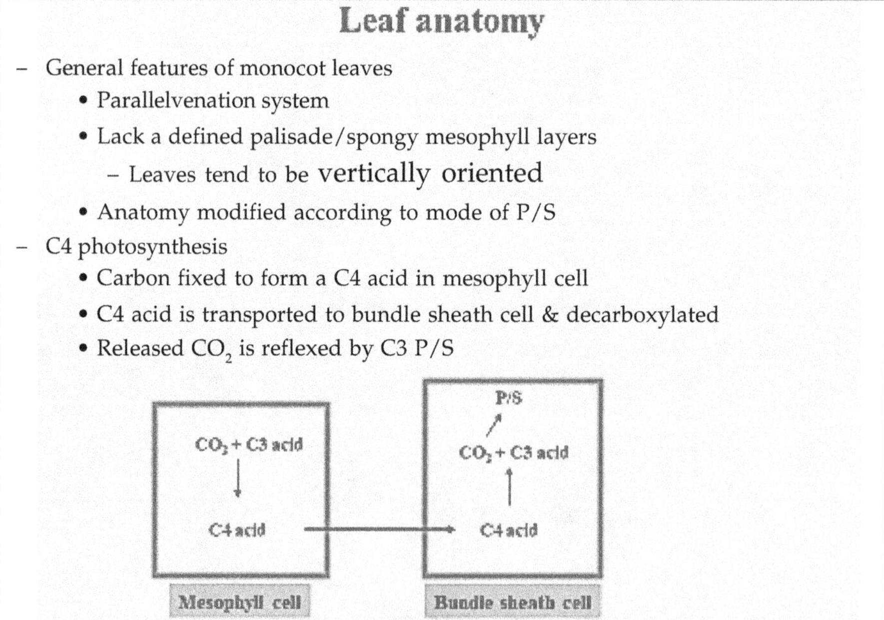

Fig. 1.25: Leaf general anatomy
Source: based on review of literature

Leaf anatomy

– Leaves in C4 plants display Kranz anatomy
  • Mesophyll and BSC form 2 concentric layers around a vascular bundle
  • Bundle sheaths are close together
– Leaves of C3 plants have well separated bundle sheaths and do not Kranz anatomy

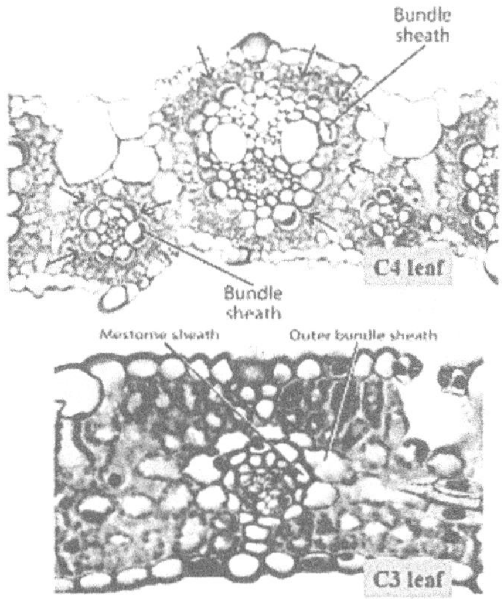

Fig. 1.26: Leaf Kranz anatomy
Source: based on review of literature

CONCLUSION

Plant morphology examines the pattern of development, the process by which structures originate and mature as a plant grows. The way in which new structures mature as they are produced may be affected by the point in the plant's life when they begin to develop, as well as by the environment to which the structures are exposed. This area of plant morphology overlaps with plant physiology and ecology. While animals produce all the body parts they will ever have from early in their life, plants constantly produce new tissues and structures throughout their life. A living plant always has embryonic tissues.A morphologist studies this process, the causes, and its result.

REFERENCES

https://en.wikipedia.org/wiki/Plant_morphology

https://www.toppr.com/guides/biology/morphology-of-flowering-plants

www.careerpoint.ac.in/download/smp_sample/Botany_Plant%20morphology.pdf

https://biocyclopedia.com/index/plant_morphology.php

https://ncerthelp.com/text.php?ques=1401+Morphology+of...Plants++Class...

https://www.askiitians.com › Revision Notes › Biology

www.sci.sdsu.edu/plants/econbot/01C-Morphology.pdf

https://www.sciencedirect.com/topics/agricultural-and-biological.../plant-morphology

https://study.com/academy/topic/plant-morphology.html

Pages: 16-25

Effect of Elements on Plants

Edited by: Dr. Prasann Kumar and Dr. Pawan Kumar 'Bharti'
ISBN: 978-93-88854-44-3
Edition: 2020
Published by: Discovery Publishing House Pvt. Ltd., New Delhi (India)

Carnivorous Plants
Fascinating and Interesting to Everyone

Prasann Kumar[1,2]*, Shipa Rani Dey[1]

GRAPHICAL ABSTRACT

Keywords: Carnivores, Everyone, Insects, Plants

INTRODUCTION

If an animal eats a plant, it is of no particular interest; but when a plant eats an animal, that is of interest. The fact that there are few flesh-eating plants make them fascinating and interesting to everyone.

[1] Department of Agronomy, School of Agriculture, Lovely Professional University, Jalandhar - 144 411 Punjab, (India)

[2] Divison of Research and Development, Lovely Professional University, Jalandhar - 144 411 Punjab, (India)

What are Carnivorous Plants?

- Carnivorous plants are plants that can eat insects and/or small animals.
- About 650 species of vascular carnivorous plants occur throughout the world (Rice, A.B., 2006).
- It belongs to 15-18 genus of 8-9 botanical families and 5 orders (Muller *et al.*, 2004).

How do Carnivorous plants get their energy?

- They get their energy the same way the other plants do…Photosynthesis.
- Darwin was the first who summarized multilateral research on carnivorous plant.
- He was the first to prove digestion of prey and to reveal that carnivorous plants showed enhanced growth if fed on insects and/or animal protein.

Why do Carnivorous plants eat insects and other small animals?

- They eat insects and other small animals because they live in places where the soil is low in nutrients.
- Carnivorous plants get the needed nutrients from their "PREY".

Fig. 2.1: Pitfall Traps (Pitcher plant)
Source: based on review of literature

Fig. 2.2: The insects and beautiful pitcher
Source: based on review of literature

Fig. 2.3: Pitfall Trap (Cobra Lily)
Source: based on review of literature

Fig. 2.4: Fly Paper Traps (Sundew)
Source: based on review of literature

Fig. 2.5: Contact with sticky
Source: based on review of literature

Fig. 2.6: Leaf slowly folds
Source: based on review of literature

Snap traps (Venus fly trap)

Fig. 2.7: Snap traps (Venus fly trap)
Source: based on review of literature

Fig. 2.8: Plants and insects
Source: based on review of literature

Fig. 2.9: Enzymes and insects
Source: based on review of literature

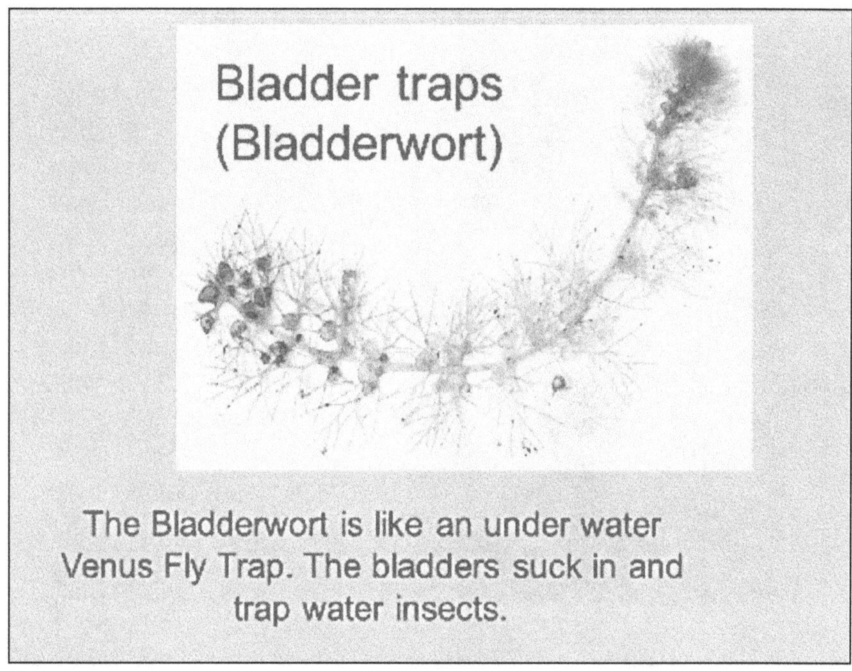

Fig. 2.10: Bladder traps
Source: based on review of literature

Plant Carnivorous Syndrome

- All plants considered carnivorous have to fulfill several criteria to separate them from other ecological plant groups.
- The criteria for carnivorous syndrome may be as follow:
    1. Capturing or trapping prey in specialized traps
    2. Absorption of metabolites (nutrients) from killed prey, and
    3. Utilization of these metabolites for plant growth and development

Ecological Characteristic of Terrestrial Carnivorous Plants and their Habitats

- The majority of terrestrial carnivorous plants grow
    1. In bog and fen soils in which they encounter persistent unfavorable condition. The soils are wet and water logged.
    2. Soil pH 3-6
    3. Anoxia
    4. Soils usually contains high proportion of decomposed materials.
    5. Very low level of macronutrients in the soils.
    6. Root: total biomass ratio is ranges from 3.4 to 23%.
    7. Root are usually short, weakly branched, and able to tolerate anoxia and related phenomena in wet soils.

8. Roots are able to regenerate easily.

9. Roots of carnivorous plants are physiologically very active per unit biomass and well adapted to endure soil anoxia.

Animals as Prey for Plants: What an Advantage

*   Ecological
*   Nutritional
*   Almost all carnivorous plants are able to capture at least some prey within a given time period.
*   It is possible to assume that it was N and P uptake from animal prey that represented the main benefit and evolutionary advantage of the carnivorous plants to which these plants from the beginning of their evolution.

Mineral Nutrition of Carnivorous Plants- General Principles

*   Terrestrial carnivorous species have considerably lower foliar tissue content of microelements than aquatic ones.
*   N(1.26% of DW), P(0.094% of DW), K(0.75% of DW) [Ellison 2006].
*   There are three critical comments should be added to the issue of interpretation of tissue nutrient content in carnivorous plants:
    (a) Leaf or shoot nutrient contents depend on leaf/shoot age.
    (b) Tissue nutrient content can remain unaffected after soil fertilization, as a result of more rapid growth.
    (c) Leaf or shoot nutrient contents depends on position of organs on carnivorous plants.

Mineral Nutrition of Carnivorous Plants-Mineral Nutrient Economy

*   The three principle processes of the mineral nutrition determine the mineral nutrient budget in terrestrial carnivorous plants
    1. Foliar nutrient uptake from prey and root nutrient uptake from soil.
    2. Mineral nutrient reutilization from senescing shoots.
    3. Stimulation of root nutrient uptake by foliar nutrient uptake.
*   A typical ecophysiological characteristic of terrestrial carnivorous plants is their extraordinarily good mineral nutrient economy, such as very efficient reutilization of N, P and K from senescing leaves/shoots and it was found to be 56-99% for N, 51-98% for P, and 41-99% for K [Adamec, 2002]

Carnivorous plants: Photosynthesis

*   All the carnivorous plants are green and able to fix CO_2 by leaves.
*   Many carnivorous plants of all taxonomic groups fix CO_2 according to the C_3 scheme of the Calvin cycle.

- Anatomical evidence in favour of the C4 type has been given in 6 Mexican succulent *Pinguicula* species

- Maximum net photosynthetic rate per unit DW or leaf area (Pmax) of leaves of terrestrial carnivorous plants is about 2-5 times lower than that of the other non-carnivorous plants.

- First Pmax of the traps is usually lower than that of the other non-carnivorous leaves of the same plants.

Ecophysiology of Aquatic Carnivorous Plants

- About 50 species of aquatic carnivorous plants are known.

- All aquatic carnivorous species are strictly rootless and therefore, they can take up mineral nutrients for their growth from the ambient medium and from captured prey only via shoots.

- Traps of aquatic species exhibit rapid movement, which are among the most rapid within the plant kingdom and represent fascinating objects for a biological study.

- Aquatic carnivorous plants usually grow in shallow standing or slowly streaming humic waters.

- The majority of aquatic carnivorous species usually grow in soft to moderately hard, acid or neutral waters.

Photosynthesis of Aquatic Carnivorous Plants

- Aquatic carnivorous plants usually grow in waters with high [CO2]>0.1mM.

- Pmax(Net Photosynthetic Rate) in aquatic species is comparable with the highest values found in aquatic non-carnivorous species.

Phylogeny of carnivorous plants: how many times in the history?

- Recent carnivorous plant evolved in 5-6 lineages from its preliminary ancestors independently on each other within evolution.

- *Palaeoaldrovanda splendens* was considered the oldest known carnivorous plant, representing the ancestral type of the recent *Aldrovanda vesiculosa*.

Concluding Remarks: Inspiration for Future Research

- Aquatic carnivorous species are ecophysiological quite dissimilar to their terrestrial counterparts.

- Carnivorous plants have evolved several times during plant evolution independently on each other.

Future Insight

- Basic properties of mineral ion uptake need to be studied in isolated roots.

- The stimulation of root nutrient uptake by foliar uptake represents the main physiological effect of carnivory but its essence is still unknown.

- What is the role of organic matter in carnivory?

REFERENCES

Adamec, L. (2002). Leaf Absorption of Mineral Nutrients in Carnivorous Plants Stimulates Root Nutrient uptake. New Phytol. 155, 89-100.

Ellison, A.M. (2006). Nutrient Limitation and Stoichiometry of Carnivorous Plants. Plant Biol. 8, 740-747.

Müller, K., Borsch, T., Legendre, L., Porembski, S., Theisen, I. and Barthlott, W. (2004). Evolution of carnivory in *Lentibulariaceae and the Lamiales*. Plant Biol. 6, 477-490.

Rice, A.B. (2006). *Growing Carnivorous Plants, Timber Press, Portland, USA.*

Effect of Elements on Plants
Edited by: Dr. Prasann Kumar and Dr. Pawan Kumar 'Bharti'
ISBN: 978-93-88854-44-3
Edition: 2020
Published by: Discovery Publishing House Pvt. Ltd., New Delhi (India)

Concept of Ideotype
An Overview

Jagdish Chand[1], Prasann Kumar[1, 2*]

ABSTRACT

Ideotype means an ideal plant, which possess all the physiological and morphological character by virtue of these character plant and able to perform good in various climatic conditions. The term ideotype of initially coined by the Donald (1968). Afterwards the concept was explorer by Donald and Hamblin (1976). Both Donald and Hamblin stated that a good ideotype is that plant which have the good and maximum harvest index. Ideotype varies from location to location, Species to species, and the also according to different climatic conditions. Ideotype plant is only an imagination of ideal plant having all the morphological and physiological characteristics because of the reason that no plant can perform their 100% ideotype characteristics due to fluctuating environmental conditions and case of dominance and deactivation of genes because of different stresses. So the finally plant we got on the field is known as plant type which possess all the characters but growth andvigour of that plant is a resultant of those character or traits which are in active condition. Donald and Hamblin (1976) proposed the concept of different types of ideotypes i.e. Isolation, Competition, and Crop ideotype. Market, climatic, edaphic, Stress and disease/pest ideotype are its other concepts.

Keywords: Ideotype, Stress, Traits, Harvest index, Plant type.

[1]Department of Agronomy, School of Agriculture, Lovely Professional University, Jalandhar - 144 411 (Punjab) (India)
[1, 2] Division of Research and Development, Lovely Professional University, Jalandhar - 144 411 (Punjab) (India)

INTRODUCTION

Ideotype is a new plant type that is supposed to perform behave in a predictable manner within a defined environment.To perform in different environment condition various physiological and morphological characters are inbuilt in the ideal plant so it can perform in a predictable manner. Characteristics that should be incorporated in plant to became the ideal plant is; Dwarfness, Synchronous tillering, Shorter Growth duration, Adaptation of seed dormancy, Disease resistance, Yield potentiality, etc. In nature plants can develop their characters accordingly but at very slow rate as we know that population of world increases day by day then we shall not depend only upon nature. Thus it is necessary to develop the ideal plants artificially or with the help of agriculture biotechnology in short period of time to cope with the food requirement of population. The concept of plant type was introduced firstly in rice by the rice breeder Jennings in (1964), while the term of Ideotype of plant was coined by the Donald in (1968).

IDEOTYPE, IDEOTYPE, AND IDEOGRAM

Ideotype

It is a new plant that is expected to perform/behave ideally in a predictable manner within defined environment.

Ideotype

It is the morphological features of the chromosome of a particular plant.

Ideogram

It is a diagrammatical representation of chromosome morphology of an organism.

NEED FOR IDEOTYPE/IDEAL PLANT

Environmental conditions vary from one location to another location so it is not possible that a single variety of any crop can perform well in all such kinds of environmental conditions. Thus, it is necessary to develop the Ideotype of crop according to the prevailing environmental conditions. Ideotype of one crop can differ according to the environmental conditions.

Feature of Ideotype

Some common feature that an Ideotype must contain:

- The high rate of photosynthesis.
- The rate of respiration must below.
- High response to nutrients.
- Disease insect/pest resistance.
- Drought resistance.

- Synchronization.
- Photo and thermo insensitivity.
- Dwarfness. etc.

Steps for Ideotype Development

Ideotype breeding consists of four major steps.

1. Development of conceptual theoretical model.
2. Selection pf base material.
3. Incorporation of desirable genotype into single genotype.
4. Selection of ideal or modal plant type

1. Development of conceptual theoretical model

Ideotype consists of various morphological and physiological traits. The values of those physiological and morphological traits are specified to develop a conceptual theoretical model.

2. Selection of base material

After the development of a conceptual theoretical model next step is to select the base material. The genotype is to be used in the planttype should have the wider adaptability. So the new plant type should be grown in wide range ofenvironmental conditions. Plant genotype should possess the capability to withstand against the frost, drought, salinity, disease and insect pest attack.

3. Incorporation of desirable genotype into single genotype

Once the desirable genotype is to the selected then combine those all genotype/traits in a single plant type with the help of different breeding methods.

4. Selection of ideal or modal plant type

This is the final step in which we get the ideal plant having all the desirable characteristics and multiply commercially the seeds of that plant and release as a variety after completing many types of trails at different locations in different research stations also on a farmers field.

IDEOTYPE OF DIFFERENT CROPS

1. **Rice:** Rice ideotype or plant type is the first time given by the Jennings in 1964, after that the term coined by Donald in 1968. Different characters of the rice plant type are: (1) Semi-dwarf stature; (2) high tillering capacity; (3) short, erect, thick and highly angled leaves (Jennings in 1964; Beachell and Jennings in 1965). Production of plant genotype starting to explore after the discovery of dwarfing genes in rice and wheat.

Fig. 3.1: Rice Plant Type

Source: http://www.google.co.in/imgres?imgurlimage

NOVEL RICE IDEOTYPE

It is proposed by the Janoria (1985). Various features of novel rice ideotype are: (1) Taller stature; (2) Tough unknown lodging; (3) All effective clumps with upright habit and well-spaced; (4) Large but stiff leaves able to maintain erect position. Janoria emphasized that semi tall plant type would require closer spacing.

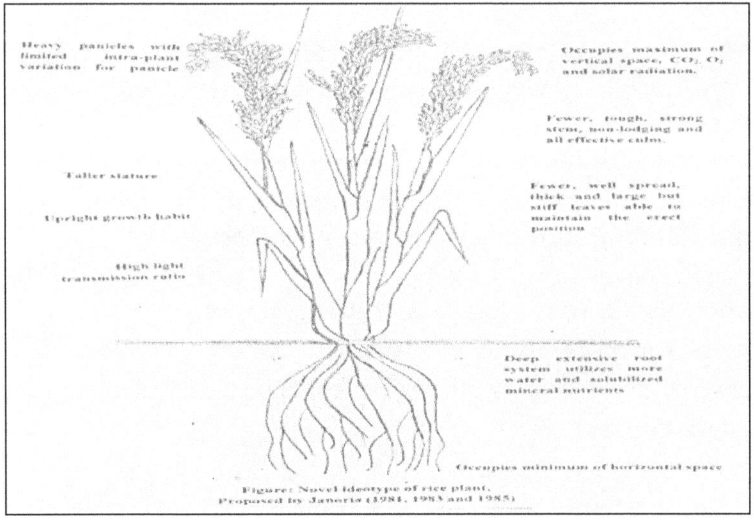

Fig. 3.2: Novel Rice Ideotype

Source: http://www.google.co.in/imgres?imgurl

2.   Maize

In 1975 Mock and Pearce both proposed ideal plant type for maize comprises of following characteristics; (1) Low tillering; (2) Large cobs; (3) Angled, leaves.

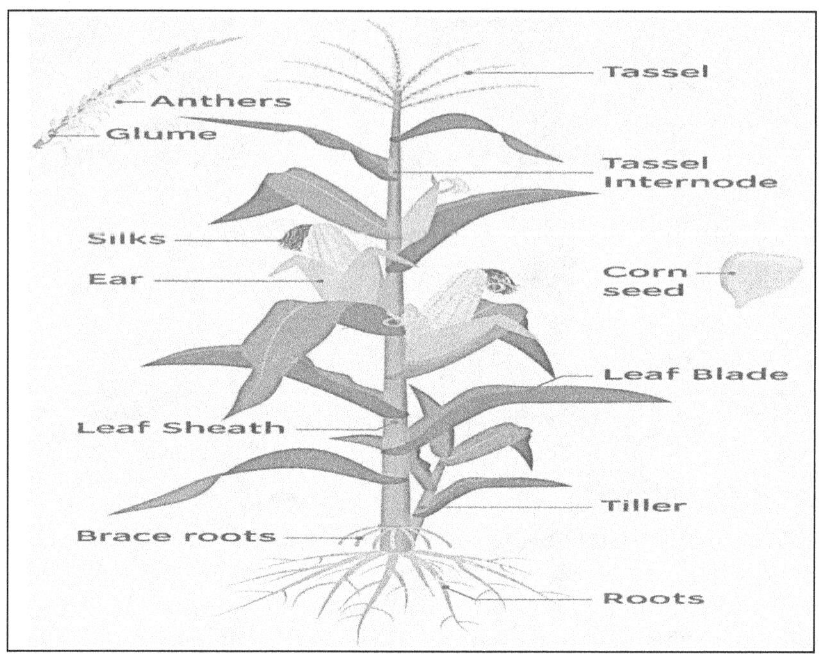

Fig. 3.3: Ideotype of maize
Source: http://www.google.co.in/imgres

3.   Wheat

Ideotype on wheat was given by Donald in 1968,withthe following main features.

1.   A short strong stem helping to plant to with stand against lodging.

2.   Erect leaves which provides better arrangement for proper distribution of light resulting in high rate of photosynthesis.

3.   Few small leaves are also important in the plant because it helps in reduction in the water loss due to transpiration.

4.   Large ear for more grains per ear.

5.   Presence of awns because they also contributes in photosynthesis.

6.   A solitary clums.

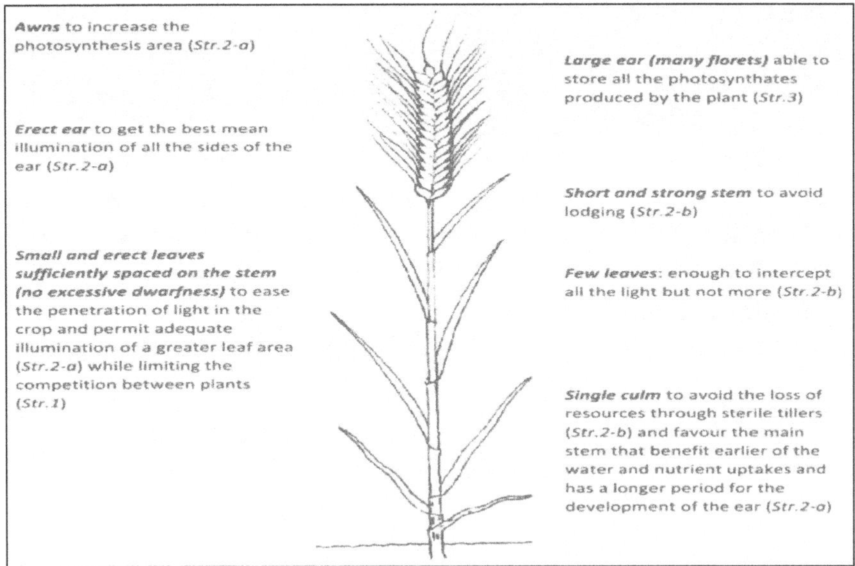

Fig. 3.4: Ideotype of wheat

Source: http://www.google.co.in

TYPES OF IDEOTYPE

Donald and Hamblin (1976) proposed the concept of different types of ideotypes i.e. Isolation, Competition, and Crop ideotype. Market, climatic, edaphic, Stress and disease/pest ideotype are its other concepts.

1.   Isolation ideotype

In this type of ideotype plant type can perform well accordingly if it is planted well-spaced and apart from each other which allow them to free tillering. This is generally happens in case of cereals.

2.   Competition ideotype

In this type of ideotype plant type perform well in heterogamous population and the competition ideotype is tall, leafy, free tillering plant having potential to dominate its neighbors and by can utilize maximum share of nutrients, water and radiation.

3.   Crop ideotype

This type of ideotype are very weak competitor and can perform well when it is surrounded by plant of same population. But its performance hinders when it is surrounded by plant is dipopulationspulation. This type is ideotype is used when crops grow at commercial level.

Other concepts of ideotypes are: It includes Market, climatic, edaphic, Stress and disease/pest.

- **Market ideotype**

  These types of ideotypes are mainly focused on market acceptability of produce by improving the traits like seed size, seed color, and cooking quality also.

- **Climatic ideotype**

  These types of ideotypes are developed that plant can survive in different climatic conditions, e.g. Heat and cold tolerance, drought resistance thermoperiod insensivity.

- **Stress ideotype**

  Includes those type of traits which are concerning for biotic and abiotic stresses.

- **Disease/pest ideotype**

  Plants are inherited to that type of traits which are responsible for disease and insect pest etc.

- **Adaphic ideotype**

  Are inbuilt with those type traits which are responsible for salt tolerance, and water logging.

  First time plant type was given by the Jennings in 1964 (on rice plant), after that the concept of ideotype was developed by the Donald in 1968, and Donald and Hamblin (1976) proposed the concept of different types of ideotypes i.e. Isolation, Competition, and Crop ideotype. Market, climatic, edaphic, Stress and disease/pest ideotype are its other concepts.

CONCLUSION

Ideotype breeding is an effective method of enhancing yield through manipulation of various physiological and morphological traits which are specified and every trait contributes in enhancing the yield of the crop.In ideotype breeding there are different barriers that hinders the development of ideotype i.e. incorporation of various desirable morphological and physiological traits into a single genotype is a difficult task. Ideotype of same crop is different from location to location and climate to climate e.g. In those areas where disease and insect pest attack are then the ideotype for that area is mainly concern for resistance against the disease and insect pest. On the other hand for same crop lodging is main problem of that area then traits which are inbuilt in plant are mainly concerning for lodging resistance. Thus, now a days environmental conditions are changing at very fast rate and the problem of salinity, insect/pest attack and other abiotic stresses are also increases, to cope up with these problems ideotype breeding is effective method for developing the new plant type which are able perform well in these types of conditions.

REFERENCES

Abbate PE, Andeade F.H. culot JP, Bindraban P.S. (1997).

Abullgasim EH (1991), Plant type concept in crop improvement.

Beachell, JennigsPR (1965) need for modification of plant type.

Donald, C.M. (December 1968). "The breeding of crop ideotype".

Evens LT (1993). Crop Evolution, Adaptation and yield, Cambridge University Press, Cambridge, U.K.

Hamblin. (1993). the ideotype concept useful or outdated, in international crop science I. Madison, WI, (USA).

Khush GS (1995), Breaking the yield frotier of rice.

Singh B.D.(2001) Plant breeding kalyani publications, Ludhiana(141008).

https://www.sciencedirect.com

https://www.researchgate.net/publications

Pages: 34-51

Effect of Elements on Plants
Edited by: **Dr. Prasann Kumar and Dr. Pawan Kumar 'Bharti'**
ISBN: 978-93-88854-44-3
Edition: **2020**
Published by: **Discovery Publishing House Pvt. Ltd., New Delhi (India)**

Three Dimensional Approach for the Mitigation of Cadmium and Lead Toxicity in Legumes

Prasann Kumar[1*2], Shipa Rani Dey[1]

GRAPHICAL ABSTRACT

Keywords: Cadmium, Density, Energy, Forage, Lead

INTRODUCTION

Legumes were known for its important source of balanced protein food for the vegetarians and poor peoples, which makes a major part of

[1] Department of Agronomy, School of Agriculture, Lovely Professional University, Jalandhar - 144 411 (Punjab) (India)

[2] Divison of Research and Development, Lovely Professional University, Jalandhar - 144 411 (Punjab) (India)

the population (Foyer *et al.* 2016). Production of the pulses varies with the crop density and adaption, prevailing agro-climatic condition. Globally, the total area under pulses has 851.91 lakh ha having production of 774.73 lakh tones. Pulses are grown in about 198 countries globally, but dry beans cultivated only in 152 countries, which consist of 35.95 percent area of the total world area. Chickpea consists of 139.81 lakh ha of the area with the production of 137.31 lakh tons. Lentil consists of 45.24 lakh ha of the area with the production of 48.27 lakh tons. Pigeon pea consists of 70.33 lakh ha of the area with the production of 48.27 lakh tons. Pea consists of 69.32 lakh ha of the area with the production of 48.90 lakh tons. Beans consist of 306.13 lakh ha of the area with the production of 245.16 lakh tons (FAO 2014).

Chickpea also is known as Bengal gram, the most important pulse crop of India. India having ranks first for the chickpea production of 98.80 lakh tons with an area of 99.27 lakh ha. Pakistan stood second having 6.29 lakh tons of production in 9.50 lakh ha area. Iran stood third having 2.62 lakh tons of production in 5.94 lakh ha area. Australia stood fourth having 6.29 lakh tons of production in 5.08 lakh ha area. Turkey stood fifth having 4.50 lakh tons of production in 3.88 lakh ha area (FAO 2014). In India, highest chickpea production recorded in Madhya Pradesh, 40.62 lakh tons production and 34.46 lakh ha of the area of the total. In terms of area 15.41 lakh ha Maharashtra stood second but for production has third 11.98 lakh tons. As Rajasthan second in production 14.47 lakh tons but area wise third 15.37 lakh ha. Highest yield recorded in Telangana 1459 kg/ha, followed by Gujrat 1201 kg/ha, West Bengal 1163 kg/ha and lowest in Karnataka 578 kg/ha (FAO 2014).

According to Aykroid and Doughty (1964) Eastern Mediterranean from where chickpea originated. Generally, Indian gram has been classified into main groups. One has "desi" or "Brown Gram" (*Cicerarientinum*) the colour of the seeds varies from yellow to dark brown. Seeds are usually small in size. The most grown legume on large scale area. The plant consists of good branching ability. Chromosome number is 2n = 14, 16. Other Kabuli or White Gram (*Cicerkabulium*) the colour of seeds are white. Seeds are attractive and bold but has production poor as compared to desi or brown gram. The height of the Kabuli plant more than the desi gram. The chromosome number is 2n = 16 (Iyengar 1939).

BOTANICAL DESCRIPTION

Chickpea belongs to the family *Fabaceae* or *Leguminosae*. The plant grows up to the height of 30-60 cm, plant consist of a well-developed root system with a strong taproot. Numerous nodules present on the root; which are helpful in fixation of atmospheric nitrogen in the presence of the Rhizobium bacteria. The stem of the chickpea greyish in appearance, well-branched with granular hairs on it. Pinnately compound types of leaves are present in chickpea, usually with one terminal leaflet. Numbers and size of the leaves vary with the type of variety. Generally, 9-15 pairs of leaves are present also consist of granular hairs. The leaves are light green or dark green in colour. Flower of chickpea are typical Papilionaceous consisting of five sepals, five petals are one size, two twigs, and two keels. Ten stamens, nine are fused to one staminal column and one free, and a carpel with an ovary. Flowers are solitary and present on the axis of the leaves (Duke, 1981; Cubero, 1987; van der Maesen, 1987). For desi type, the flowers are of purple/ violet and for Kabuli flower are white in colour. The anthesisstarts from 9 a.m. or 10 a.m. and may continue up to 3 p.m. (Daba *et al.* 2016). The flowers self-pollinated, but 5-10 percentcross-pollinated by the insects (Purseglove 1968). The pod has a length of about 2cm and generally contains two seeds. 50-150 pods produced by each plant. Seeds are round, wrinkled and having a pointed edge like a beak. Seed colour may vary from white, light fawn brown, dark brownish and with a bluish tinge. The coat of the seeds may be puckered or smooth and wrinkled. Cotyledons have a yellow in colour and thick in size (Singh 1983).

Chickpea a cool season crop and also grown in the rainfed region and in irrigated areas. Chickpea plant has well suited for the area having an annual rainfall of 600-900 mm and the temperature should be between 21 and 29 during the day time and in the night-time temperature between 18 to 21 (Duke, 1981; Muehlbauer *et al.*, 1988; Smithson *et al.*, 1985). In India, different varieties of chickpea are grown, according to the region. High yielding varieties of chickpea in India such as JH-74, Vijay, Pusa-1053, GPF-2, Pusa-372, KWR-108, GNG-416, PBG-1, BDN 9-3, BBG-1, Pusa-391, etc. Some desi or small seeded varieties which are grown in India such asAvrodhi, Pant G-186, Gaurav, Pusa-362, Pusa-372, Haryana Chana-1, BR-78, RS-11, Radhey, etc. For kabuli varieties which are grown in India such as C-104, L-550, L-144, Pusa-1003, Pusa-1053 (IPGA 2017).

According to Singh and Singh (2018), the formation of root nodulation in chickpea helps in nitrogen fixation in the presence of Rhizobium. The common cropping system consists of; Kharif fallow-chickpea, Rice-chickpea, Maize-chickpea, Pearl millet-chickpea, Sorghum-chickpea (Hajjarpoor *et al.* 2018). The requirement of fertilizer very less NPK (18-46-0). Chickpea commonly sown as rainfed crop and require very less irrigation. Sowing of the crop generally done in the first and second-week October, crops mature within 110-130 days (Singh 1983).

Chickpea has a rich amount of protein, mineral, and folate. Chickpea ranked second after soybean seed in protein content; also contain a good amount of dietary fiber and a good source of carbohydrates for the patient or people suffering from diabetes insulin sensitivity (Singh *et al.* 2017). In chickpea, poly-saturated fats present in a low amount. Consumption of chickpea makes the bone strong because have iron, potassium, calcium, magnesium, manganese, zinc and vitamin-k. inchickpea, low sodium salt present which helps in the control of blood pressure (Jukanti *et al.* 2012). According to International Crops Research Institute, In India, chickpea seeds produced at Hyderabad consist of the highest protein amount 21.1per cent, 61.5 percent total carbohydrate, 4.56 percent fat and 6.1 percentfiber. The seeds also contain a rich amount of minerals like calcium niacin and iron (Rebello *et al.*). The green seeds of chickpea used as salad and the mature seeds used for preparing different dishes around the globe (Muehlbauer and Sarker 2017). Fully matured and dried seeds turned into flour known as gram flour, used for the preparation of a variety of popular dishes and rich in protein content, so used in a variety of shake bars (Chandra-Hioe *et al.* 2016). Climate change had not the only cause of stress in plants; both factors biotic and abiotic are responsible for the inducing stress in plants (Marx *et al* 2019). These factors are severely affecting the productivity and distribution of plants (Mehrabi *et al.* 2019). In the arid and semi-arid region, heavy metals are one of the major factors responsible for the abiotic stress cause reduction in yield (Mahdi *et al.* 2019). The degradation of natural resources has perhaps one of the worst things that humanity has ever done in its progress and civilization journey. From a long time, both, biotic and abiotic stress affecting the land and water resources continuously, due to anthropogenic activity (Lajayer *et al.* 2018).

Heavy metals are natural elements of the world's crust, yet their geochemical and biochemical balance has changed drastically through indiscriminate human activities (Li *et al* 2019). The soil the primary recipient came on the contact with a waste of from all the industries, a chemical used in agriculture. Density criteria for the heavy metals range from above 3.5 g/cm3 to above 7 g/cm3(Duffus 2002). Any substance added into the soil which can cause an adverse effect on the soil functioning and ability to yield a crop knows as soil contamination. Due to its toxicity and capacity to accumulate, they are considered as an important source of environmental contamination (Hesse *et al.*, 2018).

Chromium, cadmium, mercury, lead, and arsenic are widely distributed in the environment among heavy metals (Roy Chowdhury *et al.* 2018; Paz *et al.* 2019). The natural factors which are responsible for the entry of heavy metals into the environment include soil erosion, mineral weathering and volcanic eruptions (Antoniadis *et al.* 2017; Lajayer *et al.* 2017). The various anthropogenic process involved in the release of toxic heavy metals in the air, water, and soil through a various process such as, tanning of leather, electroplating of metals, printing, thermometers, glass, batteries and metallurgy, dust from old paint which contains lead (He *et al.*, 2016; Harvey *et al.* 2015). However, heavy metals have slow degradation rate due to which they can remain in the environment for a long time; which leads to accumulation of heavy metals leads to contamination (Hesse *et al.*, 2018). The mobility of these heavy metals through several activities in the atmosphere such as, surface runoff and blowing winds have increased accumulation the upper soil, contaminating air and water which has resulted in chronic illnesses of living organisms in these areas (He *et al.*, 2016). Road dust, roadside area and plants growing in these affected regions are subject to receive high amounts of heavy metals, from both dangerous gas emissions from motor vehicles and toxic chemicals transported (Liu *et al.*, 2018). Phytotoxic effect on plants due to heavy metals contamination results in chlorosis, inhibited photosynthesis, inhibited growth, reduced biomass and finally death of the affected plant (Asatl *et al.* 2016). So, it is important to reduce the metal uptake by plants and resist the entry of metals into the food chain which slowly reaching the highest trophic level (Kamran *et al.*, 2017).

Cadmium one of the most toxic heavy metals having an upper limit is 14.157 µg/g (Kumar *et al.*, 2018i). Effects of Cd, according to Sharmila *et al.* 2017, when mustard exposed to Cd_2+ effects the growth of the plant and reduces the activity of photosystem II with a rise in the level of proline. Affect the oxidative phosphorylation in mitochondria and water uptake (Malik *et al.*, 2018); Linear increase in amount and production of MDA and H_2O_2 during stress in roots of chickpea (Kar., 2018; Zhao *et al.*, 2016),); inhibits the plant growth by stimulating ROS (Hussain *et al.*, 2019); affects the leaves, shoot, Significant reduction in amount of nitrogen, phosphorous and chlorophyll were observed with an increase in concentration of Cadmium (Shareef *et al.*, 2018; Kumar *et al.*, 2018); affects the translocation and storage of sugar in sweet sorghum (Tra *et al.*, 2016); reduces the internodal space and internodes number in maize (Kumar 2018a).

Lead (Pb) is one of the non-essential trace elements that mainly accumulate due to anthropogenic activities in agricultural soils (Gottesfeld *et al.* 2018). The upper limits of leads are 61.87 µg/g (Kumar *et al.*, 2018i).The increased levels of Pb in the soil increase the concentration of Pb in plants growing in these soils and ultimately increases the risk of Pb toxicity in food crops (Xiong *et al.* 2013; Naseri *et al.* 2015; Lai *et al.* 2018). Lead toxicity induces the effects chlorophyll, affects concentration and catabolism of IAA, stimulates ROS production and also POD activity, reduced total nitrogen and total phosphorus in the plant reduction in gemmation (Sarkar *et al.*, 2018).Also,reduction in the relative water content (RWC) and net photosynthetic rate (Sadeghipour 2016).

Polyamines (Pas) are those compounds which consist of two or more primary amine group, have low molecular mass and present in free form; i.e. putrescine, spermidine, andspermine (Masson *et al.* 2017. Polyamines are present in almost all living organisms and also in the plant). Polyamines are helpful in growth and development, also respond during abiotic or biotic stress, the Pas are present in trace amount like putrescine but in mammal's spermidine and spermine are present (Chen *et al.* 2018a). In addition, the exogenous use of Pas has an option to increase the potential for stress tolerance in plants. Polyamines increase the amount of chlorophyll during the cadmium toxicity, total soluble sugar, total soluble protein and increases water uptake by making a barrier against heavy metals (Kumar *et al.*, 2018; Kumar *et al.*, 2018b; Aldesuquy 2016). Many studies showed that Pas play an important role in defending the plant against both the biotic and abiotic stress like metal toxicity, drought, chilling stress, oxidative stress, and salinity (Li *et al.*, 2018).

The symbiosis of plant root with fungi occurs in various forms known as mycorrhiza. Arbuscularmycorrhizal fungi (AMFs) are major soil microorganisms that are key to enabling plant nutrient uptake, particularly in low-input farming, vegetation, and rhizoremediation processes, in various agroecosystems (Chen *et al.* 2018). In general, mycorrhizal fungi enhance the balance of mineral nutrients, particularly rare nutrients, stimulate their absorption when the number of nutrients was low and prevent their absorption at high levels. AMF helps in absorption of nutrients and water during, stimulates the production of antioxidants during metal toxicity (Ferrol *et al.*, 2016; Sarkar *et al.*, 2018; Miransari, 2017).

SALICYLIC ACID AND ITS ROLE FOR THE MITIGATION OF HEAVY METALS TOXICITY

Salicylic acid (SA) a compound which has been used to reduces the heavy metals toxicity in plants, which helps in regulation of plant growth. Reduces the heavy metals uptake, protects the membrane integrity and provide stability and by scavenging the reactive oxygen species which activates the antioxidant defenses mechanism and improves the photosynthesis (Liu, Z., *et al*, 2016). Exogenous SA treatment mitigated Cd toxicity by increasing the relative water content (RWC), chlorophyll, proline, and endogenous SA contents along with a decline in malondialdehyde (MDA), hydrogen peroxide (H_2O_2), and superoxide anion radicals (O_2-) (Alamri *et al.*, 2018). Many studies focused on the use of exogenous SA in crops to increase abiotic resistance, which was good for crop growth (Faried *et al.*, 2016; Gondor *et al.*, 2016; Khan *et al.*, 2015;Alamri *et al.*, 2018). Metals and metalloids those having an atomic weight between 63.4.8 and 200.59 g per mol and density over 4.5 gcm^{-3} generally known as heavy metals. The biological half-life of heavy metals very high means they can persist in the environment for a longer period. Heavy metals include cadmium (Cd), lead (Pb), cadmium (Cd), mercury (Hg), cobalt (Co), iron (Fe), zinc (Zn), silver (Ag), chromium (Cr), nickel (Ni) and arsenic (As) were considered as extremely harmful (Wu *et al.*,, 2016; GjorgievaAckova, 2018) to human, plants and environment. A pollutant, any substance that has a negative effect on the living being, but a required in traces for the development of living beings because has a highly concentrated form in the environment. Some of the metals like iron (Fe), zinc (Zn) and copper (Cu) well known as a micronutrient and used in plant growth life cycle. Heavy metals present in the free state in the environment, due to an increase in their level now they are entering the food chain. Heavy metals present in earth crust as rock solid, the natural processes were not only the sources of introduction of these metals to the environment. Natural processes like volcanic eruptions, wind-blown dust particle, aerosols, forest fires involve in additions of heavy metals to the environment. Mainly anthropogenic activities responsible, which leads to the contamination of natural resources. Since from industrialization period starts the use of chemicals containing such component increased. Anthropogenic activities include the production of PVC products, as colour pigment, nickel-cadmium batteries, electronics, cosmetic products, electroplating, fly-ash, tannery, steel smelting, mining, sewage sludge, fossil fuel combustion, burning of coal, organic and inorganic fertilizers, refineries, pesticides, fungicides and many others process involves in additions of heavy metals to environment. An. M, *et al.*, (2019) conducted an experiment on a test station at Shihezi University, China.

CADMIUM AND ROLE OF ANTI-OXIDANT FOR THE MITIGATION OF TOXICITY

The effect of four liquid modifiers (inorganic polymer compound modifier, organic-inorganic composite modifier, an organic polymer compound, andpoly-acrylate compound modifier) on plant growth, cadmium content, photosynthetic parameters and antioxidant enzymes in cotton under Cadmium stress (mg Kg^{-1}). The result showed that the Cd-treated soil increases the Cd content in cotton plant and reduction in plant height, chlorophyll fluorescence parameter, antioxidant enzyme activity, net photosynthetic rate, and biomass. On another hand, application of modifier reduces the Cd in plant and increase in antioxidant, biomass, plant height, also increase in gas exchange and photosynthetic pigment content, SOD, POD and catalase activity in leaves of cotton but the reduction in malondialdehyde content. Hence liquid modifier showed a positive role in alleviating Cd stress in cotton.Chandrasekhar and Ray (2019) conducted a pot experiment on the response of *Ecliptaprostrata*(L.) L., *Phyllanthusniruri* and *Scopariadulcwas* L. to check phytoremediation of $PbNO_3.5H_2O$ in the soil. It was found that the after the enzymatic activities E. *prostrata* having 12480µg/g of dry weight in root and 7228µg/g dry weight in shoot and tolerance of E. *prostrata* to lead stress and have lead hyper-accumulation ability for the phytoextraction. El-Meihy *et al.*, (2019) conducted a pot experiment to alleviate the toxic effect of heavy metal on Sorghum plant to improve the plant growth by using three heavy metal tolerating bacterial strains (*Alcaligenesfaecal was* MG966440.1, *Alcaligenesfaecali* MG257493.1, and *Bacillus cereus* MG257494.1). Found that the bacterial strain was useful in the reduction of heavy metal uptake and improves the growth characteristics by the application of HTM-PGPB.Lv *et al.,* (2019) conducted a field experiment effect of three treatment (Zn or ZnMn or ZnP) on six rice cultivars, on the Cd concentration. Found all three treatment significantly increase the Zn concentration in rice grain, but ZnMn was the much effective. Hence, conclude that the cultivator and Zn fertilizer can be used to minimize the Cd concentration in rice grain. Nabaei and Amooaghaie (2019) studied the impact of seed pre-soaking with melatonin and sodium nitroprusside (SNP) (as a NO donor) was evaluated on seed germination and seedling growth of *Catharanthusroseus* (L.) G. Don under both normal and Cd stress conditions. Results showed that 200 µM Cd reduced the relative seed germination, root elongation tolerance, and seed germination tolerance index. The melatonin and SNP improved the seed germination, germination rate, seedling length, and vigor index under Cd stress in a dose-dependent manner and the maximum biological responses obtained by 100 µM melatonin and 200 µM SNP. However, 200-400 µM melatonin and 400 µM SNP negatively influenced the seed germination indices and seedling establishment. The cadmium suppressed the amylase activity and contents of soluble and reducing sugars in germinating seeds; thereby it reduced seed germination. Cd stress also decreased subsequent growth of seedlings and increased electrolyte leakage in them. These Cd-induced inhibitory effects were ameliorated by applying both melatonin and SNP. Importantly, melatonin, as well as SNP, was able to markedly boost the NO content in seeds. The addition of the specific scavenger of NO (cPTIO) reversed the protective effects conferred by melatonin, but inhibition of melatonin biosynthesis by p-CPA could not alleviate effects elicited by SNP completely, suggesting that NO plays a role a downstream signal in melatonin-mediated germination responses especially under cadmium stress. Rady *et al.,* (2019) conducted an experiment to analyze the effect of exogenous application of polyamine under lead (2.0mM) stress on growth and productivity of wheat. The seeds of wheat were soaked in 0.25mM Spm, 0.50 Spd or 1.mM put, showed bettergrowth and yield attributes, RWC, MSI, leaf pigment and nutrient uptake compared to seeds soaked in water under 2.0mM lead stress. Among the polyamines, put showed the best result and thus it was recommended the soaking of wheat seed under lead stress.

REVIEW OF WORK BASED ON TOXCITY OF METALS

Rehman *et al.,* (2019) conducted an experiment to study the effect of salinity on Cadmium uptake, tolerance, and phytoremediation potential of Conocarpus. The one-month-old plant was exposed to Cd (0, 8.9, 44.5, 89 and 178µM) alone or combined with NaCl (0, 100, 200mM) in Hoagland's nutrient solution. It was found that the reduction in shoot and root biomasses, Low water content and chlorophyll content more in a combination of Cd and Saline stress compared to Cd alone. Uptake of potassium ion reduced in Cd combined with saline or alone Cd. The uptake was increased in the presence of salinity, oxidative stress increased the production of H_2O_2 and MDA content. The tolerance of Conocarpus during the Cd stress reduced in the presence of salinity because of increased uptake of toxic ions and due to an infestation of oxidative stress. Saeed *et al.,* (2019) conducted an experiment to evaluate the role of zeolite and Enterobacter sp. MN17 on Cd uptake, growth, physiological and biochemical responses of *Brassica napus* on Cd-contaminated soil. A sandy clay loam soil in plastic pots was spiked with Cd (0 and 80 mg kg-1) and amended with zeolite (0 and 10 g kg-1). Seeds of B. *napus* were inoculated with Enterobacter sp. MN17. Both inoculated and non-inoculated seeds of B. *napus* were sown and plants were harvested after 60 days of growth and data were collected. Although the sole application of zeolite and seed inoculation reverted adverse effects of Cd in B. *napus* plants, the combined use resulted in even higher growth and physiological responses compared to control plants. The combined use under Cd stress increased plant height, root length, dry biomass of shoot and root up to 32%, 57%, 42%, and 64%, respectively compared to control. The different physiological attributes (photosynthetic rate, chlorophyll content, transpiration rate, stomatal conductance) of B. *napus* were improved from 6% to 137%. Moreover, the combined use of zeolite and seed inoculation on Cd-contaminated soil reduced the stress to plants as antioxidant activities decreased up to 25-64%, however, enzyme activities were still higher than plants grown on normal soil. Root and shoot analysis of B. *napus* for Cd content depicted that zeolite and bacterium decreased Cd uptake from soil. It is concluded that combined use of zeolite and strain MN17 reduces Cd uptake from soil and improves physiological and biochemical responses of B. *napus* which is helpful to alleviate Cd toxicity to plants. Wang *et al.,* (2019) reported that foliar application of melatonin (100μmol per liter) significantly alter the Cadmium tolerance at tobacco leaves. Less accumulation of cadmium and increase in growth inhibitors and photoinhibition compared to control. The application of melatonin reduces the oxidative damage by direct scavenging and improves the activity of antioxidants. Melatonin causes modulation of genes like IRTI, HMAH, Narmol, and HMA3 could be responsible for the reduction in cadmium uptake. Yahaghi *et al.,* (2019) studied the screen bacterial strains most effective in increasing alfalfa growth and metal accumulation in the presence of toxic levels of lead (Pb) and zinc (Zn). Results show that, compared to root and shoot growth, alfalfa seed germination is less sensitive to high levels of Pb and Zn. Pb and Zn concentrations of 4.4 and 7.9mM, respectively, were required to give rise to a 50% reduction in vitro seed germination. Root growth in alfalfa seedlings is, however, completely suppressed at a Pb concentration of 4 mM or a Zn concentration of 6 mM in the agar plate medium. Inoculation of the bacterial strains capable of producing indole-acetic acid and siderophore positively affected the plant growth parameter in the metal contaminated mediums. Root and/or shoot growths of alfalfa seedlings are significantly stimulated by the seven inoculated bacterial strains investigated, among which *Bacillus filamentosus* YSP110 is found to be the most effective. Inoculation of alfalfa plants with B.*filamentosus* strain YSP110 grown in a vermiculite medium is also seen to increase Pb accumulation in plant root and shoot by 18.0 and 72.4%, respectively. *Bacillus cereus* YSP4 is the bacterial strain most effective in stimulating root and shoot growth in alfalfa seedlings cultured in a Zn-contaminated medium. Compared to the non-inoculated plants, alfalfa seeds inoculated with B. cereus YSP4 also exhibit increased Zn accumulation in their roots and shoots by 43.2 and 48.7%, respectively. Ahmad *et al.*, (2018) conducted a pot experiment on faba beans to investigate the effect of SA on NaCl stress (50mM and 100mM). 100mM causes maximum reduction in shoot and root length, also reduction in lead pigments and leaf relative water content (LRWC) with an increase in NaCl concentration. However, the application of SA on NaCl stressed seedling enhances the length and dry weight of shoot by 57.1% and root by 67.2%), also increase in leaf pigment and LRWC. H_2O_2 and MDA concentration in NaCl stressed seedling was more but in SA+ NaCl the reduction in H_2O_2 and MDA content. Application of SA reduces Na+ accumulation and enhances Ca2+ and k+ uptake during NaCl stress in seedlings of faba bean. Alamri *et al.*, (2018) suggested that the application of SA was directly or indirectly involved in improving the physiological process, which helps wheat to overcome from the oxidative damage caused by Pb toxicity. Amin *et al.*, (2018) reported that both crops sesame (*Sesamumindicum* L.) and guar (*Cyamopsistetragonoloba* L.) able to tolerate the 1000mg per kg concentration of Pb. The amount of Pb present in roots was significantly causing the reduction of biomass in both plants. Translocation factor (TF), bioaccumulation coefficient (BAC) and bioconcentration factor (BCF) showed that C.tetragonoloba was more efficient for the phytoremediation of soil consisting of high Pb concentration. Dutta *et al.*, (2018) has reported that inoculation of the *endophytic bacterium* (HR1 isolate) was isolated from the root nodule of Vigna mungo known as Klebsiellapneumoniae selected for Cd (II) tolerance. It was found that the bacteria have great potential as plant growth parameter with capabilities of Indole acetic acid, phosphate solubilization, siderophore production and able to stand in Cd (II) concentration up to 10μg/mL. Improved shoot and root length, germination percentage, and biomass compared to non-inoculated. Concluded that the bacterium had a potential of heavy metal scavenging of Cd (II) and a good plant growth promotor. Feng *et al.*, (2018) conducted a pot experiment on mitigating the effect of Sulphur on Cadmium uptake and toxicity on Tobacco using exogenous application of S1 and S2 having 47% and 38% total S respectively. It was found that the 1mg and 5mg CA kg^{-1} soil increase Cd level and accumulation, but a decrease in plant height, biomass and photosynthetic rate with more effect in Cd2 treatment S2 fertilizer reduces the Cd toxicity and improved photosynthesis. Concluded that exogenous application of sulphur fertilizer to lowers the Cd accumulation in leaves of tobacco and can safely grow in Cd affected soil. Garg and Bharti (2018) conducted an experiment to study the role of SA (0.5mM) seed promisingin the formation of arbuscular mycorrhizal (AM) symbiosis with *Rhizo glomus intraradices* and effect on nutrient uptake, growth, sugar metabolism and ion-homeostasis under salt stress. SA promotes root colonization by increasing the number of arbuscular and vesicles during salt stress. AM symbiosis showed good root biomass, the ratio between root and shoot, nutrient uptake than SA, but SA maintains the equilibrium and carbohydrate metabolism. Concluded that the priming of seed with SA improves the AM symbiosis which can be used for growing chickpea under salt stress. Kaur *et al.*, (2018) conducted an experiment to analyze the synergistic role in *Brassica juncea* seedlings during Cd stress. Cd concentration (0 and 0.6mM) and citric acid (0.6mM) and four concentration of castasterone (0, 0.01, 1 100nM) were taken. Due to Cd plant induced H$_2$O$_2$ and superoxide ion (O$_2$$^-$) production, reduction in photosynthetic pigment level, changing in Carbohydrate content. Citric acid was most effective inameliorating Cd-induced toxicity by reducing H$_2$O$_2$ and O$_2$$^-$ by 29.5% and 12.1% respectively. Improved photosynthetic pigments, chlorophyll (47%) and carotenoid (34%). It was suggested that the citric acid and castasterone are more effective alleviating Cd-induced toxicity and physiological damage by antioxidant and organic acids. Khan *et al.*, (2018) studied the role of exogenously applied salicylic acid (SA) and putrescine (Put) on the phytoremediation of heavy metal and on the growth parameters of chickpea grown in sandy soil. The SA and Put have applied alone as well as in combination with plant growth promoting rhizobacteria (PGPR). SA increased the proline content of tolerant variety while decreasing the lipid peroxidation and proline content of the sensitive variety but decreased the stimulating effect of PGPR in proline production. Interactive effects of PGPR and PGRs is recommended for inducing phytoremediation in chickpea plants under drought stress. Kumar and Dwivedi (2018) conducted a pot experiment on maize variety BIO-9544, to study the effect of putrescine and glomus mycorrhiza on cadmium toxicity reference to sugar and protein. Found that the T17 (0.15% Cd (NO$_3$)$_2$ + 5mM Putrescine + mycorrhiza) showed asignificant increase in total sugar content by 4.22%, 5.03% and 4.18% with respect to T12 (0.15% Cd (NO$_3$)$_2$)

and concluded that Pu[+] and mycorrhiza can be used against Cd-induced toxicity. Kumar (2018a) reported that the combined application of putrescine and mycorrhiza in maize crop under cadmium toxicity. The combination was suitable for mitigating Cadmium toxicity linked to internal nodal length and node number. Kumar P. (2018b) conducted a pot experiment, in which mycorrhiza and putrescine were applied as the ameliorative agents for Cd toxicity. The combination of mycorrhiza and putrescine showed a better result for the mitigation of Cd casing toxicity in plant height and leaf number per plant. Kumar P. (2018c) reported that there was a significant increase chlorophyll an in treatment T17 (0.15 % Cd $(NO_3)_2$ + 5mM Putrescine + mycorrhiza) with respect to T12 (0.15 % Cd $(NO_3)_2$). Also, chlorophyll b in T17 has a significant effect with 10.90%, 7.09% and 8.05% increase with respect to T12. Natarajan *et al.*, (2018) conducted a pot experiment tomato by using increasing concentration (10, 25, 50, 75 and 100mg Kg^{-1}) of cadmium in soil. The Cd treatment plant shows reduced growth in root and shoots length and biochemical component such as protein (except phenol and proline) content compared to control. Shoot length was higher compared to root in Cd-treated plant, but proline and phenol content in the root was higher compared to shoot. Osmolovskaya *et al.*, (2018) conducted an experiment to study the effect of cadmium at concentrations of 1 and 10 iM on biomass increment, mineral nutrient elements (potassium, calcium, and magnesium) accumulation, and oxalic acid pools in organs of *Amaranthuscruentus* L. plants growing under water culture conditions was investigated. It was established that cadmium in the tested concentrations did not exert any pronounced damage effect on amaranth plants, which was in part shown to be associated with its predominant accumulation in roots and minimization of its transfer into young leaves. It was demonstrated that, in sublethal concentrations, this metal exerted growth response in the above ground amaranth organs expressed in the stimulation of young leaves' growth, while simultaneously inhibiting growth processes in mature leaves. The results obtained are discussed in the context of the determination of plant growth response to the effect of cadmium by certain metabolic changes whose functional manifestations consisted in carbon metabolism intensification and increase in water-insoluble oxalate content in amaranth leaves. The simultaneous observed increase in Ca^{2+} and Mg^{2+} levels in young and mature amaranth leaves were considered as additional evidence in favor of accelerating leaves' ontogenesis pace under the effect of sublethal doses of cadmium. Sarkar *et al.*, (2018) reported that the inoculation of arbuscularmycorrhizal fungi (AMF) with Pb increases the total dry mass, IAA, chlorophyll content, total phosphorous and nitrogen. Whereas, the H_2O_2 concentration, POD and IAA oxidase activity were less compared to non-inoculated. Results were remarkable the use of AMF with M. *sacchariflorus* for the removal of Pb from the soil. Sinisha and Puthur

(2018) reported that the cadmium and zinc reduction in the shoot length, chlorophyll, andcarotenoid, increase in MDA content, accumulation of proline, the rise in amino acids and sugar on a seedling of rice when treated with $ZnSO_4$ and $CdCl_2$ The selected 12 rice cultivar showed changes in biochemicals during the $ZnSO_4$and $CdCl_2$ stress. Cultivar JY showed the least tolerance and Varsha showed the highesttolerance during the Zn and Cd toxicity. Tahjib-Ul-Arif *et al.*, (2018) conducted an experiment to study the potential roles of salicylic acid (SA) in the improvement of maize tolerance to salinity and evaluated the resultant effects on yield-associated parameters and yield. The results showed that maize plants grown under salinity alone exhibited severely compromised growth performance, and consequently yield loss, which could be attributed to reduced plant height, decreased photosynthetic efficiency, and elevated levels of the lipid peroxidation product malondialdehyde in maize leaves. On the other hand, foliar application of SA minimized the detrimental effects of salinity in salt-exposed plants, leading to better growth performance and yield when compared with SA-free salt-stressed plants. SA-mediated beneficial effects were particularly evident in the enhancement of photosynthesis-related parameters, including photosynthetic rate, carboxylation efficiency, water use efficiency, and chlorophyll content (SPAD value). Exogenous SA also contributed to the reduction of membrane damage under salinity, as reflected by significantly decreased levels of malondialdehyde in the leaves of maize exposed to salt stress. Furthermore, activities of enzymatic antioxidants like ascorbate peroxidase and catalase in maize leaves were significantly enhanced following SA application in salt-exposed plants, indicating a protective role of SA against salt-induced oxidative stress. Finally, clustering and principal component analysis revealed that the antioxidant capacity and photosynthetic efficiency were intimately associated with the salt and SA treatments. The result showed that foliar application of SA is a viable option in alleviating the adverse effects of salinity on growth performance and yield of maize, as well as other economically important crops cultivated in salt-affected areas. Tohidi *et al.*, (2018) conducted an experiment by using four different concentration of Ni (0, 60, 120, and 180mg kg^{-1} soil), and two levels of mycorrhiza (inoculated and non-inoculated) on wheat. The reduction in seed number per spike, test weight, chlorophyll a and b and seed yield per plant due to Ni stress, also increase in catalase (CAT) enzyme activity. Whereas mycorrhiza treated plant showed a significant increase in seed per spike, test weight, chlorophyll a and b, and also reduction in catalase. The application of mycorrhiza showed a reduction in Ni stress in wheat. Yi *et al.*, (2018) reported that the beneficial effects of exogenous spermidine (Spd, a kind of polyamine) on plant growth and development under salt stress have been widely reported; however, little information is available on the effects of Spd on the combined treatment of CO_2 enrichment and iso-osmotic salt stress. the effects of exogenous Spd (0.25 mM) on plant growth, chlorophyll content, water status, osmotic adjustment, and the antioxidant system were investigated under CO_2 enrichment (800 ppm) and iso-osmotic salt stress [150 mmol/L NaCl and 100 mmol/L Ca $(NO_3)2$] in tomato (*Solanumlycopersicum* L.). Ali (2017) conducted a pot experiment to investigate the effect of SA to enhance the tolerance of mung bean plant to aluminum (0.0, 1.0 or 10.0mM) stress. The aluminum causes a reduction in growth (length, the dry and fresh mass of shoot and root), water content, water use efficiency, photosynthesis rate, and chlorophyll content. Also causes an increase in antioxidant enzymes (CAT, SOD, proline, and POD) in shoot and root by aluminum toxicity. Application of SA results in good growth and stimulation of antioxidant caused due to aluminum toxicity. Chen *et al.*, (2017) reported that the concentration of ROS (e.g. O_2^- and H_2O_2) content was significantly decreased in metal plus hemin treatment. Also, the reduction in the root issue of rice seedling. Found that the hemin increases the concentration of antioxidant enzymes and hemin reduces the accumulation of heavy metal, resulting in improved pigment synthesis, plant growth, and photosynthetic attributes. Jung *et al.*, (2017) reported the change in ROS and antioxidant level in rice seedling treated with Cadmium and sulphur. At 30µM Cd inhibited plant growth, causing an increase in the level of superoxide, H_2O_2, and MDA content. Application of sulphur to Cd-stressed seedling reduces the Cd-induced oxidative stress by Glutathione (GSH) ascorbate (AsA) cycle, increase in cysteine sulphur assimilation in the treated plant. Hence, the application of sulphur results in restrict Cd translocation from root to stem and leaves. Kumari *et al.*, (2017) recorded that cadmium severely affects the seed germination and seedling growth when compared to control, also reduction in total chlorophyll content at high concentration of Cadmium. Velez *et al.*, (2017) studied the presence of chromium in soils not only affects the physiological processes of plants but also the microbial rhizosphere composition and metabolic activities of microorganisms. Hence, the inoculation of plants with Cr(VI)-tolerant rhizospheric microorganisms as an alternative to reduce Cr phytotoxicity was studied. In this work, chickpea germination was reduced by Cr(VI) concentrations of 150 and 250 mg/L (6 and 33%, respectively); however, lower Cr(VI) concentrations negatively affected the biomass. On the other hand, its symbiont, *Mesorhizobiumciceri,* was able to grow and remove different Cr (VI) concentrations (5-20 mg/L). The inoculation of chickpea plants with this strain exposed to Cr(VI) showed a significantly enhanced plant growth. In addition, inoculated plants accumulated higher Cr concentration in roots than those non-inoculated. Wani *et al.*, (2017) conducted an experiment to investigate the effect of foliar spray of 24-epibrassinolide (EBL) on nitrogen metabolism, antioxidant system, photosynthetic characteristics and

 Effect of Elements on Plants

chlorophyll fluorescence in two varieties (PDG-4 and GNG-1581) of *Cicer arietinum* L. under cadmium (Cd; 50 µM) and/or NaCl (100 mM) stress. It was found that the exogenous application of EBL as foliar spray significantly alleviated the inhibitory effects on photosynthesis and increased total chlorophyll content, net photosynthetic rate, stomatal conductance, internal CO_2 concentration, transpiration rate and maximum quantum yield of PSII under Cd and/or NaCl stress. In addition, EBL application also enhanced the activities of nitrogenase, glutamate synthase, glutaminesynthetase and glutamate dehydrogenase enzymes under both stresses- and stress-free conditions. Moreover, application of EBL also increased antioxidant enzyme activities and the proline content in both stresses- and stress-free plants. The EBL could alleviate the combined stress induced harmful effects on photosynthesis and nitrogen metabolism through an increase in the antioxidant system that leads to improved growth of plants. Aldesuqay H.S (2016) report that the wastewater stream causes a remarkablewas in heavy metal toxicity and saturation water deficit. External application of Spermidine and Spermine could defend the plant against heavy metal in wastewater by improving growth vigor, water uptake and reduction in translocation of heavy metals from root to leaves till reach to grains. Alyemeni *et al.*, (2016) conducted a pot experiment with 0, 25, 50 or 100mg of cadmium per kg of soil. At 30 DAS, chickpea plant was sprayed with 20mM proline and control plant sprayed with the double distilled water (DDW). Proline application partly overcome with the increasing amount of damage caused by the increase in the concentration of the cadmium in the soil. Found that, in treatment with 25mg Cadmium after application of proline significantly increase the nodulation parameter, carbohydrates and leghaemoglobin, leaf nitrogen and root nitrate content. But treatment with 100mg cadmium the proline was not much effective. Bahraminia *et al.*, (2016) conducted an experiment in poly-house to study the effectiveness of AM fungi in phytoremediation of lead (Pb) contaminated soil by Vetiver Grass from lead levels (500, 200, 400 and 800mg kg^{-1}) as Pb $(NO_3)_2$. Shoot and root dry weight reduced with the increase in the Pb, whereas in mycorrhiza inoculated the shoot and root dry weight increased significantly. The mycorrhizal inoculation increases lead extraction, uptake, and movement efficiencies. Increase in lead concentration reduces the lead uptake, but inoculation of AM fungi increases lead translocation. Chen *et al.*, (2016) conducted two experiments to study the effect of SA on photosystem II and antioxidant system in wheat. In the firstmethod, the roots were immersed in the Hoagland's nutrient solution containing 0, 0.25 and 2.5 mM SA and in the second method the foliar application was done on two-week-old seedling with the same concentration of SA. There was an increase in antioxidant enzymes in low concentration of SA treated with 2.5mM, showed reduction in antioxidant enzyme, quantum yield of PSII and the photochemical quenchingcoefficient in first method. It was concluded that the effect of SA on antioxidant and PSII depends on concentration and method of application. Imtiaz *et al.*, (2016) conducted an experiment to elucidate the effects of vanadium (V) on photosynthetic pigments, membrane damage, antioxidant enzymes, protein, and deoxyribonucleic acid (DNA) integrity in the following chickpea genotypes: C-44 (tolerant) and Balkasar (sensitive). Changes in these parameters were strikingly dependent on levels of V, at 60 and 120 mg V L^{-1} induced DNA damage in Balkasar only, while photosynthetic pigments and protein were decreased from 15 to 120 mg V L^{-1} and membrane was also damaged. It was found that photosynthetic pigments and protein production declined from 15 to 120 mg V L-1 and the membrane was also damaged, while DNA damage was not observed at any level of V stress in C-44. Moreover, the antioxidant enzyme activities such as superoxide dismutase (SOD), catalase (CAT), and peroxidase (POD) were increased in both genotypes of chickpea against V stress; however, more activities were observed in C-44 than Balkasar. The results suggest that DNA damage in sensitive genotypes can be triggered due to exposure to higher vanadium. Kuramshina *et al.*, (2016) reported that the presence of cadmium in plant seeds inoculated with *Bacillus subtills*increases the activity of POD, catalase and non-protein thiols content, but a decrease in lipid peroxidation. It was found that the seed inoculated bacteria reduces the metal content in plant shoot. Pirasteh-Anosheh *et al.*, (2016) conducted a field trial for three years in a row to study the effect of different concentration of SA (0, 0.2, 1.0, 1.2 and 2.0 mM) on grain and biological yield, also the Na^+, Cl^-, Ca^{2+}, Mg^{2+} and K^+ on barely under salinity stress. It was found that there was a reduction in storage factor (SF), grain and biological yield under salt stress. Application of SA at higher concentration increases the SF for Cl^- and Na^+ but reduces the K^+.this showed that the SA helped in the storage of Cl^- and Na^+ ions in the root system. This suggested that SA improves the ions transport in barely during the salt stress. Piršelová *et al.*, (2016) conducted an experiment to investigate the effect of Cd (5mg per kg soil) and arsenic (5mg per kg soil) on plant growth of two soybeans (*Glycine max* (L.)) cultivars (Merr. CVS. Bólyi 44 and Cordoba). It was found that the impact of arsenic on Cordoba was more, reduction in the rate of fluorescence on old leaves (UL decrease of 5.6%). Similarly, Bólyi 44 variety TL2showed the most sensitive response (decrease of 10.7%); while Cordoba variety bL2 leaves show more tolerance (decrease of 1.2%). Results suggested that the Genotypic differences in cadmium and arsenic defense strategy across the various types of leaves. Sadeghipour (2016) reported that the lead toxicity significantly reduces the chlorophyll content, relative water content (RWC) and net photosynthetic rate but increase in lipid peroxidation and catalase, superoxide dismutase (SOD), glutathione reductase, ascorbate peroxidase and proline content. Different concentration of nitric oxide (NO) significantly decreases the lead toxicity by increasing the SOD, CAT, glutathione reductase, ascorbate peroxidase activity and also proline accumulation. However (0.5 and 1.0 mM) was more effective in lead stress, 0.5mM was much effective. Sakouhi *et al.*, (2016) conducted an experiment to study the Impact of exogenous calcium and ethylene glycol tetra acetic acid (EGTA) supplement on chickpea (*Cicer arietinum* L.) germinating seeds exposed to cadmium stress for 6 days was studied. Ca and EGTA late treatment (3 days) alleviated growth inhibition and decreased Cd accumulation as well as lipid peroxidation and protein carbonylation in both root and shoot cells. Exogenous effect or application relieved Cd-induced cell death which was associated with a constant level of ATP, which was considered as an apoptotic-like process. Redox balance was examined through the study of the redox state of pyridine nucleotide couples $NAD^+/NADH$ and $NADP^+/NADPH$ as well as their related oxidative [NAD(P)H-oxidase] and dehydrogenase (glucose-6-phosphate dehydrogenase, 6-phosphogluconate dehydrogenase, and malate dehydrogenase) enzyme activities. The ameliorative effect of Ca and EGTA on the growth of Cd-exposed chickpea seedlings that occurs through the protection of sensitive cell sites from Cd-induced oxidation, namely membrane lipids, and proteins, rather than the improvement of recycling capabilities of the cellular reducing power. Wu *et al.*, (2016) conducted an experiment to investigate the beneficial role of selenium (Se) in protecting oilseed rape (*Brassica napus* L.) plants from cadmium (CdC2) and lead (PbC2) toxicity. Exogenous Se markedly reduced Cd and Pb concentration in both roots and shoots. Supplementation of the medium with Se (5, 10, and 15 mg kg^{-1}) alleviated the negative effect of Cd and Pb on growth and led to a decrease in oxidative damages caused by Cd and Pb. Furthermore, Se-enhanced superoxide free radicals (O_2^-), hydrogen peroxide (H_2O_2), and lipid peroxidation, as indicated by malondialdehyde accumulation, but decreased superoxide dismutase and glutathione peroxidase activities. Meanwhile, the presence of Cd and Pb in the medium affected Se speciation in shoots. Yang *et al.*, (2016) conducted a pot experiment to investigate the influence of sulphur on Fe plaque formation and lead accumulation in rice (*Oryzasativa*) under two levels of Pb (0 and 600mg kg^{-1}). Combined with four different concentration of sulphur also added (0, 30, 60 and 120 mg kg^{-1}). Hence, found that the sulphur application significantly reduces the lead accumulation in grains and rice straw. Excessive sulphur supply results in more monosulfide toxicity and reduction in Fe plaque formation on the root surface in a flooded condition. Excessive supply of sulphur results in a decrease in the availability of Pb and the accumulation of Pb to rice plant. Yu *et al.*, (2016) conducted an experiment to study the effects of three concentrations (0.001, 0.01, and 0.1 mg/L) of exogenous spermidine (Spd) on the O_2^- production rate, malondialdehyde (MDA) content, antioxidant enzyme activities, leaf photosynthesis, chlorophyll content, chlorophyll fluorescence, and light response curve parameters were investigated in the seedlings of two tomato cultivars: low-light-stress-tolerant 'Zhongza 9' and sensitive 'Zhongshu 6'. Low-light stress of 150 mol m-2 s-1 resulted in an increase in the O2 production rate, MDA content, and peroxidase activity, whereas the superoxide dismutase and catalase activities decreased.

CONCLUSION

Exogenous Spd effectively ameliorated these effects. The net photosynthetic rate (Pn), maximal photochemical quantum efficiency of photosystem II (Fv/Fm), light saturation point, net photosynthetic rate at light saturation point (Amax), and dark respiration rate (Rd) simultaneously decreased under low light, but the chlorophyll content, particularly the chlorophyll b (CHL b) content, markedly increased when compared to the normal-light (control) plants. Exogenous Spd diminished the decrease in leaf Pn and Fv/Fm and induced a further increase in the CHL b content and decrease in Rd and chl a/Chl b under low-light stress. It was found that exogenous Spd could improve plant tolerance by alleviating the membrane lipid peroxidation and photosynthetic inhibition resulting from low light. However, the optimal SPD concentration generally differed in the two cultivars.

REFERENCES

Arnon, D.I., Copper Enzyme Polyphenoloxides in Isolated Chloroplast in *Beta vulgaris, Plant Physiology*, 24, 1-15, 1949.

Aebi, H., Catalase in vitro. *Methods of Enzymology*, 105, 121-126, 1984.

Bradford, M.M. (1976). A Rapid and Sensitive method for the Quantitation of Microgram Quantities of Protein Utilizing the Principle of Protein-dye Binding. Analytical Biochemistry, 72(1-2), 248-254.

Chamberlain, J.E., Chantry and Wright, A.J.,The Spectral Transmission at infra-red wavelengths of Michelson Interferometers with Dielectric film Beam-dividers, *Infrared Physics*, 6(4), 195-203, 1996.

Dhindsa, R.H., Plumb-Dhindsa, R. and Thorpe, T.A., Leaf Senescence Correlated with Increased Level of Membrane Permeability, Lipid Peroxidation and Decreased Level of SOD and CAT, *Journal of Experimental Botany*, 32, 93-101, 1981.

Heath, R.L. and Packer, L., Photoperoxidation in isolated Chloroplasts. I. Kinetics and Stoichiometry of Fatty Acid Peroxidation, *Archives of Biochemestry and Biophysics*, 125, 189-198, 1968.

Jana, S. and Choudhuri, M., Glycolate Metabolism of Three Submerged Aquatic Angiosperms during Aging, *Aquatic Botany*, 12, 345-354, 1981.

Premchandra GS, Saneoka H, Ogata S (1990). Cell Membrane Stability, an Indicator of Drought Tolerance as Affected by Applied Nitrogen in Soybean. J. Agric. Sci. Camb. 115: 63-66.

Pages: 52-61

Effect of Elements on Plants

Edited by: Dr. Prasann Kumar and Dr. Pawan Kumar 'Bharti'
ISBN: 978-93-88854-44-3
Edition: 2020
Published by: Discovery Publishing House Pvt. Ltd., New Delhi (India)

Effect of Nitrogen and Phosphorus on Pearl Millet with Respect to its Growth and Development

Prasann Kumar[1*2], Shipa Rani Dey[1]

GRAPHICAL ABSTRACT

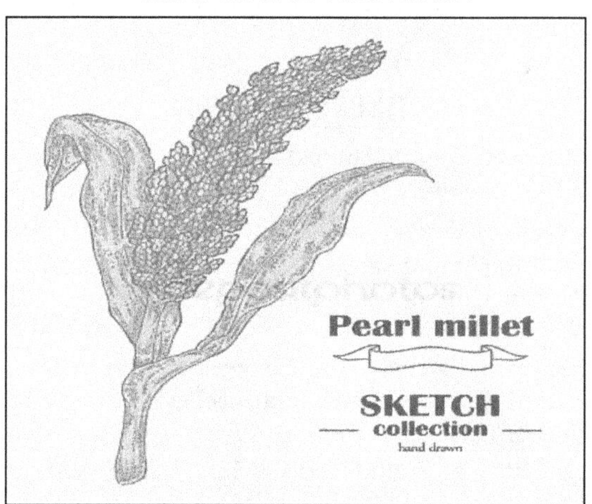

Keywords: Effect, Growth, Nitrogen, Phosphorus, Millets

INTRODUCTION

Rao *et al.* (1991) conducted an experiment on finger millet and found that the increasing levels of nitrogen increase plant height significantly up to the level of 75 kg N/ha. Keshva and Jat (1992) reported that all the

[1] Department of Agronomy, School of Agriculture, Lovely Professional University, Jalandhar - 144 411 (Punjab) (India)
[2] Divison of Research and Development, Lovely Professional University, Jalandhar - 144411 (Punjab) (India)

growth attributing character and green fodder yield of pearl millet showed increasing trend with increase in phosphorus level. Application of P at 60 kg/ha showed a significant increase of 14.3 and 8.2% in total green fodder yield over 0 and 20 kg P_2O_5/ha, respectively.

EFFECT ON TILLER AND PLANT HEIGHT

Lal *et al.* (1992) conducted and experiment on pearl millet and concluded that application of N greatly improve the plant height and number of tillers/plant. Number of tillers per plant increase significantly up to 80 kg N/ha. However no measurable difference was found between 40 and 80 kg N/ha for plant height. Kavimani *et al.* (2000) laid an experiment on pearl millet and asserted that there was significant increase in plant height due to FYM application and N levels, but when FYM and nitrogen application was combined the effect was more pronounce. Chaudhari *et al.* (2002) conducted an experimenton growth and yield of pearl millet cv.MH 179 in Jobner, Rajasthan, India and reported that plant height, number of tillers, dry matter accumulation increased with 16 and 19 kg/ha. Muniratham and Gautam (2002) revealed that nitrogen application markedly influence all the growth parameter of pearl millet. The dose of 90 kg N ha^{-1} applied in two equal splits resulted in taller plants more tiller per plant and dry matter per plant (18.76 gram). Eltelib *et al.* (2006) reported in a study the effect of nitrogen and phosphorus application on growth. Nitrogen was applied at the rates of (0, 40 and 80 kg/ha) while phosphorus levels were (0, 50 and 100 kg P_2O_5/ha). The parameters studied were plant height, number of leaf per plant, stem diameter and leaf area index. Result showed that addition of nitrogen fertilizer significantly increase plant height, stem diameter and LAI. Phosphorus fertilizer application has no significant effect on growth.

NITROGEN UPTAKE AND ITS EFFECT ON PEARL MILLETS GROWTH

Jakhar *et al.* (2006) conducted an experiment on pearl millet at Anand Agriculture University to study the influence of levels of nitrogen application on growth, yield and nitrogen uptake and reported that with increasing levels of nitrogen up to 200 kg N/ha, the leaf area per plant, dry matter per plant increased. Rathaur and Singh (2006) revealed that increasing N levels resulted in significant increase in growth parameters i.e. plant height, leaf area per plant and dry matter accumulation per plant in pearl millet hybrid HHB-94. Verma *et al.* (2006) conducted a field experiment to evaluate the effect of nitrogen (20, 40, 60 and 80 kg/ha) and mulching treatments. Results revealed that application of nitrogen at 60 or 80 kg/ha recorded the highest value for the different growth character i.e. plant height, dry matter accumulation and number of tillers per plant in pearl millet. Chaudhary and Gautam (2007) conducted an experiment in New Delhi and reported that are the growth parameter increase with different combination of nitrogen and phosphorus. Bagla *et al.* (2008) conducted field trials in

Hisar to study the effect of various combinations of organic and inorganic sources of nutrient on growth and yield of pearl millet. Number of tillers/ m row length, dry matter accumulation and leaf area index were significantly higher in treatment where 50% dose of the recommended nutrients was supplied through chemical fertilizer and 50% through FYM which proved better than the treatment where all the nutrient supply was through chemical fertilizer alone. The grain and stover yields of the crop were also found to be the highest with same treatment concluding that FYM can replace 50% requirements of the chemical fertilizer to meet the nutrient needs of pearl millet. Onasanya *et al.* (2009) conducted an experiment on maize crop and reported that application of 120 kg N/ha + 0 kg P/ha and 60 kg N/ha + 40 kg P/ha significantly increase the growth of maize than other treatment. Sheta *et al.* (2010) reported that the yields of green forage and dry matter yield of pearl millet increased by application N, K and S. The increase in yield was also supported by increasing growth parameters i.e. plant height and number of tillers per meter row length.

EI-Lattif, EAA (2011) showed in an experiment that growth parameters and forage yield were significantly affected by sowing dates and fertilization treatments.

RESPONSE OF PEARL MILLET TO DIFFERENT N AND P LEVELS ON YIELD ATTRIBUTES AND YIELD

Bishnoi and Agarwal (1980) stated that the grain yield of bajra continued to increase with the increase in the levels of nitrogen up to the maximum dose and the difference between two success levels were found to be significant. Increase in the grain yield of bajra with increasing rate of nitrogen associated with the increased number of ears per plant in the present investigation. Kurlekar *et al.* (1980) conducted a field experiment on *Pennisetum typhoids* hybrid BJ-104 grown in Kharif seasons given combinations of 0-60 kg N, 0-30 kg P_2O_5 and 0-30 kg K_2O kg ha^{-1}. Average grain yield was highest (2.3 t ha^{-1}) with 60 kg N + 30 kg P_2O_5 + 15 kg K_2O ha^{-1} compared with 1.1 tonne ha^{-1} without N, P and K.Upasani and Sharma (1980) revealed that nitrogen treatment caused significant variation in the grain and stover yield. Grain yield due to 20 and 40 kg N ha^{-1} were comparable to that without N application. Similarly 20, 40 and 60 kg; 40, 60, and 80 kg; 80 and 100 kg N rates were comparable among themselves in this respect. The lowest stover yield was recorded at control and highest from 100 kg N ha^{-1}. Nitrogen rates of 20 and 40 kg ha^{-1} were at par in this respect. Kadrekar and Bhosale (1981) observed that the levels of nitrogen had significant effect on the grain yield of finger millet. The yield increased significantly with every increase in the level of nitrogen up to 100 kg N ha^{-1} over the control. The various levels of phosphorus influenced the grain yield up to 50 kg P_2O_5 ha^{-1} significantly. Taneja *et al.* (1981) reported that the application of 40 and 80 kg P_2O_5 ha^{-1} increased grain and stover yield which may be due to favorable effect on growth and yield attributes of bajra crop. Kaushik and Pal (1983) found that the nitrogen fertilization brought about significant increase in grain and stover yield. The highest grain yield of 38 q ha^{-1} was obtained on an average, with 120 kg N ha^{-1}. Rao *et al.* (1984) reported that the nitrogensignificantly influenced at all stages of crop growth. All the yield attributing characters were also significantly influenced due to nitrogen addition. There was significant increase in nitrogen level up to 90 kg ha^{-1}. Maximum straw yield was obtained with 120 kg N ha^{-1} which was significantly superior to rest of the treatment. The grain yield increased up to 90 kg N ha^{-1} and further increase in nitrogen level increased straw yield without additional increase in grain yield. Dhillon *et al.* (1987) observed that pearl millet responded significantly to applied P up to 30 kg ha^{-1}. Singh (1987) conducted field experiment on kharif frenchbean on a sandy loam soil of medium nitrogen and high phosphorus status. Green pod yield of frenchbean increased with increase in the rates of N up to 60 kg ha^{-1}. Crop responded to P_2O_5 up to 40 kg ha^{-1}. The optimum does of N and P_2O_5 were 67.3 and 79.7 kg ha^{-1}, respectively. Nimje and Seth (1988) conducted experiment on maize and observed that the various yield attributes like, number of cobs plant^{-1}, length and girth of cob, number of grain cob^{-1}, grain yield cob^{-1}, 1000 grain weight responded to nitrogen application up to 120 kg ha^{-1} and significantly increased grain yield of maize during both the years. Hooda *et al.* (1991) reported that bajragrown at Hisar, was given 12 different fertilizer treatment including various combination of NPK fertilizer, FYM and green manure. Bajra crop was given 0-100 percent of recommended NPK fertilizer. Highest yield was with 100 percent of recommended does (120 kg N + 60 kg P_2O_5 + 60 kg K_2O ha^{-1}). When 25% of NPK replaced by FYM green manure, yield remained same while at 50% NPK replacement, yield remained less than highest. Rathee *et al.* (1991) revealed that grain, and stover yields and yield contributing characters such as length of ear, 1000 grain weight and dry matter accumulation plant^{-1}, increased significantly with successive increase in N levels. Subhian (1991) conducted an experiment consisting of the treatment of 3 levels of each of N (40, 80, and 120 kg ha^{-1}), P_2O_5 (0, 40 and 80 kg ha^{-1}) and K_2O (0 and 40 kg ha^{-1}) with all 18 combination of N, P, K along with control (N_0P_0 and K_0) plot in each block. The yield increased with an increase in level of N up to 120 kg N ha^{-1} and P_2O_5 application up to 40 kg ha^{-1}. Potassium application did not show any significant influence on the grain yield. Sridhar *et al.* (1991) conducted studies on hybrid maize with 4 fertility levels on sandy loam soil which were low in available N and medium P and K. They reported that level of N_{180}, P_{90} and K_{60} resulted in significantly higher values of all yield attributes viz. cob plant^{-1}, cob length, cob girth, cob weight, grain cob^{-1} and test weight. This level of fertility also produced significantly maximum yield of 38.86 q ha^{-1} grain and 92.04 q ha^{-1} stover which were 4.55 and 11.00 q ha^{-1} higher, respectively, over next dose of N$_{120}$, P$_{60}$ and K$_{40}$ kg fertility level. Srivastava and Singh (1992) find out increase in the maize grain yield by more than 6 q ha^{-1} due to the application of 80 kg N ha^{-1} over the control and further increased by 4.5 q ha^{-1} when 40 kg P$_2$O$_5$ ha^{-1} was applied along with the N dose. Nimje and Gandhi (1993) asserted that the nitrogen fertilization to sorghum crop significantly increased the grain, stover, and weight of grain/ear and 1000 – grain weight, the effects were significant up to 80 kg ha^{-1}. Stover yield, however, increased significantly as the higher doses of N increased. Billore *et al.* (1994) reported that application of 120 kg Nha^{-1} gave significantly higher grain yield. Application of P was effective in all the years. Phosphorus @ 40 and 80 kg ha^{-1} resulted in substantially higher yield than no phosphorus application. Application of K enhanced the yield. Paradkar and Sharma (1994) showed that application of 100 kg N ha^{-1} obtained grain yield of 27.1 q ha^{-1}, but when applied 100 kg N + 50 P produced the yield of 42.3 q ha^{-1} (35.30%), and 100 kg N + 50 kg P$_2$O$_5$ +40 kg K$_2$O ha^{-1} produced, the grain yield of 50.3 q ha^{-1} (15.90%). Kumpawat and Rathore (1995) conducted a fertilizer studies on hybrid maize in sandy loam soil and found that maize responded significantly up to 120 kg N and 60 kg P$_2$O$_5$ ha^{-1} but no response to applied potassium. Singh and Verma (1996) observed that the grain and stover yields increased significantly with increasing N and P fertilization. Nitrogen @ 100 kg and phosphorus 50 kg gave the highest grain and stover yields followed by N$_{80}$, P$_{40}$ for grain and stover yield during both the years. Singh *et al.* (1996) observed that the grain and stover yields increased significantly with increasing N and P fertilization. Nitrogen @ 100 kg and phosphorus 50 kg produced the highest grain and stover yields followed by N$_{80}$ P$_{40}$ for grain and stover yield during both the years. Gautam and Kaushik (1997) observed the response to nitrogen application. A dose of 60 kg N ha^{-1} produced as high average 23.9 q ha^{-1} of grain yield which was significantly superior to grain yield obtained at 0-30 kg N ha^{-1}, but did not differ significantly with the grain yield obtained at 90 kg N ha^{-1}. Stover yield of pearl millet linearly increased up to 60 kg N ha^{-1}. Dahiya *et al.* (1998) reported that the yield attributes viz. effective tillers, length of ear head, number of grains per ear head and 1000-grain weight, as well as grain and stover yields of bajra increased with the increasing levels of fertility up to recommended dose of N$_{120}$ and P$_2$O$_5$ 60 kg ha^{-1}. Khistaria *et al.* (1998) conducted field experiment with cropping sequence of pearl millet where as grain and fodder yields were significantly increased by fertilizer application. Maximum grain (15.19 q ha^{-1}) and fodder (60.17 q ha^{-1}) yield of pearl millet were recorded when 100% recommendation dose (80 kg N + 40 kg P$_2$O$_5$ ha^{-1}) was applied. Limon-Ortega *et al.* (1998) observed that the *Pennisetumglaucum* was influenced by N rates from 0 and 78 kg ha^{-1}. Grain yield of bajra crop was enhanced by N application with adequate seasonal precipitation. Mishra *et al.* (1998) applied 50 to 100 per cent recommended dose of fertilizers against control. They reported that increase fertility level was not significant on 1000-grain weight of maize. In this study, grain and stover yields were significantly maximum at 100 per cent recommended levels of N_{80} P_{40} N_{40}. Raskar (1999) observed that in the sorghum crop the effect of various levels of phosphorus was significant and the magnitude being 18.93, 21.29, 21.63 and 22.53 qha^{-1} respectively, at 15, 30, 45 and 60 kg P_2O_5 ha^{-1} respectively. Similarly grain and stover yield increased significantly up to 60 kg P_2O_5 ha^{-1}. Verma and Rajput (1999). Asserted that grain yield of pearl millet increased significantly with increasing levels of nitrogen up to 120 kg N ha^{-1} during 1991-92, 1992-93 and up to 80 kg N ha^{-1} in 1990-91. On an average, application of nitrogen increase the grain yield by 74, 109 and 120 percent with 40, 80 and 120 kg N ha^{-1} respectively over control. Marked response of phosphorus application was observed up to 40 kg P_2O_5 ha^{-1} only this might be attributed to more phosphorus fixing capacity of soil of experimental plot. Ray *et al.* (2001) Find that grain and stover yield was significantly increased by increasing dose of nitrogen and phosphorus. The combined application of N and P did not show any significant effect on grain yield of finger millet, although the application of N along with @ 60 kg P ha^{-1} gave higher yield, it was at par with grain yield recorded by single application of N @ 60 kg ha^{-1}. Rathore and Sharma (2004) revealed that the application of increasing levels of N up to 80 kg ha^{-1} and P at 20 kg ha^{-1} significantly increased plant height, number of tillers m^{-1}, number of panicle m^{-1}, grain panicle^{-1} and grain and straw yields of foxtail millet. Singh and Kang (2005) revealed that the highest green fodder yield was recorded with the application of 150 kgN ha^{-1} in conjunction with recommended rate of FYM 25 tonnes ha^{-1} which was significantly higher than the FYM 25 tonnes ha^{-1}, N 50 kg ha^{-1}, FYM 25 tonnes + 50 kg N ha^{-1} and FYM 25 tonnes +100 kg N ha^{-1} during all the three years. Tanweer *et al.* (2011) conducted an experiment during Kharif season of 2009 to find out the response of maize cultivars of varying six N and P rates (0-0, 200-100, 250-125, 300-150, 350-175 and 400-200 kg/ha) were tried on two maize hybrid (YH-1898 and YH-1921) for growth and yield. Results showed that all fertilizer rates significantly increased the plant height, 1000-grain weight, grain number per ear, grains weight per ear and grains yield of both hybrids over control.

RESPONSE OF PEARL MILLET TO DIFFERENT LEVELS OF N AND P ON NPK CONCENTRATION

Payne *et al.* (1995) a field experiment was conducted in Sahel, to study the measured pearl millet N and P uptake and compared the efficiency with which N and P are used for growth under varied soil P availability.

Plant P concentration decreased strongly with plant age; added P increased stem and leaf P concentration. Plant N concentration also decreased with age, but decreased with added P.Kumpawat and Rathore (2003) a field experiment was conducted in Bhiwara, Rajasthan, to study the effect of preceding grain legume crops viz, cowpea, black gram, green gram and soyabean, with a rainy season fallow on the nitrogen requirement of succeeding wheat and their influence on growth and yield attributes, nutrient content and uptake. Nitrogen content and uptake by grain and straw increased significantly up to 160 kg N ha^{-1}, while phosphorus content and uptake only up to 120 kg N ha^{-1}. Lakhana and Gupta (2005) a field experiment was conducted in Jobner, Rajasthan, to study the response of pearl millet to nitrogen and thiourea. The nitrogen concentration in straw and phosphorus concentration in both grain and stover increased significantly with the application of 90 kg N ha^{-1}, over the lower levels. The chlorophyll content, grain yield, nitrogen content in grain and total uptake of nitrogen increased up to 60 kg N ha^{-1}. Sumeriya *et al.* (2005) reported thatapplication of N$_{80}$ + P$_{40}$ kg ha^{-1} significantly registered nitrogen content per cent in grain fodder. Singh *et al.* (2006) Afield experiment was conducted in Hisar Haryana, to study the effect of nitrogen levels on grain, stover yield, nitrogen concentration and its uptake in grain and stover of some pearl millet hybrids during kharif 2003. The highest and lowest N content and uptake in grain was recorded with significantly highest grain yield. N content and uptake in stover did not differ significantly among various pearl millet hybrids. Increasing levels of N application brought about significant improvement in nitrogen content by rain fed pearl millet. Islam *et al.* (2006) reported that concentration of P and S increased with increasing doses P and S in wheat and rice plants using three levels of P (0, 17.6, 35.2 kg ha^{-1}) and three level of S (20. 30.40 kg S ha^{-1}) for each crop. Singh *et al.* (2006) an experiment was conducted in Hisar, to evaluate varying rats of nitrogen + phosphorus on grain yield nutrient content and nutrient uptake of pearl millet. Variety HHV-94 recorded significantly higher N and P content in grain and stover. Sammauria and Yadav (2010) conducted an experiment in split plot design at Bikaner and they observed that effect of phosphorus level (0, 8.7, 17.5 and 26.2 kg ha^{-1}). Application of 26.2 kg P ha^{-1} significantly increased the content of pearl millet. Jakhar *et al.* (2011) a field experiment was conducted at College Agronomy farm, B.A. College of Agriculture, Anand Agriculture University, Anand to study the influence of levels and time of application of nitrogen on growth, yield and nitrogen uptake by pearl millet (*Pennisetum glaucum* L.) during summer. Nitrogen content in grain and stover were increased in the treatment except the treatment 50% basal + 25% foliar spray at 30 DAS + 25% foliar spray at 60 DAS (S5) as compared to other treatments of 50% basal + 25% top dressing at 30 DAS + 25% foliar spray at 45 DAS (S3) and 50% basal + 25% top dressing at 30 DAS + 25% foliar spray at 60 DAS (S$_4$).

RESPONSE OF PEARL MILLET TO DIFFERENT LEVELS OF N AND P ON NPK UPTAKE

Lal (1980) find out that application of 120 kg N and 60 kg P_2O_5 ha^{-1} significantly increased the grain and stover yields. However, the economical dose was 106.2 kg N and 54.0 kg P_2O_5 hs^{-1}. The application of potassium did not give any response. The levels of N and P significantly influenced the uptake of nitrogen, phosphorus and potassium. On an average, 120 kg level of N removed 133.69 kg N, 27.98 kg P and 169.37 kg K ha^{-1}. At 60 kg rate of P_2O_5 the uptake of N, P and K was 117.91 kg, 24.69 kg and 152.44 kg ha^{-1} respectively. The increasing level of potassium did not influence N and P uptake, but K uptake was significantly increased. Sharma (1983) reported that results indicated the significant increase in plant height, number of leaves plant^{-1} 500-grain wt. and nitrogen uptake with each successive increase in the level of fertilizer. Addition of FYM (12 t ha^{-1}) along with fertilizer levels up to 60 kg N, 30 kg P_2O_5 ha^{-1} significantly improved the growth characters and nitrogen uptake as compared to the fertilizer levels without FYM. Munda *et al.* (1984) Studied nutrient uptake pattern of hybrid pearl millet. This character was highly influenced at all the stages of growth by the levels of N and P, average uptake at maturity remained at 80.6, 7.3 and 169.0 kg ha^{-1} of N, P and K, respectively. Nitrogen and phosphorus uptake at maturity were increased by 36.6 and 65.2% due to 120 kg N and 60 kg P_2O_5 ha^{-1}, respectively over their zero levels. Potassium uptake also increased by 35.10 and 40.5% due to 120 kg N and 60 kg P_2O_5 ha^{-1}, respectively, over no application of N and P. Saini *et al.* (1985) find out N and P content in plant at different growth stages. In grain and straw these uptake increased in pearl millet with increasing rate of both applied N (0-120 kg ha^{-1}) and P_2O_5 (0-40 kg ha^{-1}). Munda *et al.* (1985) reported that application of N and P increased the uptake of N, P in pearl millet crop. Singh and Thakare (1986) studied the varietal difference in yield and nitrogen uptake in response to nitrogen rates. Most cultivars responded significantly up to 75 kg N ha^{-1}. Gaur *et al.* (1992) observed that the application of 120 kg N ha^{-1} increased the grain and stover yield by 10.8 and 11.1%. Nitrogen uptake in grain and stover by 39.0 and 32.6%, respectively, over 80 kg N ha^{-1}. Niranjan and Arya (1993) find out the highest green forage, dry matter, yield and N, P, K uptake were obtained with 100% recommended dose of inorganic fertilizer (60 kg N ha^{-1} + 40 kg P_2O_5 ha^{-1}) in forage and sorghum. Patel *et al.* (1994) conducted field experiment in summer groundnut and rainy season pearl millet crop sequence and reported that nitrogen had direct as well as residual effect on N, P and K uptake by both the crops. Direct effect of P application was noticed for N, P and K uptake by both crops, whereas its residual effect on N was observed in pearl millet crop. Venkatesh *et al.* (2002) reported that application of 60 kg P_2O_5 with 5 tones FYM and 2 tones lime ha^{-1} resulted in a significant increase in the phosphorus uptake in maize. Basavariappa *et al.* (2002) observed that 60 kg N ha^{-1} regertersd higher and uptake followed by 30 kg ha^{-1} and 0 kg ha^{-1} The values were obtained for nitrogen uptake found 43.63, 34.63 and 28.41 kg ha^{-1}. Phosphorus uptake showed similar trend along with potassium uptake. Patel and Rajgopal (2002) showed that incremental doses of P increased N and P uptake up to the highest P level 60 kg P$_2$O$_5$ ha^{-1}. The maximum value of nitrogen uptake was 88.4 and 122.9 kg ha^{-1} and phosphorus was 14.7 and 20.5 kg ha^{-1} during 1996-97, 1997-98 respectively. Khanda and Mahapatra (2003) conducted an experiment to study the effect of combined application FYM (5, 10 and 15 tone ha^{-1}) and inorganic fertilizer (75 and 100% NPK) and reported that combined application of NPK and FYM enhanced the uptake of N, P and K significantly. Arivazhagan and Ravichandran (2005) reported that the nutrient uptake in grain and straw of rice increase with the increase in the level of N and K.Tong *et al* (2007) observed that N fertilization with the rate range of 0-210 kg ha-1 significantly increased total N uptake. N content in plant increased with N rate. Karmal *et al.* (2008) bineal field experiments were conducted as C.C.S., Hisar during Kharif 2003-04 to study the effect of four levels (0, 60, 120 and 180 kg N ha^{-1}) of nitrogen. They explained that N, P and K uptake increase with increasing level of N.

CONCLUSION

Incremental doses of P increased N and P uptake up to the highest P level 60 kg P$_2$O$_5$ ha^{-1}. The maximum value of nitrogen uptake was 88.4 and 122.9 kg ha^{-1} and phosphorus was 14.7 and 20.5 kg ha^{-1} during 1996-97, 1997-98 respectively.

REFERENCES

Arora, S.K., & Patel, A.A. (2017). Effect of Fiber Blends, Total Solids, Heat Treatment, whey Protein Concentrate and Stage of Sugar Incorporation on Dietary Fiber-fortified Kheer. *Journal of Food Science and Technology*, 54(11), 3512-3520.

BISEN, P.K. Promising Partnership of Indian Youth in Development and Agricultural Entrepreneurship.

Bishnoi, K.C., & Agarwal, S.K. (1980). Response of Hybrid Bajra to Irrigation and Levels of Nitrogen. *Indian Journal of Agronomy*, 25(4), 729-730.

Choudhary, R.S., & Gautam, R.C. (2007). Effect of Nutrient-management Practices on Growth and yield of Pearl millet (Pennisetum glaucum). *Indian Journal of Agronomy*, 52(1), 64-66.

Eltayeb, A.E., Kawano, N., Badawi, G.H., Kaminaka, H., Sanekata, T., Morishima, I.,... & Tanaka, K. (2006). Enhanced Tolerance to Ozone and Drought Stresses in Transgenic Tobacco Overexpressing Dehydroascorbate Reductase in Cytosol. *Physiologia Plantarum*, 127(1), 57-65.

Gupta, S.K., Rai, K.N., Singh, P., Ameta, V.L., Gupta, S.K., Jayalekha, A. K.,... & Verma, Y.S. (2015). Seed Set Variability under High Temperatures during Flowering Period in Pearl millet (Pennisetum glaucum L.(R.) Br.). *Field Crops Research*, 171, 41-53.

Habiyaremye, C., Matanguihan, J.B., D'Alpoim Guedes, J., Ganjyal, G.M., Whiteman, M. R., Kidwell, K.K., & Murphy, K.M. (2017). Proso millet (Panicum miliaceum L.) and its Potential for Cultivation in the Pacific Northwest, US: A Review. *Frontiers in Plant Science, 7*, 1961.

Jukanti, A.K., Gowda, C.L., Rai, K.N., Manga, V.K., & Bhatt, R.K. (2016). Crops that Feed the World 11. Pearl Millet (Pennisetum glaucum L.): An Important Source of Food Security, Nutrition and Health in the Arid and Semi-arid Tropics. *Food Security, 8*(2), 307-329.

Kadrekar, S.B., & Bhosale, R.J. (1981). Nitrogen and Phosphorus Response of Finger Millet under Rainfed Conditions. *Indian Journal of Agronomy.*

Kaushik, A., Nisha, R., Jagjeeta, K., & Kaushik, C.P. (2005). Impact of Long and Short term Irrigation of a Sodic Soil with Distillery Effluent in Combination with Bioamendments. *Bioresource Technology, 96*(17), 1860-1866.

Kumar, A., Arya, R.K., Kumar, S., Kumar, D., Kumar, S., & Panchta, R.A.V.I.S.H. (2012). Advances in Pearl Millet Fodder yield and Quality Improvement through Breeding and Management Practices. *Forage Research, 38*, 1-14.

Kurlekar, V.G., & Khuspe, V.S. (1980). Correlation and Regression Studies in H-4 cotton (Gossypium hirsutum). *Research Bulletin of Marathwada Agricultural University, 4*(4), 52-55.

Mohan, S., Singh, M., & Kumar, R. (2015). Effect of Nitrogen, Phosphorus and Zinc Fertilization on yield and Quality of Kharif Fodder-A Review. *Agricultural Reviews, 36*(3), 218-226.

Munirathnam, P., & Gautam, R.C. (2002). Response of Promising Pearlmillet (Pennisetum glaucunt) Cultivars to Levels and Time of Nitrogen Application under Rainfed Conditions. *Indian Journal of Agronomy, 47*(1), 77-80.

Rao, S.V., Raju, M.V.L.N., Reddy, M.R., & Panda, A.K. (2004). Replacement of Yellow Maize with Pearl millet (Pennisetum typhoides), Foxtail millet (Setaria italica) or Finger Millet (Eleusine coracana) in Broiler Chicken Diets Containing Supplemental Enzymes. *Asian-australasian Journal of Animal Sciences, 17*(6), 836-842.

Rathore, S., Singh, K., & Kumar, V. (2016). Millet Grain Processing, Utilization and its Role in Health Promotion: A Review. *International Journal of Nutrition and Food Sciences, 5*(5), 318-329.

Srinivasarao, C.H., Venkateswarlu, B., Lal, R., Singh, A.K., Kundu, S., Vittal, K.P.R., ... & Patel, M.M. (2014). Long term Manuring and Fertilizer Effects on Depletion of Soil Organic Carbon Stocks under Pearl Millet Cluster Bean Castor Rotation in Western India. *Land Degradation & Development, 25*(2), 173-183.

Upasani, R.K., & Sharma, H.C. (1980). Response of Pearl-millet to Nitrogen Fertilization under Rainfed Condition. *Indian Journal of Agronomy, 25*(4), 727-728.

Effect of Elements on Plants
Edited by: Dr. Prasann Kumar and Dr. Pawan Kumar 'Bharti'
ISBN: 978-93-88854-44-3
Edition: 2020
Published by: Discovery Publishing House Pvt. Ltd., New Delhi (India)

Fluorine and its Effect on Crops

Prasann Kumar[1*2], Shipa Rani Dey[1]

ABSTRACT

Fluorine belongs to the halogen group of element in the periodic table and is a natural constituent of the environment and is one of 92 naturally occurring elements. It isa chemical element, a greenish, very toxic and reactive gas, composed of diatomic (two atoms) molecules, F2. When a molecule of fluorine picks up a couple of extra electronsfrom somewhere, forms two fluoride (F) ions.

Keywords: *Agriculture, Crop, Electronegativity, Fluoride, Helium, Neon.*

INTRODUCTION

It is a typicallithophilic, the most reactive and the highly electronegative element (element has extraordinary tendency to get attracted by positively charged ions like calcium) of all chemical elements and is never encountered in nature in the element form. It is a pale yellow gas which is extremely reactive. As a result it is never found free in nature but only combined with otherelements as compounds called fluorides. Fluorine readily forms compounds with allelements except two, helium and neon. Despite being the thirteenth most abundantelement with an average concentration of 0.032% by weight in the earth's crust, it is notan essential nutrient for any living thing.The main natural sources of inorganic F in soil are weathering and dissolution ofrocks and minerals, emissions from volcanoes and marine aerosols. Naturalcontamination of groundwater

[1] Department of Agronomy, School of Agriculture, Lovely Professional University, Jalandhar - 144 411 (Punjab) (India)
[2] Divison of Research and Development, Lovely Professional University, Jalandhar - 144411 (Punjab) (India)

sources of F are derived by the solvent action of water onthe rocks and the soil of the earth crust as dissolved salts is a major constraint mainly inregions characterized by arid and semiarid climates (Rao and Mamatha, 2004).In water it reacts with some of the other elements and turns into salts and gets deposited on the soil as sediments. Though, irrigation water quality, in general, is assessed through EC, SAR and RSC, the predominance of specific ion like F will not be known unless analyzed separately. The existence of a strong relationship between F- and ground water composition may serve as a proxy indicator of the potential problem of fluoride as fluorosis. This high concentration of fluoride affects all the life forms in the soil. So periodical measurement and control of the concentration of F is very important to avoid both biological and environmental damage. Fluorides are mainly present in neutral and acid igneous rocks (850-1000 mg kg-1). F could be found in a number of minerals, of which fluorite (CaF2), apatite [Ca5(Cl,F,OH)(PO4)3], topaz – Al2(F,OH)2SiO4 are stable. F can replace hydroxyl ions in different minerals and, consequently, forms fluorapatite (Ca10(PO4)6 F2), which is a common F mineral in the sediments and soils. The same trend leads to an increase of its content in primary minerals (amphiboles and micas), as well as in clay minerals (illites). Besides the principal F containing mineral in a soil, there are also other minerals, such as: fluorspar, cryolyte (Na3AlF6), AlF3 and Al2(SiF6)2 (Natarajan and Murthy, 1974). The average content of total F for "world soils" amounts to 320 mg kg-1. The lowest amounts are found in sandy soils in humid climate, while the highest ones are found in soils with high clay content and soils formed on igneous rocks. For most soils, the content of total F ranges from 150 to 400 mg kg-1 F (Pendias and Pendias, 1984). In India totally 29 states have been reported as F affected areas but severe problem occurred in the states of Telangana, Andhra Pradesh, Tamilnadu, Gujarat, Rajasthan and Madhya Pradesh (Kishore and Hanumantharao, 2010). The F content in groundwater of Indian aquifers varies from <1 to 25 mg L-1. Higher F content in ground waters not only poses problems to human health but also has negative impact on crop production. The granitic rocks of Nalgonda region possess F content (325 to 3200 mg kg-1) higher than the world average concentration of F in granitic rocks (810 mg kg-1). The major rock type of this area is granite gneisses. Assessment of the granite gneisses from Nalgonda showed the presence of F containing minerals such as fluorite (0-3.3%), biotite (0.1-1.7%) and hornblende (0.1-1.1%) (Reddy *et al.*, 2009). Since some F compounds in the earth's upper crust are soluble in water, F is found in both surface waters and groundwater. In surface freshwater, however, F concentrations are usually low (0.01 to 0.3 mg L-1). In groundwater, the natural concentration of F depends on the geological, chemical and physical characteristics of the aquifer, the porosity and acidity of the soil and rocks, the temperature, the action of other chemical elements and the depth of wells. Because of the large number of variables, the F concentrations in groundwater can range from 1.0 mg L-1to more than 35.0 mg L-1. During the decomposition of igneous rocks, F forms bonds with silicates, which leads to its high content in the residuum. Under natural conditions, fluorapatite and phosphorite have very low solubility, while cryoliteand similar minerals are easily soluble. Clays and phosphorite absorb fastly the soluble F. Clay minerals, soil pH andCa, P and Al concentrations in soil control F content in a soil solution. Adsorption of F ina soil is highest at acid and neutral reaction (pH=6-7). Anthropogenic sources of F into the environment include the coal combustion and waste from various industrial processes, including steel manufacture, primary Al, Cu and Ni production, phosphate ore processing, petroleum refining, glass, brick and ceramic manufacturing, and glue and adhesive production (Sloof *et al.*, 1989), use of chemicals such as, Hydrogen fluoride (HF), Calcium fluoride (CaF2), Sodium fluoride (NaF), Fluorosilicic acid (H2SiF6), Sodium hexafluorosilicate (Na2SiF6), Sulfurhexafluoride (SF6), *etc.* Production of Phosphate fertilizers by using rock phosphates (3.5% F) are the major sources of F contamination of agricultural soils. The uses of Fcontainingpesticides as well as the fluoridation of drinking-water supplies also contribute to the release of F from anthropogenic sources (Low and Bloom, 1988). F can form complex ions with aluminum (AlF2+, AlF2 +, AlF4 -), so it can control the activity of Al3+ ions in a soil solution. Under ordinary conditions, F has a low mobility in a soil and does not accumulate in upper soil horizons, especially in acid soils, which is more soluble and susceptible to greater leaching. F content in different soils is determined by its concentration in a parent material, while its distribution in soil profile depends on the rate of mineral decomposition, pH and content of the clay fraction (Omueti and Jones, 1980). Endemic fluorosis caused by F in the environment is a global geochemical disease. At present Telangana state is facing major problem with F pollution because ground water is used as drinking and an irrigation source, a natural occurrence of excessive amounts of F levels in ground water. Nalgonda is the worst effected district with a presence of excess F in ground water in the state of Telangana. In spite of continuous efforts by the government, external support agencies, NGOs and private enterprises the problem still remains unsolved. There are 59 mandals with 1175 Gram panchayats and about 3100 habitations in the district. Nalgonda, Prakasham, Khammam, Anantapur districts of Telangana and Andhra Pradesh are facing F hazards. Plants take it up from the soil and from the air. From the soil, F is transmitted through fine hair rootlets into the stems, and some reaches the leaves. Plants absorb more F from sandy than from clay soil and more from wet and acid soils than from dry and alkaline ones. High concentrations of F in the irrigation water causes necrosis and chlorosis of leaves, reduction in growth of root and shoots, and ultimately reduces the yield of crop. In addition, F in mesophyll cells disturbs mineral metabolism, reduces chlorophyll pigments, and alters other morphological and physiological parameters such as height, number of leaves, biomass productivity, fruiting, and yield of the plant (Gautam and Bhardwaj, 2010). Concentration of F in plants is very low and has no correlation with its total content in a soil. Because of that, so far fluorine toxicity to animals and plants has not been recorded. It is generally believed that the F contaminates drinking water source andtransfer of F from soil to plant parts by accumulation and enter into food chain. Earlier it was observed that food was not a rich source of F, but it is now documented that certain types of food can have high F content in Telangana by continuous practice of irrigation using ground water containing high F.

SOURCES OF FLUORIDE

The main sources of F are water, air, soil and rocks. F is estimated to be thirteenth in abundance among the elements of the earth. Fluorides are released into the environment naturally through the weathering and dissolution of minerals. Higher F content in ground waters not only poses problems to human health but also has negative impact on crop production. The existence of a strong relationship between F and ground water composition may serve as a proxy indicator of the potential problem of F.

FLUORIDE CONTENT AND OTHER PARAMETERS OF IRRIGATION WATER

The concentrations of F in the ground water samples in different states of India are reviewed. The groundwater quality of SwetaNadi, Vellar River by Suresh *et al.* (2014) reported that the pH ranged between 6.80 and 9.50 with a mean of 8.42 and EC was found to be from 330 to 3870 with a mean of 1594.26 µS cm-1. And also other parameters like Ca+2, Mg+2, Na+, HCO3 -, CO3 2-, SO4 2-, RSC and SAR varies from 14 to 136, 19 to 258, 10 to 598, 73 to 573, 0 to 72, 10 to 528, -18.81 to 3.14 mg L-1 and 0.21 to 9.98, respectively with the mean values of 73.71, 82.79, 155.15, 277.74, 16.77, 84.72, -3.70 mg L-1 and 3.12, respectively. Kishore and Hanumantharao (2010) analyzedthe concentration of F in water samples belonging to 22 villages of Tipparthy revenue sub division of Nalgonda district. The F concentration was found to be from 1.4 to 4.5 mg L-1, 1.57 to 3.02 mg L- 1 and 1.06 to 3.02 mg L-1, in hand pump, bore well and open well water samples respectively. 14 water samples from bore well, 19 from hand pump, 5 samples from open well water was fallen within the range of 1.50 to 4.50 mg L-1 concentration of F ion, but only one from bore well, 3 from open well water samples having less than 1.5 mg L-1 concentration. Especially higher concentrations were observed in bore well and hand pump water. The higher concentration of F ion in all water sources may arise due to the nature of rock and soil formation. F is found in all natural water at different concentrations depending on the geology, chemistry, physical characteristics and climate of the area. In groundwater, however, low or high concentrations of F can occur, depending on the nature of rocks, and the occurrence of F bearing minerals. High F concentrations may be expected in groundwater from calcium poor aquifers and in areas where F bearing minerals are common (Weinstein and Davison, 2004). Reddy *et al.* (2009) reported that the granitic rocks of Nalgonda region possess total F content (325 to 3200 ppm) higher than the world average concentration of F ingranitic rocks (810 ppm). The major rock type of this area is granite gneisses.Assessment of the granite gneisses from Nalgonda showed the presence of F containing minerals such as fluorite (0.0 to 3.3%), biotite (0.1 to 1.7%) and hornblende (0.1 to 1.1%). Most of the ground water in parts of Nalgonda district is alkaline in nature (6.3vto 9.3). Higher alkalinity of ground water activates leaching of F and thus increase concentration of F ions in ground water. Brindha *et al.* (2010a) reported that the F concentrations in groundwater samples varied from 0.1 to 8.8 mg L-1 in Nalgonda district. Nearly 29.5% of the groundwater samples have F content greater than that of the maximum permissible limit of 1.5 mg L-1 while 15.8% of the samples possessed F less than the minimumvrequired limit of 0.6 mg L-1. Possible source of F in groundwater are weathering andvleaching of F bearing minerals from the basement granitic rocks of this region under alkaline environment. The total F concentration in granite rock samples collected from a nearby area to be ranging from 242 to 990 mg kg-1. The surface, subsurface and thermal water samples were analyzed by Sharmav(2003) and identified the F concentration ranging from 0.2 to 18 ppm in the states of Jammu and Kashmir, 0.2 to 6.5 ppm in Himachal Pradesh, 0.2 to 0.6 ppm in Haryana,v0.35 to 15 ppm in Bihar, on an average 12 ppm in West Bengal, 15 to 20 ppm in Chattisgarh, 8.2 to 13.2 ppm in Orissa and 0.7 to 6.0 in Maharashtra, indicating that except in Haryana, the concentration of F is very high up to 20 ppm. Probable source of high F in Indian water seems to be that during weathering and circulation of water in rocks and soils, fluorine is leached out and dissolved in groundwater. A study of the water quality condition of Tonk district, Rajasthan was conducted by Yadav *et al.* (2009) and revealed that the ground water of Tonk district is contaminated with fluorides by natural F rich rock salt system. The 110 villages of Tonk district have high F concentration in water (i.e. >1.5 mg L-1). It has been observed that 58.19% of villages have F concentration of water ranging from 1.5 to 3.0 mg L-1 and 30% villages have 3.0 to 6.0 mg L-1 of F, while 12% village have more than 6.0 mgL-1 of F. The geochemical study was carried by Gautam *et al.* (2011) in 27 villages of Eastern, South Eastern and Southern zone of Nawa tehsil in Nagaur district of Rajasthan. The F concentration in the three different zones ranged from 0.64 to 14.62mg L-1 where 13.04% samples were found within permissible limit while 86.96% had F beyond permissible limit (> 1.5 mg L-1). It was found that among the three different zones south-eastern zone was under serious F contamination where F concentration ranged between 1.10 to 14.62 mg L-1. In the eastern zone F concentration was recorded from 1.52 to 5.13 mg L-1 whereas in the southern zone it was found between 0.64 to 3.63 mg L-1. Rao and Mamatha (2004) reported that the groundwater with high F content is found mostly in calcium-deficient groundwater in many basement aquifers, such as granite and gneiss. Seventeen states in India have been identified as endemic to fluorosis due to abundance in naturally occurring F-bearing minerals. Three major sources of F are fluorspars, rock phosphates and phosphorites. Because of differences in geo-chemical conditions in aquifers and differences in contact period between groundwater and F-bearing rocks, the F content in groundwater of Indian aquifers varies from < 1 ppm up to 25 ppm. Yet, another factor contributing to excess F in groundwater is the over-exploitation of groundwater resources for agricultural and drinking water purposes. In Patan district of Gujarat, the F values were found to be from 1.88 to 6.80 ppm in winter, 1.89 to 6.84 ppm in summer, 1.88 to 6.84 ppm in monsoon and 1.82 to 6.81 ppm in post monsoon. Maximum value was observed during summer and minimum value was observed during post-monsoon in almost all the groundwater samples (Paya and Bhatt, 2010). The variation of F is dependent on a variety of factors such as amount of soluble and insoluble F in source rocks, the duration of contact of water with rocks and soil temperature, rainfall, oxidation- reduction process (Mahapatra *et al.*, 2005). Excessive F concentrations were reported by Meenakshi and Maheshwari (2006) in ground waters of more than 20 developed and developing countries including India where 19 states are facing acute fluorosis problems. In India, it was first detected in Nellore district of Andhra Pradesh in 1937. It has been observed that low calciumand high bicarbonate alkalinity favour high F content in groundwater. Water with high F content is generally soft and having high pH.Weathering of rocks and evaporation of groundwater are responsible for high F concentration in groundwater of Agra as reported by Sharma *et al.* (2011). Based on the concentration of F, the groundwater samples obtained from the study area have beenclassified into four groups as low (0.1 to 0.6 mg L-1), medium (0.6 to 1.5 mg L-1), high (1.5 to 3 mg L-1) and very high (> 3 mg L-1). It was found that the concentration of F in 80% of the total 180 groundwater samples did not fall within the desirable range of 0.6 to 1.5 mg L-1 of F. F in groundwater of this region is mainly due to dissolution from Fbearingminerals like fluorspar, fluorite etc. Raju *et al.* (2009) identified 47% of samples had high F content than the maximum permissible limit (1.5 mg L-1) in Kachnarwa region of Sonbhadra district, Uttar Pradesh. The highest F concentration was found to corroborate with low calcium values and high sodium content in the groundwater. Weathering and leaching of fluorine- bearing minerals in rock formations under alkaline environment lead to the enrichment of F in the groundwater. Ramanaiah *et al.* (2006) determined F concentrations varied between 0.5 and 9.0 mg L-1 in surface and ground water samples in eight villages of Prakasham district, which is the second-most severely affected district after Nalgonda district. Groundwater samples contained high concentrations of fluorides compared to open well and pond water samples, which could be a major source of F in water since the geological formation of this area consists of fluorite and fluoropatite. Brindha *et al.* (2010b) analyzed F concentration in groundwater collected from 45 wells in Nalgonda and reported that the F concentration in groundwater ranged from 0.1 to 8.8 mg L-1 with a mean of 3.1 mg L-1. About 52% of the samples collected were suitable for human consumption. However, 18% of the samples were having less than the required limit of 0.6 mg L-1, and 30% of the samples possessed high concentration of F, *i.e.,* above 1.5 mg L-1. Weathering of rocks and evaporation of groundwater are responsible for high F concentration in groundwater apart from anthropogenic activities including irrigation which accelerates weathering of rocks. The use of water containing relatively low (< 3.1 mg L-1) levels of F for crop irrigation generally does not increase foodstuff F concentrations (Schamschula *et al.*, 1988). However, this is dependent on plant species and F concentrations in soil and water. Kabasakalis and Tsolaki (1994) showed that F concentrations in vegetables irrigated with water containing 10 mg L-1 F were increased compared with F concentrations in vegetables grown with irrigation water containing low Fconcentrations (0.15 mg L-1). They also commented that F has a tendency toaccumulate in the vegetable leaves rather than in the fruits. According to Murthy (1974) investigation, the F content in both surface vagu(canal) and ground water around Huzurabad of Karimnagar district of Telangana as 3.8 and 5.5 mg L-1, respectively. Krupanidhi (1973) reported that maximum concentration of F in groundwater of Anantapur district of Andhra Pradesh as 12 mg L-1. Singh and Dass (1993) have reported very high F contents (1.5 to 13.0 mg L-1) in the groundwater of areas surrounding Delhi. Rao (1974) observed that the F content of well waters of Nandigama, Krishna district of Andhra Pradesh varied from 1.0 to 8.0 mg L-1- and the areas were underlain by granites and gneisses intruded by dolerites. Adhikary *et al.* (2014) found that the F was varied between 0.22 and 5.12 with mean of 0.89 ppm, in groundwater samples of Delhi. F concentrations of Vellar river water were varied between 0.06 and 1.42 with the mean value of 0.89 (Suresh *et al.*, 2014). The investigation conducted by Munusamy *et al.* (2014) in Nellore district of Andhra Pradesh in the region of Udayagiri Taluk villages having high F concentration in drinking water. They are

4.01 (Turkapalli), and 4.00 (Pakeerpalem), 6.74 (Varikuntapadu), 2.92 (Bijjampalli), 2.37 (Masipeta), 2.98 (Singareddypalli), 3.47 (Bodabanda), 5.12 (Kolangadipalli), 4.43 (Gangireddypalli) and 3.12 ppm (Basinepalli). The F contamination in the South-Eastern part of Rangareddy district, in Andhra Pradesh. The endemic district of Andhra Pradesh has indicated that the F rich ground water present in the wells located downstream water and close to the surface water is getting low F. F concentration in 8 villages of surface and groundwater samples containing thirty eight samples varied from 0.5 and 9.0 mg L-1 (Munusamy *et al.*, 2014). Munusamy *et al.* (2014) explained about various factors that govern the release ofF in to water from F-bearing minerals are (i) the chemical composition of the water, (ii) the presence and accessibility of F minerals to water, and (iii) the contact time between the source mineral and water. Overall water quality (e.g., pH, hardness, and ionic strength) also plays an important role by influencing mineral solubility, complexation and sorption/exchange reactions. Jinwal and Dixit (2008) reported that ground water with pH was found to bealkaline in nature in most of the samples ranged between 7.0 to 8.5 and 7.1 to 8.5 inpost and pre-monsoons, respectively in Bhopal area. EC was found varying from 240 to 1490 mmho cm-1 and 357 to 1150 mmho cm-1 in post and pre-monsoon, respectively.Alkalinity, hardness and chloride concentrations was found in the range of 40 to 528, 72 to 380 and 18 to170 mg L-1, respectively in post monsoon and 68 to 584, 140 to 620 and 26 to 206 mg L-1, respectively in pre monsoon. The sulphate and sodium contentswere under the limit prescribed by BIS in both the seasons. Alkaline water may decrease the solubility of metals. The alkalinity varies in accordance with the fluctuation in the pollution load. Subramanian *et al.* (2011) reported that the hydro-chemical parameters of groundwater in Tirunelveli district were found to be neutral to alkaline in nature with pH ranging from 7.1 to 8.6 with an average of 7.82 and 7.74 in pre and post-monsoons, respectively. Ca+2, Mg+ 2 and chloride concentration was found in the range of 31 to 344, 4 to 150 and 25 to 1106 mg L-1, respectively in post monsoon and 8 to 477, 7 to 347 and 25 to 1489 mg L-1, respectively in pre monsoon. A study was carried out by to assess the F contamination and hydrogeochemical characterization of groundwater indicated that quality of groundwater samples in terms of total soluble salts (ECiw) was in the range of 1.28-11.40 and 1.16- 8.19 dS m-1 in pre and post monsoon seasons, respectively. F concentration ranged from 0.14 to 3.28 mg L-1 and 0.12 to 3.25 mg L-1 with mean values of 1.21 and 1.20 mg L-1 in pre and post monsoon seasons, respectively (Gurjar *et al.*, 2013). The spatial variation of groundwater quality index indicates that overall quality of Delhi groundwater is acceptable for irrigation and drinking, while highly polluted groundwater zones are mainly found at the Western part. Approximately,

76.44 and 89.14% area of Delhi have groundwater suitable for irrigation and drinking purposes, respectively (Adhikary *et al.*, 2014). FAO (2003) proposed modified groundwater quality index for irrigation water. The maximum permissible limit for electrical conductivity is 3 dS m-1, sodium adsorption ratio is 20, bicarbonate is 8.5 me L-1, chloride is 10 me L-1 and magnesium/calcium ratio is 3 to determine overall water quality for irrigation.

INTERACTION OF FLUORIDE WITH OTHER PARAMETERS OF WATER

A strong negative correlation between Ca and F in the groundwater thatcontains Ca in excess of that required for the solubility of F minerals. If calcium is present in higher concentrations it is most effective in reducing the F concentrations. Due to low F solubility, hardness showed negative correlation with F content. Increasing concentration of F in the ground water causes decrease in hardness, while alkalinity increased (Gautam *et al.*, 2011). The toxicity of F is also influenced by high ambient temperature, alkalinity, Caand Mg contents in the water. Rock minerals weather to form Ca and Mg carbonates, which serve as good sink for F ions. However, it is the leachable state of F ions that determines the water F levels. The leachability is governed by pH of the draining solutions and dissolved carbon dioxide in the soil (Latha *et al.*, 1994). Saxena and Ahmed (2001) observed that the pH value of groundwater varies from 7.0 to 7.7, indicating an alkaline condition which favours the solubility of fluorine bearing minerals. In acidic medium, F is adsorbed on clay and in alkaline medium, it is desorbed and thus alkaline pH is more favourable for F dissolution activity. Generally, high concentration of sodium will increase the solubility of F-bearing minerals in the water. Ramanaiah *et al.* (2006) studied the relation between F concentration and other physicochemical parameters of Prakasham district. They reported that the TDS showed good correlation (r2 - 0.61) followed by EC (r2 - 0.36), total hardness (R2 - 0.12), chloride (R2 - 0.06) and sulfate (R2 - 4 × 10-5). The principal ions contributing TDS are carbonate, bicarbonate, chlorides, fluorides, sulphates, nitrates, sodium, potassium, calcium and magnesium. Another factor significantly contributing to excess F concentration in the ground water samples may be attributed to the depletion in water table. Brindha *et al.* (2010b) analyzed F concentration in groundwater collected from 45 wells in Nalgonda and reported that the pH of groundwater of this area varied from 6.3 to 9.3 with a mean of 7.5. The pH of groundwater shows slight increase withincrease in F concentration. This indicates that the F content of groundwater will vary due to the changes in alkalinity, i.e., carbonate and bicarbonate content. Also, the F content of groundwater has an inverse relationship with calcium and magnesium content. The average F content and its relation with its chemical composition in semiarid tracts of Northern

Karnataka were reported by Hebbara *et al.* (2010). The results indicated that the average F content increased with increasing pH (r=0.26) while remained independent of soluble salt content. The cations viz. Ca+2 and Mg+2 showed inverse relationship with F. Calcium was more significantly related to F (r = -0.20) than Mg+2 (r = -0.13), while F content remained largely unaffected by the Na+ content. The F content increased with increasing SAR, probably due to increased solubility. Groundwater with higher pH, SAR and RSC values are likely to have a higher F content in irrigation water while a higher Ca may decrease the F content. Paya and Bhatt (2010) observed relationship between F and other ionic properties and found that F is inversely related with Ca2+ and positively related with HCO3-, whereas the correlation coefficient between F and other ions is very poor during both seasons. The positive correlation of pH with F indicates that alkaline groundwater is likely to have a higher amount of F, suggesting that the pH of the groundwater is more important in determining the concentration of F. The high F groundwater is generally associated with high bicarbonate values and low calcium contents. Groundwater in the sodium bicarbonate (Na–HCO3) type always has very high F contents. The combination of F and sodium forms water-soluble salt, the content of F ion increases relatively due to the containment of sodium in groundwater, the opportunity for sedimentation of calcium fluoride (CaF2) is greatly decreased (Gupta *et al.*, 2005). Rao (2003a) identified the possible sources of F as weathering and leaching of F bearing minerals under the alkaline environment. A high rate of evapo-transpiration, comparatively low rainfall, intensive irrigation and heavy use of fertilizers, alkaline environment, longer residence time of water in the weathered aquifer zone and low rate of dilution are favorable factors for the dissolution of fluorine bearing minerals and thereby increase of F concentration in the groundwater. A significantly positive correlation has been observed between F and sodium. More over the decreasing trend of calcium concentration is indicative of calcite precipitation which increases F solubility in groundwater thus in turn increasing F concentration in ground water. A positive relationship with pH indicates towards apossible leaching of F under high alkaline conditions of water. This is because of the similarity between the ionic radius of fluoride (F-) ion and hydroxyl ion (OH-) thereby replacing each other at higher pH (Chakrabarty and Sarma, 2011). In dilute solutions at neutral pH, dissolved fluorides are predominantly present as the F ion. As the pH decreases below 5.5, the proportion of F ions decreases, and the proportion of non-dissociated hydrogen fluoride increases. However, if sufficient aluminium is present in solution, aluminium–fluoride complexes (AlF2+, AlF2+ and AlF3) generally dominate below pH 5.5 until 1.0, where hydrogen fluoride begins to dominate as pH decreases further (Parker *et al.*, 1995). Thergaonkar and Kulkarni (1971) reported that a positive correlation occurred between the alkalinity and fluorides of ground waters and that probability of occurrence of alkalinity/fluoride ratio of the range 50 to 100 associated with 2.0 to 4 .0 mg L-1 of F. In high F waters, there existed positive linear relationship between F and HCO3-, negative relationship between F and Ca+2, Mg+2 (Ramgopal *et al.*, 1981). Rajgopal and Tobin (1991) suggested that in general, the F content of ground water increases with depth.

FLUORIDE STATUS AND OTHER PROPERTIES OF SOIL

F represents about 0.06 0.09 per cent of the earth's crust. The average crustal abundance is 300 mg kg 1. F is found at significant levels in a wide variety of minerals, including fluorite (CaF2), cryolite (AlF6Na3), hornblende-Ca3 Na (Mg, Fe)6 (Al, Fe)3 (Si4O11)4 (OH)4 F2), mica ((K, Na, Ca)2 (Al, Mg, Fe)4 6 Si8)O20(OH,F)4), apatite(Ca5(PO4)3F), and others. Fluorite is a common F mineral of low solubility occurring in both igneous and sedimentary rocks (Fawell *et al.*, 2006). F is a component of most types of soil with total concentrations ranging from 20 to 1000 µg g-1 in areas without natural phosphate or F deposits and up to several thousand micrograms per gram in mineral soils with deposits of F (Davidson, 1983). The clay and organic carbon content as well as the pH of soil are primarily responsible for the origin and/or retention of F in soils. F in soil is primarily associated with the soil colloid or clay (Omueti and Jones, 1977). Available F concentration in soil samples was also quite variable from village tovillage. It was maximum (1.82 mg kg-1) in Jagatpur and minimum (0.75 mg kg-1) inBarwala village in Alipur block of Delhi with a mean value of 1.31 mg kg-1 in pre monsoon and 1.29 mg kg-1 in post-monsoon season. Wide variation in F concentration in the soils suggests possible contribution from both point as well as non point sources. Although there is no firm evidence yet, brick kilns appear to be a major point source for very high level of F in groundwater as well as irrigated soils. The higher values of F in irrigated soils may be due to natural presence of F in the soils (Gurjar *et al.* 2012). The main natural source of inorganic fluorides in soil is the parent rock. During weathering, some F minerals (Cryolite or Na3AlF6) are rapidly broken down, especially under acidic conditions. Other minerals, such as fluorapatite (Ca5 (PO4)3F) and calcium F are dissolved more slowly. The mineral fluorophlogopite (mica; KMg3 (AlSi3O10) F2) is stable in alkaline and calcareous soils. However, its solubility is affected by pH and the activities of silicic acid (H4SiO4), aluminium, potassium and magnesium ions (Okibe *et al.*, 2010). Reddy *et al.* (2009) recognized the high concentrations of F (up to 7.6 mg kg-1) in Wailapally granitic aquifer of Nalgonda District. Average water soluble F concentration in different profiles varies from 0.5 to 10 mg kg-1 and within the profile the variation is 2-4 times the average concentration. Average water soluble F in the depth profile at Dubbagadda Tanda is 0.5 mg kg-1, although it increases slightly with depth (0.2-0.8 mg kg-1). Total F concentration in the profile average is 626 mg kg-1 F with relatively little variation. Therefore water soluble F represents less than 0.1% of the total. F concentration in the groundwater around this site is 3.7 mg L-1. Begum (2012) analyzed water and soil samples from 5 agricultural locations across Mysore district that represented different soil types in the region. Mean water extractable soil F concentration from a depth of 5 to 20 cm in each location was in the range, sandy (3-1.9 mg L-1), black (4-2.3 mg L-1), laterite (4.5-3.6 mg L-1), alluvial (9-6.3 mg L-1) and red loam (11.2-7.9 mg L-1). F in the groundwater in the experimental location is in the range 25.5 mg L-1 for sandy soil and 1.5 mg L-1 for loam soil. Factors that influence the mobility of inorganic fluorides in soil are pH and the formation of stable aluminium and calcium complexes. In acidic soils, concentrations of inorganic fluorides were considerably higher in the deeper horizons. The low affinity of fluorides for organic material results in leaching from the acidic surface horizon and increased retention by clay minerals and silts in the more alkaline deeper horizons. This distribution profile is not observed in either alkaline or saline soils. The fate of inorganic fluorides released to soil also depends on the chemical form, rate of deposition, soil chemistry and climate (Mishra *et al.*, 2009). A geochemical survey conducted by Jakovljevic *et al.* (2002) in soils of Northern Pomoravlje and revealed that the highest average amount of total F was found in alluvial soils (391mg kg-1) than other soils. The available F content was very low (<1 mg kg-1) being mostly less than 0.2% from its total amount. So it could be concluded that there was no danger from F accumulation in the plants. The total and available F contents have mostly been in the positive correlation with soil pH and the mechanical fraction silt + clay. Highly acid soils normally contain high amounts of Al and Fe hydroxides.

CONCLUSION

When F is added to these soils, OH- ions are released in relatively higher concentrations than from soils containing fewer amounts of these hydroxyl minerals. Accordingly, HF addition is expected to be less effective in decreasing the pH of these acid soils. On the other hand, alkaline calcareous soils have high content of carbonates which can neutralize the added H+ ions. Expectedly, the addition of P decreased the pH for the three (acid, neutral and alkaline) soils. It appears that H3PO4 addition along with HF has an accumulative effect on H+ concentration in these soils. This suggests the absence of any interaction between P and F in soils that may enhance or inhibit each one effect on the pH (Jackson, 1969). Phosphorus addition released a part of the native F from the acid, neutral and alkaline soils. The amount of F released ranged from 0.135 to 1.860 mg kg-1 soil. The magnitude of F released from the soils followed this trend: alkaline soil > acid soil >neutral soil. This trend could be explained by the effect of P addition on the pH of the three soils. The amount of F released is decreasing with the increase in P addition. This effect could be explained by reactions between P and F and the formation of insoluble F minerals. The results show that most of F added to the soils was sorbed by the solid phase. The amount of F sorbed ranged between 74.0 and 96.3%. The alkaline soil shows relatively higher F sorbing capacity than the acid and neutral soil. The formationof insoluble F minerals may be enhanced by the addition of P to the soils (Elrashidi *et al.*, 1998).

REFERENCES

Brindha, K., Rajesh, P., Murugan, P and Elango, L. 2010b. Fluoride Contamination in Groundwater in Parts of Nalgonda District, Andhra Pradesh, India. *Environmental Monitoring Assessment*. DOI 10.1007/s10661-010-1348-0.

Chakrabarty, S and Sarma, H.P. 2011. Fluoride Geochemistry of Groundwater in Parts of Brahmaputra Flood Plain in Kamrup District, Assam, India. *Archives of Applied Science Research*. 3(3): 37-44.

Chakraborti, D. 2000. Fluorosis in Assam, India. *Current Science*. 78: 1421-1423.

Chapman, H.D. 1965. Cation-exchange Capacity. In: C.A. Black (ed.). Methods of Soil Analysis - Chemical and Microbiological Properties. *Agronomy*. 9: 891-901.

Chatterjee, M.K and Mohabey, N.K. 1998. Potential Fluorosis Problems Around Chandidongri, Madhya Pradesh, India. *Environmental Geochemistry and Health*. 20: 1-4.

Chaudhary, D.R., Ghosh, A and Patolia, J.S. 2006. Characterization of Soils in the Tsunami Affected Coastal Areas of Tamil Nadu for Agronomic Rehabilitation. *Current Science*. 91(1): 99-104.

Chaudhary, V., Sharma, M and Yadav, B.S. 2009. Elevated Fluoride in Canal Catchment Soils of Northwest Rajasthan, India. *Fluoride*. 42(1): 46-69.

*Chesnin, L and Yien, C.H. 1951. Turbidometric Determination of Available Sulphates. *Soil Science Society of America Proceedings*. 14: 149-151.

Chhabra, R., Singh, A and Abrol, I.P. 1980. Fluorine in Sodic Soils. *Soil Science Society of American Journal*. 44: 33-36.

Chinoy, N.J. 1992. Studies on Effects of Fluoride in 36 Villages of Mehsana District, North Gujarat. *Fluoride*. 25: 101-110.

Cholak, J. 1959. Fluorides: A Critical Review. The Occurrence of Fluoride in Air, Food and Water. *Journal of Occupational Medicine*. 1: 501-511.

Choubisa, S.L., Sompura, K., Bhatt, S.K., Choubisa, D.K., Pandya, H., Joshi, S.C and Choubisa, L. 1996. Prevalence of Fluorosis in some Villages of Dungarpur District of Rajasthan. *Indian Journal of Environmental Health*. 38: 119-126.

Cooke, J.A., Jhonson, M.S and Davison, A.W. 1976. Uptake and Translocation of Fluoride in *Helianthus annuus* L. grown in Sand Culture. *Fluoride*. 11: 76-88.

Das, S., Mehta, B.C., Samantha, S.K., Das, P.K and Srivastava, S.K. 2000. Fluoride Hazards in Groundwater of Orissa, India. *Indian Journal of Environmental Health*. 1: 40-46.

Effect of Elements on Plants
Edited by: Dr. Prasann Kumar and Dr. Pawan Kumar 'Bharti'
ISBN: 978-93-88854-44-3
Edition: 2020
Published by: Discovery Publishing House Pvt. Ltd., New Delhi (India)

Heavy Metal Stress
An Overview

Poonam Kumari[1], Prasann Kumar[2]

ABSTRACT

Heavy metals are metallic elements having high density as compared to water Heavy metals uptake, by the plants using phytoremediation technique, this is a very convenient way to remediate environment from these heavy metals. Toxicity is a function of solubility. In soluble compounds as well as the metallic form often exhibit negligible toxicity. The ligands depends upon the toxicity of metals. Treating heavy metals with this phytoremediation technique gives a brief information which shows the uptake mechanisms of heavy metals on plants this will give some description about the heavy metal uptake by plant, and also provide knowledge of arsenic (As), lead (Pb), Mercury (Hg) toxicity in plants.

Keywords: *Agriculture, Contamination, Degradation, Environment, Phytoremediation, Trace.*

INTRODUCTION

Heavy metals are mostly contaminated in the environment and causes harmful effect to the environment. These heavy metals are difficult to remove, for that various techniques are used in fate to get rid from these heavy metals. Nowdays, a very effective and improved technique is used to remove the active and in active metals from the affected environment, soil, water etc. This technique is environmental friendly. Heavy m. and

[1]Department of Agronomy, School of Agriculture, Lovely Professional University, Jalandhar - 144 411 (Punjab) (India)

[1,2] Division of Research and Development, Lovely Professional University, Jalandhar - 144 411 (Punjab) (India)

that technique is known as phyto remediation. Heavy metals are those elements whose density is five times greater than that of water, has high atomic weight and these metals occurs naturally. It is spread due to its use in agriculture, household, industrial purposes which effects the surrounding environment as well as health of animals as well as human beings. Gender, age are the main factors on which the toxicity of element depends. Elements show high toxicity are arsenic, chromium, cadmium, lead, and mercury. Heavy metals are also known as trace elements because they are present in trace concentrations (ppb to less than 10ppm) in various environmental conditions. The heavy metal releases physiological and biochemical functions in human beings and plants. With translocation, bio accumulation processes occurs in phyto remediation helps in declining the toxicity of heavy metals from plants. (Hinchman *et.al*,1995).

TOXICITY

Toxicity is characterized as the degree at which compound substances or blend of substances can harm a life form. It can allude with the impact on entire living being, for example, plant, microscopic organisms, creature (David S.Cloud). Impact of poisonous quality are portion dependent. Substantial metals are characterized as the components having thickness more prominent than 5 g cm^{-3}. Some substantial metals to be specific, cobalt (Co), copper (Cu), iron (Fe), manganese (Mn), molybdenum (Mo), nickel (Ni) and zinc (Zn) are viewed as fundamental for plants). Metal solvency and bioavailability to plant is primarily impacted by the concoction properties of soil, for example, soil pH, stacking rate, cation trade limit, redox potential, soil surface, earth substance and natural issue (Williams *et al.* 1980; Logan and Chaney 1983; Verloo and Eeckhout 1990). By and large, higher the mud or potentially natural issue and soil pH, the metals will be undoubtedly soil with longer home time and will be less bioavailable to plants. Soil temperature too is a significant calculate representing varieties metal amassing by harvests (Chang *et al.* 1987). Fermentation of the rhizosphere and exudation of carboxylates are viewed as potential intends to improve metal gathering. Overwhelming metals are caught by root cells of the plants after their assembly in the dirt, and their development in the dirt depends mostly upon: (I) dissemination of metal components along the focus slope which is framed because of take-up of components and subsequently consumption of the component in the root region; (ii) capture by roots, where soil volume is dislodged by root volume in the wake of developing, and (iii) progression of metal components from mass soil arrangement down the water potential angle (Marschner 1995). The take-up of metals, both by roots and leaves, increments with expanding metal fixation in the outer medium. In any case, the take-up has no straight connection with expanding fixation. This is chiefly on the grounds that the metals bound in the tissue cause immersion that is administered by the rate at which the metal is taken up. The take-up productivity of metals by the plants (or gathering factor) is most elevated at their low fixations in the outer medium. The vast majority of the metal components are insoluble in the vascular arrangement of plants and unfit to move unreservedly, -418.36thus as a rule structure sulfate, phosphate or carbonate accelerates immobilizing them in apoplastic (extracellular) and symplastic (intracellular) AQ1 compartments (Raskin *et al.* 1997).

SOURCES OF HEAVY METALS

The toxic elements can be air borne or may reach soil through native rocks mining operations or get applied to agricultural land as impurities of agricultural inputs such as fertilizers manures fungicides waste water and sludge, and their addition through aerial sources native rocks or mining operations are largely localized. In soil toxic elements interact with both organic and inorganic matter may become available to vegetation and subsequently to the animals/human beings consuming that vegetation it is at this point the metal toxicity should be realized. The effect is visible in form of reduced crop yield and sick animals not only crop plant exhibit response to potentially toxic elements but also the behavior of elements in the soil plant system varies considerably.

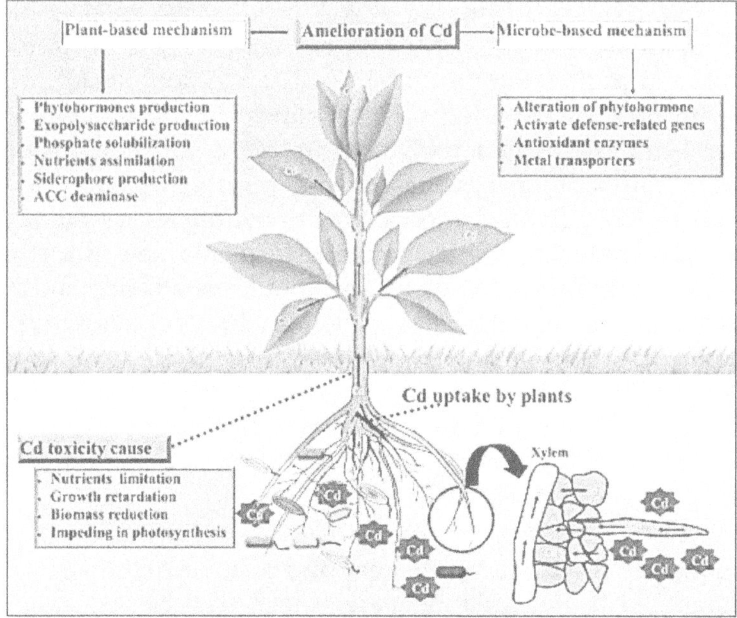

Fig. 7.1: Cadmium and its transportation

Source: researchgate.net

Cadmium: High levels of cadmium in soil >1mg/kg presently found in some mining and industrialized areas such as Orrisa are largely the result of emission in the past when smelters were operating under less stringent conditions and when cadmium was not recovered during zinc production uptake of Cd by plants from soil. Soil pH is a factor which controls the amount of Cadmium in the soil solution. In applied fertilizers present heavy metals temperature and soil organic matter exert a profound influence on cd uptake of plants. Certain increase in the pH of soil reduces the availability of cd to crop plants. in soil containing free CaCo availability of cd may be reduced due to adsorption of Cd^2 on surface of CaCo or due to effect increased soil ph. although incidence of itai-itai diseases in the jintsu valley of japan occurred because of the high Cd-content of rice reducing soil conditions hinder the uptake of Cd by rice. Anaerobic conditions during the grain filling stage depress the Cd-content of grains.

Lead: Lead having 82 atomic number and 207.2 atomic mass. Wide variations in Pb levels in the soils have been reported ranging from less than 100mg/kg to well over 11 000mg/kg naturals levels of lead in surface soils are usually below 50 mg/kg. The accumulations of Pb in soil is through atmosphere or it accumulates in various ways through additions from sewage and different kind of industrial wastes. The amount of lead present in soil, affects the mineral adsorption, soluble solids precipitation and the formation of organometallics complex compounds as well as the chelates which are found in organic matter of soil. Lead is converted as high cation absorbed rapidly to lead sulphate at the soil surface. Lead surface relatively less soluble and could leach through the soil if it is not transformed further. In soils with ph5. Undisturbed soil has almost 5% of organic matter and the upper layer is retained with lead upto 2-5 cm.Lead produce toxic responses in soil because it is present in a very high amount in soil. The toxic responses like polymerization as well as hydrolysis are already decided in the soil. For reducing the lead uptake in plants, the soil should have high organic matter, and p- content, soil should be alkaline and have high cation exchange capacity.It means that if sludge and sewage waters are used in soils that this will caused very less harm to soil because of the soil is rich is phosphorus. In water the inorganic salts of lead $^{2+}$ such as non-soluble in water. Atomic number of lead is 82 having specific gravity 11.34, melting point 327.5°C, atomic weight 207.19, boiling point 1740°C and is silvery grey or bluish in colour.

204, 206, 207, 208 are the atomic weights of the isotopes of arsenic. Lead is considered as a trace element and is found worldwide in many forms. +2 and +4 is the oxidation state of lead and the two electrons from the four electrons can ionized easily because its valance shell has four electrons. With industrial wastes, gases, vehicles exhaust, dust, the soil and plants gets contaminated with lead. If lead is present in large amount so, it is harmful to the human beings. Soil if exposed to lead, it remains in soils for long term because it is non-biodegradable in nature.

Mercury: Mercury is an element having atomic number 80 and atomic weight 200.59. Considerably,behavior of hg in the soil is controlled by adsorption desorption processes. Mercury is strongly held by the soil and the adsorption sites for the element never approach saturation before another toxic element becomes hazardous. It is available in many forms Mercury has shine nature, silvery-whitish in colour and is naturally occurring metals. Mercury compensates with the elements that is chlorine, sulfur, and oxygen and converted into inorganic mercury compounds and salts, they are mostly present in white crystal and powdered form. Mercury and carbon combined together to form compounds associated with organic mercury.[7]. Mercury having lowest melting point that is -390°C among all the pure metals. Among all pure metals the melting point of mercury is lowest that is -390°C.Among all the pure metals, mercury is the only one purest metals that is present in the liquid form at room temperature. Mercury also have low boiling point that is 357°C and it vaporizes easily [8].

Nickel: Nickel having atomic number 28 and atomic weight 58.69. Nickel is attached with the soil particles having iron and manganese when it is released in the environment.4 to 80 mg nickel is found in every 1 kg of soil. The pollution caused by nickel also affects the microbial activity in soil and its fertility. Nickel is mainly present in the soil nearby its ores or industries. When it is exposed to environment it affects the atmosphere and the soil as well. Nickel content ranges from 50-100 mg/gram is toxic to plants.

Chromium: Chromium having atomic number 24 and atomic weight 51.9, it is silvery metallic in color. The one important aspect of chromium is that it is immobile in soil, therefore the loss due to leaching is less. Chromium is essential for human being, somehow, it is mobile when present in the form of di chromates and chromates. Chromium has acidic basic oxidation states like+4, -2,-1, 0, +1, +2,+3,+4,+5,+6. Chromium shows a low soil- plant transfer factor.

Arsenic: Arsenic having atomic number 33 and atomic weight 74.9, silvery grey, crystalline in nature, specific gravity 5.73, melting point 817oC, boiling point 613Oc. Arsenic builds up in the soil environment through natural processes of weathering of arsenic bearing rocks of use of arsenic, contaminated groundwater for irrigation or through a host of anthropogenic activities such as mining operations, smelting of base metal ores, combustion of coal and application of arsenical pesticides. The arsenic content of contaminated soils varies widely. In general soils overlying sulphide ores deposits or derived from shales and granites and those surrounding geothermal activity, have high arsenic contents. The toxicity of arsenic compounds in the soil environment determined by its oxidation state and its presence in the organic/inorganic combination. The arsenic are highly soluble, mobile and toxic than arsenates. The arsenic content in soil decreases as addition of organic matter especially farmyard manure.

HEAVY METAL UPTAKE BY PLANTS

Cadmium, Zinc, Mangnese, Cobalt, Nickle and Lead can concentrate in the plants species upto100 to 1000. They are taken up by excluder plants. The microorganisms, bacteria and fungi which lives in rhizosphere, relates in plants. They mobalizes metallic ions. They helps in exterminate organic contaminates more efficiently then inorganic compounds [11, 12]. Phyto remediation techniques are used the uptake of heavy metals which include phyto extraction, Phyto stabilization, Rhizofiltration, Phytovolatization, Rhizosphere biodegradation, Phyto degradation.

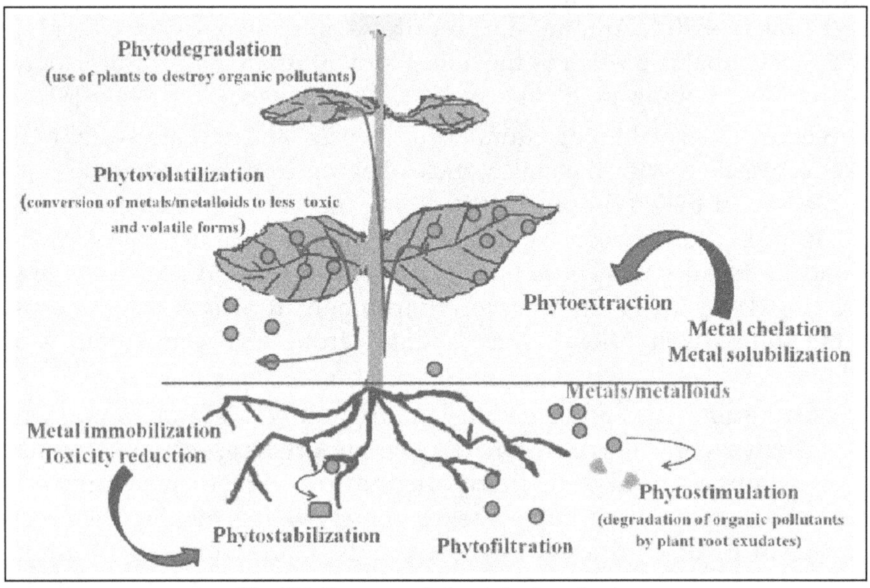

Fig. 7.2: Heavy metal uptake by plants
Source: //images.app.goo.gl

PHYTOEXTRACTION

The phenomenon of absorption and transportation of adulterant by below ground portions to the shoot portion which are collected and then burned for collecting energy, by recycling process. [9, 11, 13].

PHYTOSTABILISATION

Phytostabilisation is the utilization of certain plant species to immobilize the contaminants in the dirt and groundwater through ingestion and amassing in plant tissues, adsorption onto roots, or precipitation inside the root zone avoiding their relocation in soil, just as their development by disintegration and flattening [9, 11, 13]. In phytostabilization, substance mixes immobilizes contaminants created by plants and them debase them. In this procedure, plant really utilizes and decimate contaminants and discharges the contaminants into air through their leaves.

RHIZOFILTRATION

Rhizofiltration is the adsorption or precipitation into plant roots or absorption into and sequesterization in the roots of contaminants that are in solution surrounding the root zone by constructed wetland for cleaning up communal wastewater [9, 11, 13].

PHYTOVOLATILIZATION

Phytovolatilization is the take-up and transpiration of a contaminant by a plant, with arrival of the contaminant or a changed type of the contaminant to the environment from the plant. Phytovolatilization happens as developing trees and different plants take up water alongside the contaminants. A portion of these contaminants can go through the plants to the leaves and volatilize into the air at relatively low focuses.

RHIZOSPHERE BIO-DEGRADATION

This is a method, in which the natural substances are released by the plants from roots, that the nutrients are available to the micro-organisms present in the soil and enhances microbiological decomposition.

PHYTO DEGRADATION

In this procedure, plant really utilizes and decimate contaminants and discharges the contaminants into air through their leaves.

Table 7.1: Metal toxicity symptoms

Sl.No.	Metals	Deficiency symptoms
1.	Deficiency or Toxicity of Copper Toxicity of Uranium Toxicity of Zinc Toxicity of Cadmium	Reduces photosynthesis Decrease in chlorophyll content Leaf chlorosis
2.	Aluminium toxicity Cadmium toxicity Copper toxicity	Causes root damage Affects cortex Affects epidermis of plants
3.	Aluminium toxicity Cadmium toxicity Copper toxicity Lead toxicity	Membrane gets injured Disbalance in lipids
4.	Cadmium toxicity Lead toxicity Uranium toxicity	Iron, Calcium, Manganese, Zinc get changed

Source: https://as-botanicalstudies.springeropen.com/articles

Stunted Growth due to Metal Toxicity: Heavy metals either retard the growth of the whole plant or plant parts (Shafiq and Iqbal 2005; Shanker *et al.* 2005). The plant parts which have the direct contact withthe contaminated soils normally the roots exhibit rapid and sensitive changes intheir growth pattern (Baker and Walker 1989).

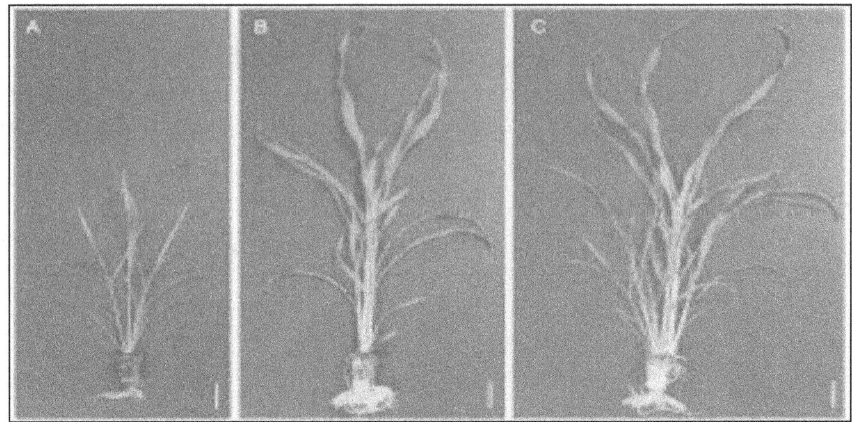

Fig. 7.3: Growth due to metal toxicity
Source: https://www.google.com/url

INDUCED SEED GERMINATION

Seed germination and early seedling development are very touchy towards changing ecological conditions (Seregin and Ivanox 2001).The germination execution and development pace of seedlings are accordingly used to evaluate the capacities of plant resilience to metal components. The higher fixations (1, 5 and 10 µM) of overwhelming metals (Cu, Zn, Mg and Na) repress seed germination and early development of grain, rice and wheat seedlings significantly contrasted with control (Mahmood *et al.* 2007). Since seed germination is the first physiological procedure influenced by harmful components, the capacity of a seed to grow in a medium containing any metal component (i.e., Cr) would be an immediate demonstrative of its degree of tolerance to this metal. (Peraltha *et al.* 2001).

These are the symptoms shown by heavy metal and these heavy metals causes several effects to the plants like cold stress, drought stress, increases pathogen attack etc. and this will affects to the crop plants and causes decline in yield.

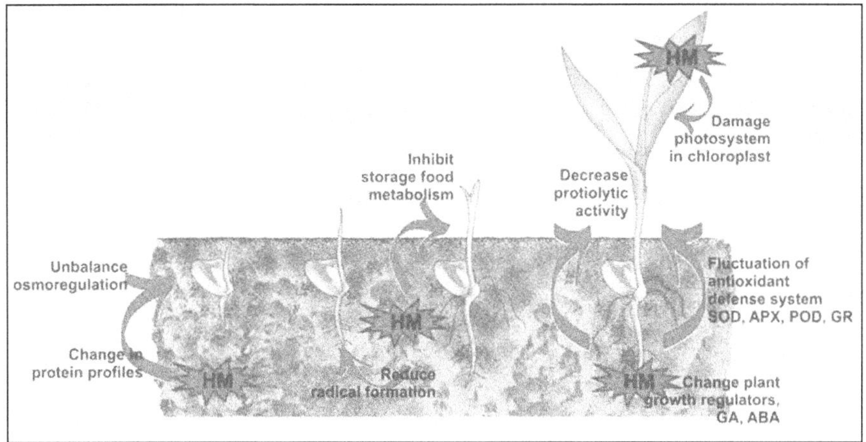

Fig. 7.4: Seed germination and metals

Source: https://www.google.com/imgres?imgurl=x-raw-image

CONCLUSION

Through our ecosystem they enter in our food chain and directly causes carcinogens diseases. Their fate in soil is too long almost 13 years of time taken up by Cadmium to leach down. Heavy metal from plants and environment are remediated through phyto remediation techniques. Techniques of phyto remedation to reduce effects of heavy metal in soil is seen very beneficial. Through the techniques of phyto extraction, Phytostabilization, Rhizo filtration, Phyto volatization, Rhizosphere bio degradation and phyto degradation.etc. Heavy metals can be easily remediated. The toxicity of Cadmium, Arsenic, Chromium, Lead, Mercury depends on several factors like Route of exposure, Dose, Gender and chemical species etc.

REFERENCES

1. D. Mohan and C.U. Pittman Jr., "Arsenic Removal from Water/wastewater using Adsorbents–a Critical Review," Journal of Hazardous Materials, Vol. 142, No. 1-2, pp. 1-53, 2007.

2. National Ground Water Association, Copyright 2001. Arsenic. What you need to knowhttp://www.ngwa.org/ASSETS/A0DD107452D74B33AE9D5114EE6647ED/Arsenic.pdf.

3. U.S. Department of Health and Human Services, Public Health Service Agency for Toxic Substances and Disease Registry. Division of Toxicology and Environmental Medicine. Arsenic 2005, http://www.baltimorehealth.org/info/ATSDR%20fact%20sheet.pdf.

4. H. Hasegawa, M.A. Rahman, T. Matsuda, T. Kitahara, T. Maki, and K. Ueda, "Effect of Eutrophication on the Distribution of Arsenic species in Eutrophic and Mesotrophic Lakes," Science of the Total Environment, Vol. 407, No. 4, pp. 1418-1425, 2009. View at Publisher·

5.   WHO Regional Office for Europe, Air Quality Guidelines, Chapter 6.1, Arsenic, Copenhagen, Denmark, 2nd Edition, 2000.

6.   WHO Regional Office for Europe, Air Quality Guidelines, Chapter 6.7, Lead, Copenhagen, Denmark, 2nd Edition, 2001, http://www.euro.who.int/document/aiq/6_7lead.pdf.

7.   J.F. Musselman and QEP, "Sources of Mercury in Wastewater, Pretreatment Corner," http://www.cet-inc.com/cmsdocuments//7%20-%20Sources%20of%20Mercury%20in%20Wastewater%20(0204).pdf.

8.   T.C. Chang, S.J. You, B.S. Yu, C.M. Chen, and Y.C. Chiu, "Treating High-mercury-containing Lamps using Full-scale Thermal Desorption Technology," Journal of Hazardous Materials, Vol. 162, No. 2-3, pp. 967-972, 2009. View at Publisher·

9.   A. Erakhrumen and A. Agbontalor, "Review Phytoremediation: An Environmentally Sound Technology for Pollution Prevention, Control and Remediation in Developing Countries," Educational Research and Review, Vol. 2, No. 7, pp. 151-156, 2007.

10. U.S. Environmental Protection Agency, "Introduction to Phytoremediation," National Risk Management Research Laboratory, EPA/600/R-99/107, 2000, http://www.clu-in.org/download/remed/introphyto.pdf.

11. L. Erdei, G. Mezôsi, I. Mécs, I. Vass, F. Fôglein, and L. Bulik, "Phytoremediation as a Program for Decontamination of Heavy-metal Polluted Environment," in Proceedings of the 8th Hungarian Congress on Plant Physiology and the 6th Hungarian Conference on Photosynthesis, 2005.

12. L. Erdei, G. Mezôsi, I. Mécs, I. Vass, F. Fôglein, and L. Bulik, "Phytoremediation as a Program for Decontamination of Heavy-metal Polluted Environment," Acta Biologica Szegediensis, Vol. 49, No. 1-2, pp. 75-76, 2005.

13. V.M. Ibeanusi, "Denise Antonia Grab in Collaboration with Larry, Jensen Stephen Ostrodka—Environmental Protection Agency. Radionuclide Biological Remediation Resource Guide, U.S. Environmental Protection Agency," 2004, http://www.clu-in.org/download/remed/905b04001.pdf

Pages: 85-106

Effect of Elements on Plants
Edited by: Dr. Prasann Kumar and Dr. Pawan Kumar 'Bharti'
ISBN: 978-93-88854-44-3
Edition: 2020
Published by: Discovery Publishing House Pvt. Ltd., New Delhi (India)

Cadmium Induced Toxicity in Legumes with special reference to *Pisum sativum* L.

Prasann Kumar[1,2*], Shipa Rani Dey[1]

GRAPHICAL ABSTRACT

Keywords: Cadmium, Dose, Economy, Food, Gap

INTRODUCTION

Pisumsativum also known as the field pea belongs to the family Fabaceae. It is an annual herbaceous plant with a life cycle of one year. It is

[1] Department of Agronomy, School of Agriculture, Lovely Professional University, Jalandhar - 144 411 (Punjab) (India)
[2] Divison of Research and Development, Lovely Professional University, Jalandhar - 144 411 Punjab, (India)

believed to have originated from the Mediterranean region of Southern Europe and Western Asia. It is cultivated throughout the world and is considered the fourth most important cultivated legume crops grown (Vidal *et al.* 2003). The largest producer of the field pea in India is Uttar Pradesh accounting 49% of the total pea produced in India (Reddy *et al.* 2010). Legume crops are rich in nutritional value provided that, Pea is one such legume crop rich in protein and low in fat content (Vadivel *et al* 2005). It is also a rich source of both soluble and insoluble fiber, and contains vitamins like VitA, Vit B6, Vit C, Vit K, etc. (Vadivel *et al.* 2005). Pea has the inherent capacity to fix atmospheric nitrogen by forming a symbiotic relationship with rhizobium bacteria and thus obtain most of the required nitrogen from it (Simm *et al.* 2002).

BOTANICAL DESCRIPTION

Pisumsativum L. is a cool-season crop which is cultivated throughout the world. It is an annual crop which can grow up to the height of 3ft tall (Pavek, 2012) It can be either determinate or indeterminate type. This herbaceous plant has alternate leaves which are pinnately compound. The leaflets are oval in shape and are sessile in nature. There are 1-4 pairs of pinnately compound leaflets at each side of the rachis and the terminal leaflet pair is modified into branched tendrils. The stipules are large which are attached to round, slender and glabrous stem. Pea can be low-growing or vining type. Vining cultivars produce tendril at the apex of the compound leaf which helps the plant coil around any available support to grow. The vining cultivars can grow upto the height of 1-2m (Pavek, 2012). Pea produces flowers, color ranging from white to reddish purple. Flowers are borne on the axillary raceme. Most pea varieties are self-pollinated. Each flower will produce a pod containing 4-9 seeds. The seeds of peas are round in shape and green or yellow in colour (Pavek, 2012). The pea seeds can be used as whole or split grains. Pea has hypogeal germination in which the epicotyl elongates and the cotyledons remain below the soil surface. Pea has a tap root system which can grow upto the depth of 3-4ft. The optimum temperature required by the plant is 13-18⁰C. High temperature is more injurious to pea plant than the frost. It can grow in a wide range of soil with the optimum pH of 5.5 to 7.0 (Hartmann *et al.* 1988).

Contamination with heavy metal is one of the major concern in agricultural soil as it possesses potential ecological threat and undesirable effect. Elements having a relative density greater than 5g cm^{-3} is termed as heavy metal (Schutzendubel and Polle, 2002). Elements like cadmium, arsenic, lead, chromium,etc are considered as heavy metals and these are very toxic in nature. These toxic elements are considered as soil pollutants which can cause both acute and chronic effect on plants grown in soil contaminated with these metals (Mallikarjuna Kunjam *et al.* 2015). These metals are very persistent and tend to remain in the soil for a very long period of time. Because of their toxic nature, non-biodegradability and lacking bio-disintegration, the bio-accumulate of heavy metals poses risk to the environment. In the past 150 years, the pollution level has increased more than 4000 times (Z. Yousefia 2018).

Cadmium is one of those heavy metals that is lustrous, silver-white, ductile and very malleable metal which is of considerable environmental and occupational concern and hasadetrimental effect on the environment and humans. It is toxic even at a concentration as low as 0.1mg to 0.2 mg. Cadmium is ranked 7th most toxic element present in the earth's crust (ASTDR 2014). Cadmium (Cd) does not have any beneficial role in plant biology and is considered toxic to plants and animals. Many times anthropogenic activities like using sewage water for irrigation and continuous phosphorus application increased the cadmium content in agricultural soil (Younis *et al.* 2016). The average concentration at which cadmium is distributed in the earth's crust is 0.1-0.5mg/kg. It always occurs in the combination with zinc. In the environment, marine phosphate and sedimentary rocks contain the highest level of cadmium which is about 15mg cadmium/kg. They are known as trace elements because it is present in trace concentration i.e, less than 10ppm. Cadmium in industries is produced as an inevitable byproduct of Zinc, Lead, Copper extraction (Wuana *et al.* 2011). They are used for the production of alloys, pigments, and batteries and as stabilizers in plastics. Cadmium toxicity in the agricultural field also increases due to continuous application of phosphorus (Singh *et al.*, 2017). The International Agency for Research on Cancer classified cadmium and its compound to be Group 1 carcinogens for humans (Henson and Chedrese, 2004). The solubility of cadmium and its compounds in water are higher in comparison to other metals, thus elevating their bioavailability for plants. Hence it can get bio-accumulated easily in the plant system. This bioaccumulation of cadmium in plants leads to several health implications when consumed. Cadmium can get accumulated in leafy vegetable, potatoes, grains, seeds etc. (Satarug *et al.*, 2003). Like any other plants, Tobacco plant can also accumulate cadmium in the plant system. Smokers get exposed to cadmium by smoking cadmium contaminated tobacco (Ashraf 2012). Cadmium remains in the soil for a very long period, they either leach in the ground water or are uptaken by the plants which then migrate into the food crops which are then consumed by the humans. Thus having detrimental effects on the environment as well as to the human body. Exposure to cadmium causes many health problems like kidney disorder, lungs problem, hypertension, fever, DNA damages in living cells, gastrointestinal irritant, pulmonary or renal injury and comatose, etc (Richter *et al.* 2017).

Cadmium toxicity induced oxidative stresses in the plants. Cadmium is bioavailable and can be easily transported inside plants as a metallo-organic complex (Jali *et al.*, 2016). According to Clemens *et al.*, 2002, the bio-accessibility of Cadmium in soil depended on its pH, concentration, redox potential, temperature and concentration of different elements. In the acidic pH condition, the solubility of cadmium increased which made it more likely to be absorbed. As cadmium and zinc share same oxidation states, therefore, zinc present in the metallothionein can get replaced by cadmium thereby preventing it from acting as a free radical scavenger within the cell (Jaishankar *et al.*, 2014). In response to cadmium stress, ROS production dramatically elevated. This increase of free radicals like superoxide, hydroxyl radical, hydrogen peroxide, etc., interfered with the metabolic activity and caused disruption of cell structure, membrane stability, and integrity. It reduced the chlorophyll content of Chl a, Chl b, Chl c, etc. (Abeer *et al.*, 2015). The toxic effect of cadmium caused chlorosis, necrosis, marginal yellowing in *Pisumsativum* (Pandey *et al.* 2012). Oxidative stress increased the production of MDA and H_2O_2 drastically (Malecka *et al.* 2014). According to the report of (Nahar *et al.* 2016), the photosynthetic activity was affected due to decreased chlorophyll content. The presence of cadmium interfered with the germination process of Pea by altering of storage protein mobilization which resulted in the reduction of free amino acids. Thus, reducing the nitrogen supplied to growing embryo (Jaouani *et al.*, 2018). Cadmium competed for the absorption sites and inhibited the phosphorus and other mineral nutrients absorption by plants (Jarvis *et al.* 1976; Afridi *et al.*, 2019). Cadmium and Zinc have an antagonistic effect on each other. Increase in cadmium concentration decreased the zinc absorption by plants. Likewise, an increase in zinc concentration inhibited the cadmium from entering into plant system (Soudek *et al.* 2016).

Mycorrhiza is a fungus having a symbiotic or mutualistic relationship with the rhizosphere or roots of the plants (Morton *et al.* 2004). They share a mutualistic relationship in which the mycorrhiza forms a network of filaments that associates with the plant roots which helps them in uptaking the mineral nutrients or water (Chen *et al.* 2019), while the mycorrhiza is benefitted by getting access to carbohydrates such as glucose and sucrose. The carbohydrates are translocated from their source to root tissues and onto the plant fungal partners. Some plant roots may be unable to uptake nutrients that are chemically or physically immobilized. For example, phosphate ions and micronutrients such as Fe, Cu, Zn, etc. (Edelstein *et al.* 2018). The mycelium of mycorrhiza fungus can, however, access many nutrient sources and make them available to the plants they colonize. Thus many plants are able to obtain phosphate without using soil as a source. Some other form of immobilization is when nutrients are locked up in an organic matter that is slow to decay. In such cases, some mycorrhizal fungus acts as a decay organism and mobilize the nutrients. Some of the fungi has shown resistance to toxicity in plants. That fungus is found to play a protective role for plants rooted in soils with high metal concentration, such as acidic and contaminated soils.

Several studies reported on improved physiological function and increased biomass in plants colonized by Arbuscular mycorrhizal fungi (AMF) compared to the counterparts not treated with AMF when grown in soil contaminated with heavy metal. The tolerating capacity of Arbuscular mycorrhizal fungi heavy metal was more for AMF isolated from heavy metal contaminated soil in contrast to AMF of others (Amir *et al.*, 2008). The plants ability to alleviate heavy metal toxicity in the presence of AMF was not necessarily because of the reduced heavy metal absorption by the plants but might have been because of the capacity of the plant to accumulate larger quantity of heavy metal in the roots and shoots of plants (Redon *et al.*, 2009; Andrade *et al.*, 2009). According to Amir *et al.*, 2013 the metal accumulated in the roots were stored in an inactive form. So, the high concentration of heavy metal in the root and shoot was not manifested as a high level of toxicity. But some studies revealed the decreased amount of metal accumulates in plant biomass. The mechanism behind it may be the ability of the mycorrhiza to bind the heavy metal in the cellwall or in the extraradical mycelium. Thus, restricting the heavy metal entering into the plant system. According to Coninx *et al.*, 2017 mycorrhiza stored the metals in vesicles and spores. It also secreted glomalin which helped in metal sequestration. Mycorrhizal fungi immobilized Cadmium and reduced its absorption in both roots and the mycorrhizosphere (Chen *et al.* 2004). Arbuscular mycorrhiza also improved the mineral nutrition of phosphorus and potassium ensuring plant growth which subsequently diluted the cadmium concentration in plant biomass.

A Polyamine is an organic compound having two or more primary amino groups NH-2. It is a group of natural compounds having an aliphatic nitrogen structure present in almost all living organisms. It plays a crucial role in various physiological functions like cell growth and development. Putrescine, spermidine, spermine, etc. are the polyamines which are generally found. The putrescine (diamine), the spermidine (triamine) and the spermine (tetramine) are ubiquitously found in plant cells whereas the occurrence of other polyamines is limited. Polyamines such as putrescine (Put), spermidine (Spd) and spermine (Spm) have regulatory roles in plant cell and is involved in mitigation of abiotic stresses (Alcázar *et al.*, 2010; Hussain *et al.*, 2011; Calzadilla *et al.*, 2014; Gupta *et al.*, 2016; Rady *et al.*, 2016). PAs are involved in many cell activities like cell division. It also promoted growth and inhibited ethylene production and has a role in plant senescence (Nahar *et al.*, 2016; Gupta *et al.*, 2016). PAs are involved in various growth and developmental processes ranging from cell division to leaf senescence and in various physiological functions (Alcázar*et al.*, 2010; Feng *et al.*, 2011; Alet *et al.*, 2012; Tavladoraki *et al.*, 2012), and also in plant tolerance to different environmental stresses (Yiu *et al.*, 2009; Jia *et al.* 2010; Hatmi *et al.*, 2015; Nahar *et al.*, 2016). The enzyme regulating polyamine metabolism is ornithine decarboxylase. Polyamine can also be synthesized from the amino acid arginine and methionine. The first step in the pathway is the production of ornithine from arginine by the mitochondrial enzyme arginase. Ornithine is then decarboxylated by ornithine decarboxylase to produce putrescine (Saha *et al.*, 2015). Polyamine is found in high concentration in the mammalian brain. The polyamines decline with the ages in the organism. According to Farooq *et al.*, 2009, Polyamines like putrescine are involved in several plant growth and developmental processes. They are recently added to the class of plant growth regulators, and also considered as a secondary messenger in signaling pathways (Kusano *et al.*, 2008). Polyamines helped the plant to cope with the abiotic stresses (Nayyer *et al.*, 2005). The external application of polyamine increased endogenous polyamine. In a polyamine cycle, PAs has the ability to interconvert with each other. Thus the polyamine pool is dynamic, changing over time (Guzman-Uriostegui *et al.* 2002). Studies revealed that the exogenous application of PAs, including Spermine, Spermidine, and Putrescine, promoted cadmium tolerance of *T. aestivum* (Rady *et al.*, 2016). In *Vignaradiata*, exogenous application of Putrescine mediated control over cadmium thereby reducing the Cd accumulation and its translocation in roots and shoots (Nahar *et al.*, 2016). In cadmium exposed *Malus*, the foliar application of Spermidine or Spermine increased in the activity of glutathione peroxidase (GPX) and superoxide dismutase (SOD) decreased generation of O^{2-} and malondialdehyde (MDA) (Zhao and Yang 2008; Rady and Hemida 2015). According to Hsu and Kao 2007, Spermidine and Spermine prevented Cd-induced increment in H_2O_2 and MDA contents, while it decreased GSH and the ascorbate peroxidase. Pal *et al.*, 2017 reported that the relationship between PAs increased the production of phytochelatins when exposed to cadmium in *Oryza sativa*.

Polyamines are low molecular weight aliphatic polycations which can readily bind with the ROS anionic species. They act as a protective shield to protect membranes and biomolecules by binding with the negatively charges surface (Wen and Moriguchi, 2015). Polyamine acts as the ROS and free radical scavengers (Sawa *et al.*, 2006; Stewart *et al.*, 2018). It also activates the anti-oxidant enzymes and reduces oxidative stress. PAs can also bind with cellular polyanions like DNA, RNA, protein which interferes with the synthesis, it alters the structure and functionality of these macromolecules (Wen and Moriguchi, 2015). Moreover, PAs act as direct or indirect ROS scavengers (Ha *et al.* 1998). It is an antioxidant which restricts the accumulation of O^{2-}, apparently by inhibiting NADPH oxidase (Papadakis and Roubelakis-Angelakis, 2005). According to Pathak 2017, increased level of polyamine in stressed plants has significant tolerance capacity as polyamine regulated the cellular ionic environment in plant and maintained the membrane integrity, it prevented the loss of chlorophyll and stimulated nucleic acid, protein, and protective alkaloids. Polyamines also protect membranes from oxidative damages as they are free radical scavengers (Pathak 2017). The tolerance mechanism of engineered plants to different environmental stress is mediated by the increased production of polyamines (Hussain *et al.* 2011; Sathe Atul *et al.* 2015).

REVIEW ON CONCERN RESEARCH

Ahmad *et al.* (2019) reported that during the stress condition plants develop a defense mechanism to cope with the situations that negative impact on plants metabolic pathway, and other physiological functions. In such responses plants produced S- rich molecules, phytochelatinis capable of mediating a varying array of cadmium stresses in plants. Some other mechanisms involved are by immobilizing heavy metal ions and by chelation as well as compartmentalization.Bali *et al.* (2019) Cadmium can stimulate the contamination of terrestrial and aquatic ecosystem. Because of its malevolent nature in plants, cadmium is one of the most extensively studied metals. Phytohormones like salicylic acid, jasmonic acid, brassinosteroids, abscisic acid, ethylene, gibberellic acid, etc. are considered to be of significant importance for ameliorating cadmium toxicity in plants.Chen *et al.* (2019) reported that the symbiotic relationship of plant root with the mycorrhiza facilitated better access to mineral by plants. It enhanced the better acquisition of plant minerals that are immobile thus enabling the plants to adapt better in environmental stress condition. AM fungi also helped in restoring the ecological balance by promoting better plant growth. Cui *et al.* (2019) reported that the two soybean genotypes HN89 and HX3 that are portrayed by their low or high Cd resilience respectively were inoculated with AM fungal advocated better root growth in case of tolerant genotype whereas no significant result was seen in the sensitive genotype. Mycorrhizal inoculation reduced the Cd uptake by the plant, thereby increasing phosphorus absorption. Dias *et al.* (2019) reported that *Pisumsativum* exposed to Pb induced oxidative stresses. It leads to higher Pb accumulation in roots of the plant in comparison to the leaves. The glutathione reductase and ascorbate peroxidase activities were more in leaves and the activity of catalase, superoxide dismutase was observed higher in case of leaves. Pb induced protein oxidation even at a very low Pb concentration. Goh *et al.* (2019) reported that the symbiotic interaction between terrestrial plant and AM fungi is regulated by the plant hormones. Increase in the cytokinin level can stimulate the AM colonization as it was observed that the increase in active cytokinin level was paralleled with expanded AM colonization while decreased cytokinin levels corresponded to reduced AM colonization. Grobelak *et al.* (2019) studies indicated that oxidative damages caused due to Cadmium stress resulted in decreased plant biomass. However, the application of organic fertilizer helped in coping with oxidative stresses. Exogenous application of nutrients, organic and inorganic like calcium and iron rich substances, etc. enhanced the antioxidant activities and provided as a shield to plants from the cadmium toxicity. Jebera *et al.* (2019) suggested that Legume crops coinoculated with cadmium-resistant, plant growth promoting bacteria (PGPB) can act as a phytoremediating plant which can scavenge metals like cadmium from cadmium contaminated soil. The study showed that PGPB promoted better plant growth by producing phytohormones and siderophores, and also symbiotically fixed nitrogen and enhance phosphorus solubilizing capacity. The association between legumes and PGPB were reported to have a positive impact on cadmium bioavailability in legumes by enhancing several mechanisms, such as bioaccumulation, precipitation, complexation, and chelation. Mongkhonsin *et al.* (2019) stated that indigenous herbaceous plant species are capable of colonizing on remediated soils and can be potentially used for phytoremediating heavy metals. Many herbaceous plant species are used as phytoextractor and phytostabilizer for heavy metals like cadmium. The mechanisms involved were immobilization, exclusion, and compartmentalization. They had the ability to adapt and synthesize phytochelatins, metallothioneins, stress proteins, and phenolic compounds to tolerate cadmium and other metals. Moreover, endophytic microorganism also enhanced the plants' tolerance mechanism. Naeem *et al.* (2019) reported that of all the heavy metals, cadmium is considered highly toxic, because it is highly soluble and mobile nature in soil and plant systems. It restricted plants physiological function through different mechanisms. For instance, cadmium competed with plant essential nutrients for absorption and translocation and adversely affected plants water status. The toxic nature of cadmium interrupts plants vital processes as it interfered with the nutrient uptake thereby making it deficient in plants. Navin *et al* (2019) reported that polyamine alleviated the abiotic stress like drought stress, osmotic stress, heat stress and also ameliorated heavy metal induced stresses. Polyamine like putrescine and spermine minimized the lipid peroxidation and modulated gluthathion to induce heat tolerance. It is also involved in the mechanism to reduce the damages caused through oxidative stresses.Quiroga *et al.* (2019) studied on the effect of arbuscular mycorrhiza association with the roots of maize to enhance the root cell water transport capacity by regulating the maize aquaporin and concluded that its symbiotic association increased the stomatal conductance, photosynthetic efficiency and higher water permeablility in AM root cell thus improving the physiological performance of plant during water stress condition. Rask *et al.* (2019) had selected different plant species *like Hordeumvulgare, Linumusitatissimum* L. and *Sorghum bicolor* L., *Matricariarecutita* L., *Sinapisalba* L. and *Dianthus deltoides* L. which were exposed to high Cd concentration. Result showed that colonization in mycorrhizal plants were increased with the increase in Cd concentration but decreased after a certain amount of threshold level reached. But in case of *Hordeum sp.* and *Linumsp*, the mycorrhizal colonization was highest even at highest cadmium concentration. Shah *et al.* (2019) reported that the cadmium uptaken by the plants might result in alteration of structure, cellular and biochemical processes inside the plant cells. The cadmium-induced toxicity resulted from the absorption and distribution in plants which significantly depended on the concentration absorbed by the plant and plant species. The toxic effect also varied among varieties of the same species. Shanmugaraj *et al.* (2019) The toxicity of cadmium causes retarded plant growth, interferes with the photosynthetic activity, alters the stomatal conductance, enzymatic activities, protein metabolism, and membrane functioning. Wei *et al.* (2019) reported that the elevated level of cadmium stipulated that both *R. communis* and *S. nigrum* were immune to high cadmium concentrations. It can accumulate cadmium in their organs. The study also showed that *S. nigrum* had higher tolerant capacity compared to *Ricinuscommunis*. Study also revealed that cadmium toxicity enhanced the uptake of calcium, copper, lead in roots whereas in both plant species calcium and magnesium were observed to b higher in leaves. It also restricted the uptake of iron and aluminium in the roots. In *Solanumnigrum* accumulation of cadmium occurred in the orders of leaf > stem > root. Xie *et al* (2019) studied on the Cd resistant fungus *Aspergillus aculeatus*and reported that the fungus had the ability to decrease the Cd concentration by 46.8% when inoculated in turfgrass growing in Cd-contaminated soil. *A. aculeatus* lowering the MDA and superoxide content. It helped in scavenging the ROS and increased the anti-oxidative enzymes. It could also increase the P solubilization and make it available for the plant for uptake. Zhang *et al.* (2019) reported that Zea mays inoculated with Rhizophagusintraradices and Glomus versiforme resulted in better biomass production. The Cd concentration were minimal in roots and shoot compared to the non-inoculated plants. Also, the colonization rates of these fungus were over 60% and not influenced by the increase in Cd concentration. Zhang *et al.* (2019) reported on the synergistic effect of AMF and biochar in the Cd created stress. Study had shown that the drastic reduction in the colonization of AMF was due to the presence of Cd. But it was seen that AMF inoculation tremendously increased contents of nitrogen and phosphorus in shoots of plant grown in the soil contaminated with cadmium. The application with both AMF and biochar resulted in the less cadmium accumulation in shoot and increased nitrogen and phosphorus in plant tissue. Asgher *et al.* (2018) reported that an increase in heavy metal toxicity lead to a decline in crop productivity. According to the study, polyamines and ethylene played a significant role in the cell signaling in response to the heavy metal stress. The synergistic effect between polyamine and ethylene helped plant against the decreasing root-shoot ratio. Benavides *et al.* (2018) reported on the effect of polyamines on cadmium and copper-mediated alterations in wheat and sunflower seedling membrane fluidity. The study showed that Cd disrupted the growth of wheat and sunflower while Cu had affected the only sunflower. Cd and Cu both increased the membrane fluidity of leaves of both plants and Cd decreased the membrane fluidity of roots. Application of polyamine partially prevented the alteration of membrane biophysical properties that were induced by the toxic cadmium and copper toxicity. Bui *et al.* (2018) reported that arbuscular mycorrhiza can colonize in the plant root which can enhance the tolerant capacity of the plant to heavy metals. *Rhizophagus irregularis* when inoculated in the root of *Daucuscarota* helped the plant acclimatize to metal stress thereby conferring the Zn tolerance capacity of the plant. This acclimatization improved the fungal growth as well as helped the plant to cope with metal stress condition. Chang *et al.* (2018) the study revealed that the maize plant inoculated with AMF which were also exposed to Lanthanum and Cadmium showed a reduction in plant biomass by 15.3% to 44.4% compared to control. It also showed that the plant that was not inoculated with AMF accumulated higher concentration of both heavy metal in shoot also the K uptake was significantly reduced. However, the increased concentration of Cd and La also decreased the colonization rate of AMF. Chen *et al.* (2018) reported that the AMF could improve plant tolerance to heavy metal contamination. The study showed that the presence of mycorrhizal colonization restricted the Cd mobilization in plant roots. Therefore the Cd content in the plant shoot was remarkably lesser. SR-µXRF imaging indicated that Cd absorbed by extraradical hyphae was translocated into intraradical fungal structures, in which arbuscules accumulated large amounts of Cd; however, plant cells without fungal structures and plant cell walls contained negligible amounts of Cd. The present results provided direct evidence for the intraradical immobilization of Cd absorbed by AM fungi, which may largely contribute to the enhanced tolerance of plants to Cd. Therefore, AM fungi havea significant role in the phytostabilization of cadmium contaminated soil. Debeljak *et al.* (2018) study showed that the maize plant grown on contaminated soil of mercury affected the plant hormone thus increasing plant biomass in comparison to arbuscular mycorrhiza. However, the exposure of mercury to plant enhanced the arbuscule formation that facilitated as a source for nutrient exchange between the plant and the fungi. Deswal *et al.* (2018) reported that *Pisumsativum* exposed to Cd^{2+}, Ni^{2+}, Pb^{2+} delayed the germination. The growth of radical was affected more compared to that of plumule. It also decreased the dry weight and fresh weight of various plant parts. However, in the case of cotyledons, the percentage of nitrogen increased with a higher concentration of heavy metals. The protein content of plumule and radical increased with the heavy metal concentration, and decreased protein content in case of cotyledons. Edelstein *et al.* (2018) reviewed that heavy metals were bioavailable and could easily be uptaken by the plants. Heavy metal could enter into plant system mainly through leaves and roots. Mycorrhiza helped in exhibiting tolerance to heavy metals as act as bio-filter by restricting the absorption of metals such as iron, nickel, zinc, and copper through roots. Gai *et al.* (2018) studied on *Cucumis Sativa* which were introduced to two AM fungal species *Glomus etunicatum* and *Glomus claroideum*. It was also exposed to different cadmium concentration. The result showed both AMF significantly increased the plant biomass with time. It also increased P uptake and decrease in Cd uptake. The extra mycelium length was affected by a higher concentration of Cd. In response to the Cd stress, the extra mycelium length grew extensive which helped in coping with the Cd stress. Out of both the fungal species, *Glomus claroideum* were better resistant to the unfavorable stress condition. Guan *et al.* (2018) revealed on the experiment conducted that the accumulation of soluble sulfide was observed to be higher due to the presence of Cadmium. However, the exogenous foliar application of sulfide in the form of NaHS diminished the toxic effect of Cadmium by decreasing the soluble Cadmium fraction in the plant. Jaouani *et al.* (2018) reported on the mechanism of action of cadmium on pea germination. The study reported that the germination process may be interfered by alteration of storage proteins mobilization which may result in a reduction in releasing of free amino acids thus reducing the nitrogen supply to the growing embryo in Cd stress. The Cd toxicity also resulted in the altered metabolic processes that affected immobilizing reserves and reduced nutrient bioavailability. Cd stress also induced oxidative stress which resulted in the production of free radicals which interacted with the enzyme and altered the activity and structure of the plant. J. Li *et al.* (2018) studied on *Medicago sativa* which was exposed to different concentration of Arsenic and also was inoculated with arbuscular mycorrhiza to observe the influence of arbuscular mycorrhiza in alleviating the toxic effect of arsenic. The study reported that the plant treated with Arsenic alone resulted in yellowing and wilting of plants whereas in plants inoculated with AM resulted in reduced phytotoxicity. Hence, it improved plant P nutrition thus increasing plant biomass and decreased Arsenic concentration in plant parts. Lam *et al.* (2018) reported that the colonization of the arbuscular mycorrhiza in the plant roots increased the phosphorus accumulation in plants. The inoculation of arbuscular mycorrhiza in spinach improved the plant growth and had the capacity to reduce the nickel accumulation but less was in case of cadmium. It also reported that the plants' ability to tolerate heavy metal and its detoxification were associated with the subcellular distribution of HMs and their chemical form. Liu *et al.* (2018) reported that the combined application of AMF and biochar had a synergistic effect on minimizing the Cd translocation and bioavailability compared to the solo application of biochar and AMF in maize. It also increased the activity of SOD, POD, and catalase. But the mitigating capacity of AMF was observed to be better than biochar in case of Cd related stress. The result showed that the combined application of AMF with biochar enhanced better maize growth and caused Cd immobilization. Biochar also improved the fungal colonization in the root. Ronzan *et al.* (2018) reported that *Oryza sativa* L. easily absorbed arsenic and cadmium by the plant root, which induced consistent damages to the root system. Auxins regulated all physiological processes, including root organogenesis. Therefore, by altering the levels and distribution of endogenous phytohormones, cadmium and arsenic-induced stress can be mitigated. However, the results based on the experiment conducted on seedlings of rice showed that arsenic and cadmium affected the cellular activity and morphological structure of the roots. They can interfere with the lateral root primordia organization and development and have a detrimental effect on a plant root. Saikat *et al.* (2018) reported that heavy metal was an environmental hazard which leads to disruption in human health and crop production. Heavy metal toxicity induced oxidative stresses. During stress, condition plant adapted several defense mechanisms such as polyamine accumulation in order to cope up with the deteriorating effect of heavy metal. Exogenous application of Pa such as putrescine, spermine, spermidine, etc. modulated antioxidative pathway to scavenge ROS and prevent its bioaccumulation, thus promoting better plant growth. Shamshed *et al.* (2018) studied on the influence of EDTA, Citric acid and cadmium accumulation and its toxicity effect on germinating and young pea seedlings. Exposure of EDTA at high concentration increased cadmium accumulation whereas Citric acid did not demonstrate cadmium accumulation by pea. Studies showed that the cadmium stress induced over production of hydrogen peroxidein roots and leaves which further decreased the pigment content and increased lipid peroxidation. Both EDTA and citric acid elevated cadmium-induced H_2O_2 production and MDA production. In comparison to the young seedlings, the germinating pea was more affected by cadmium stress. Spagnoletti *et al.* (2018) had reported on the toxicity effect of arsenic on the physiological and biochemical activities of the plant. However, AMF had the ability to alleviate the toxicity of arsenic by enhancing the plant biomass thus diluting the arsenic concentration. AMF could sequester arsenic in its hyphae thereby minimizing the translocation of this metal into other plant parts. AMF helped in the better mobilization of phosphorus making it available for the plant to uptake and decreased absorption of arsenate by roots by repressing arsenate and phosphate transporters. Tajti *et al.* (2018) reported that the exposure of cadmium had tremendously decreased the growth and development of wheat seedlings. Both the putrescine and spermidine did not have any effect on the growth parameter but alleviated by the Cd-induced reduction of the shoot. Plant treated with spermidine and putrescine in combination helped increase the proline content and other antioxidant activities. Wang *et al.* (2018) According to the study, high doses of zinc oxide, nano particles, cadmium significantly increased zinc concentration in plant root and also inhibited the enzymatic activity of soil. The presence of zinc oxide, nano particles, cadmium had a phytotoxic effect on the plant. But the inoculation of AMF helped in mitigating the damaging effect induced by zinc oxide, nano particles and cadmium. Zhan *et al.* (2018) reported on the study conducted on two arbuscular mycorrhiza namely *Funneliformis mosseae* and *Diversispora sputum* to determine the effect on growth, anti-oxidant activity and absorption of phosphorus, sulfur, lead, zinc, cadmium, and arsenic by maize growing in heavy metal-polluted soils. It was observed that both the AMF had amelioration effect on the heavy metal. H_2O_2 and MDA production decreased whereas the production of catalase and SOD were increased. *F. mosseae* remarkably improved the plant chlorophyll content, plant height and plant biomass. AMF increased the retention capacity of the maize to accumulate heavy metal in its root and reduced its translocation. Zhu *et al.* (2018) According to him, when exposed to cadmium stress condition, *C. crepidioide*s resulted into better tolerant as they had accumulated a higher amount of cadmium in its shoot, whereas, in case of *A. conyzoides* the cadmium accumulation in its shoot were significantly lower, due to which it exhibited reduced plant growth. In the aerial plant part of *C. crepidioides* the cadmium concentration accumulate exceeds the threshold level. So, it is considered as hyperaccumulator of cadmium. The mechanism behind the better tolerant capacity and higher accumulation of cadmium in *C. crepidioides* was due to the higher production of free amino acids, especially for Glutamine and Asparagine, in *C. crepidioides* compared to *A. conyzoides*. Basu *et al.* (2017) reported that the symbiotic association of mycorrhiza with plant root helped in alleviating the abiotic stress by regulating the antioxidant enzyme during salinity stress. It coped with drought stresses by regulating the stomatal conductance and enhancing the water use efficiency. During heavy metal stresses, mycorrhizal fungi helped in better nutrient uptake of nitrogen and phosphorus and also helped in the synthesis of organic acids. The mycorrhiza also immobilized the heavy metals in its hyphae. The glomalin produced by AMF helped in decontaminating the metals in soil. Coninx *et al.* (2017) reported on the response of mycorrhiza on coping with the metal stress condition by chelation of the metal and by producing organic acid. Mycorrhiza also helped in retaining the metal in its spores and also stored the metal in the vesicles thus restricting their further mobility in plant parts. Arbuscular mycorrhiza also promoted the secretion of glomalin which helped in the sequestration of metal. Fuego *et al.* (2017) the study reported that the plant *Betulapubescens* were grown in two different industrial area with varying concentration of heavy metal. The plant grown in lesser metal polluted soil resulted in more uptake of metals in the plant system contrasting the plant growing in heavily metal polluted soil with lesser metal accumulation and showed increased biomass production suggesting cell wall to be the main detoxification mechanism for metal sequestration. Gupta *et al.* (2017) reported that under cadmium toxicity *Arabidopsis thaliana* showed a reduction in the growth of the plant. Study revealed that the concentration of H_2O_2 and lipid peroxidationincreased in response to time. Magda *et al.* (2017) reported that treating the plant with putrescine and Cd in combination resulted in increased accumulation of Cd in plant roots. The result also reported that the combined application of both treatment induced more oxidative stress in both leaves and roots suggesting that Cd and putrescine in combination has an additive effect. It also resulted in increased polyamine synthesis. Pathak (2017) reported that certain plants had a remarkable ability to endure and mitigate the extensive concentration of heavy metal contamination. Plants exposed to cadmium nitrate exhibit phototoxic responses. Likewise, Putrescine enhanced the tolerance of plants to environmental stresses. Increment in polyamines enhanced the cellular ionic processes, strengthened membrane integrity, improved chlorophyll content and revitalize protein, nucleic acid and protective alkaloids. Placek *et al.* (2017) stated that the soil pH had a role in increased concentration of Cadmium in the soil as in acidic soil condition the chemical compound can easily be broken down making it more mobile and bioavailable. However, at alkaline pH the metal was inaccessible. Rahman *et al.* (2017) reported that the Cd toxicity can be ameliorated from pea seedling and may be associated with the Cd sequestration in roots of the pea plant thus reducing the translocation of the Cd in the shoots. The other coping mechanisms involved in diminishing the Cd-induced stresses are by increasing the activity of the antioxidants like SOD, POD, CAT, GR activity,etc along with elevated S-metabolites like cysteine, methionine, glutathioneetc to scavenge the ROS in pea plant. Rizwan *et al.* (2017) reviewed on the toxic effect of Cadmium on the leafy vegetable. He reviewed that the leafy vegetable had the ability to accumulate a large amount of Cd in their biomass. The toxic effect of Cd lead to the decrease in seed germination, plant growth, chlorophyll content etc. however the plants response on the stresses might induce the enzymatic activity to cope with the related stresses. The plants also had the ability to sequester Cd in the cell wall of the roots and the leaf vacuoles. Such sequestration might help in detoxifying the Cd toxicity. Shanying *et al.* (2017) reviewed that the increased cadmium concentration inhibited plant growth by producing ROS, which induced certain modification to antioxidant enzymes activities. It also disturbed the physiological functions by affecting of structural and biochemical processes. Cadmium-induced stresses caused decreased seed germination and lowered the nutrient availability. Dhawi *et al.* (2016) studied on sorghum plant that were grown in heavy metal contaminated soil. Sorghum was subjected to plant growth promoting bacteria and mycorrhiza. Plants exhibited better shoot and root biomass that were exposed to these bacteria and fungus alone or in combination. Increase in phosphorus and potassium uptake by plants were observed. It also increased the concentration of Ca, Mg, S in roots and shoots. Also, there was a significant increase in root metabolic activity. Gong *et al.* (2016) reported that the introduction of Cd to *Boehmeria nivea* resulted in Cd accumulation in the biomass. It also increased the H_2O_2 and MDA content and inducing Cd causing oxidative stresses. However, the exogenous application of calcium and spermidine helped in reducing the oxidative stress caused and decreased the Cd accumulation and enhanced the activity of SOD and POD. Hristozkova *et al.* (2016) reported that AMF helped marigold in tolerating heavy metals. The AMF inoculation of increased the accumulation of secondary metabolites thereby increasing the antioxidant capacity. Jali *et al.* (2016) reported that Cadmium was phytotoxic affecting the physiological, morphological, biochemical and molecular activities. At low concentration, it could induce secondary metabolites that could help the plant resist against oxidative damage caused by cadmium whereas at high concentration plants might die. Jiang et al. (2016) reported on the soil exposed to cadmium in which *Lonicerajaponicum* were grown. Two AMF *Glomus versiforme* and *Rhizophagus intraradices* was introduced. The result showed that the colonization of these two AMF increased the activity of the anti-oxidants. But lower production of MDA and Glutathione were observed. Plants inoculated with either of these AMF showed better root and shoot growth and improved P nutrition. In the case of *Rhizophagus intraradices* the Cd accumulation was higher in roots and lower in a shoot which indicated the possibilities of producing plant from Cd-contaminated soil. Leal *et al.* (2016) reported that Arbuscular mycorrhiza had the capability to rehabilitate better compared to other mycorrhizal fungus in the heavy metal contaminated soil. The spore count, species richness of arbuscular mycorrhiza was better than glomalin. Li *et al.* (2016) reported that *Elsholtzia splendens* was a Copper tolerant plant. But the increased concentration of heavy metal lead to decrease in germination rate, seedling growth and fresh weight of radicle. But the addition of AMF in the soil helped *E. splendens* in coping with the stress condition and facilitated rapid adaptation to Cu thus increasing the radicle length, germination rate as well as germination index. Murtaza *et al.* (2016) reported that the irrigation water containing Cd tend to decrease the plant biomass whereas the application of Zn and Cu increased the biomass production. The Cd concentration in the plant biomass increased due to the Cd contaminated irrigation water. The study also reveal that the application of Zn decreased the Cd concentration in plant biomass due to its antagonistic effect and could therefore reduce the Cd toxicity in plant biomass. Nahar *et al.* (2016) reported that cadmium is a toxic metal which caused abiotic stresses and was an environmental hazard. Cadmium-induced stress caused an increase in Cd accumulation in roots and shoots of mung bean. It also deteriorated the plant growth and its chlorophyll content. Cd toxicity induced oxidative damages but the application of putrescine in Cd-stressed plant helped in ameliorating the oxidative stresses by enhancing the enzymatic and non-enzymatic antioxidants. Polyamine also enhanced the glyoxalase system in detoxifying the metal-induced methylglyoxal toxicity and promoted better growth of the plant. Nahar *et al.* (2016) reported that the exogenous application of spermine diminished the accumulation and translocation of Cd in mung bean. It also counteracted the cadmium causing oxidative damages by increasing the activity of anti-oxidant enzyme as well as non-enzymatic antioxidants. Exogenous application of spermine also enhanced the level of the endogenous free polyamine thus alleviating the toxic effect of Cd in seedlings of mung bean. Oukarroum (2016) reviewed that polyamines get accumulated under abiotic stress condition. It had involvement in cellular defense against oxidative damages through the inhibition of lipid peroxidation and scavenging free radicals. The study also revealed that the exogenous application of polyamine helped enhance the endogenous polyamine. Exogenous application of polyamine diminished the oxidative stresses and helped restore the normal physiological processes. It also modulated the antioxidant pathways and enzymatic activities. Rady *et al.* (2016) reported that the wheat plant treated with lead showed reduced growth characteristics. However, the application of polyamines like putrescine, spermine, spermidinealleviated the toxic effect the lead had on plant and enhanced better plant growth thereby increasing the plant biomass. The study revealed that the pre-treatment of putrescine by soaking the seeds helped in mitigating the Pb inducing stresses and lead to increased yield. Rizwan *et al.* (2016) reported that cadmium toxicity in paddy affected the seed germination, growth and mineral nutrient. It caused oxidative stress and genotoxicity. The stress caused by cadmium toxicity can be alleviated by exogenous application of microbes, selection of low cadmium accumulating cultivars, etc. Sharma *et al.* (2016) stated that phytoremediation can be used for hyperaccumulating the metals in plants organ. This method of ameliorating metal from soil can be enhanced by introducing the plants to certain metal resistant bacteria that is associated with better plant growth and can also bind metals in plant tissues. Studies also suggested on the inoculation of cadmium-resistant plant growth promoting rhizobacteria to increase agricultural production which will inhibit the metal accumulation in plant tissues. Using microorganisms may promote plant growth in soils contaminated with cadmium with minimum or no accumulation of cadmium in edible parts of plants. Soudek *et al.* (2016) according to them, the application of polyamine decreased the Cd accumulation in the roots of the plants but it had a lesser influence on the shoot of the plant. Polyamine did not show a significant difference in the case of Zn accumulation in the plant when compared to the control plant. But some plant exhibited in the Cd and Zn concentration as both metals have an antagonistic effect on each other. Thus the presence of Zn decreased the Cd uptake by the plant and vice-versa. Wu *et al.* (2016) reported on the enhancement of tolerance of a plant to Chromium toxicity by inoculation of arbuscularmycorrhizal fungi. The study revealed that the amount of extracellular polymeric substance produced on the surface of AM fungi due to the Chromium stress helped in reducing and immobilizing chromium. The study showed the accumulation of chromium in the cell wall of mycorrhizal root and the hyphae and other fungal structure was the underlying mechanism of immobilizing the chromium. Abeer *et al.* (2015) reported on the Cadmium inducing stress on Tomato plant. Cd stress had an influence on plant biomass which was observed to have drastically declined compared to control. Cd-induced stress also reduced the chlorophyll content of Chl a, Chl b. Chl c by 50.11%, 31.7%, 43.7% respectively. Production of H_2O_2 and lipid peroxidation increased due to the Cd related stresses but colonization of AMF helped in reducing their production of 90.5% and 16% respectively. The MSI of the plant also dropped by 43.75%. AMF enhance the activity of anti-oxidant which further helped in minimizing the oxidative stress damage. Fiala *et al.* (2015) reported that the grapevine was treated with different concentration Cadmium which elevated the ROS production and also disrupted the cell viability by disturbing the plasma membrane integrity. The production of superoxide and H_2O_2 were observed even in low Cd concentration. Hediji *et al.* (2015) explained on the possibility of biological abnormalities caused by the cadmium. The reported demonstrated that the increased absorption of cadmium by plants lead to the deficient in the essential mineral nutrient. Thus, the plants exhibits reduced plant growth and biomass. Thiruvengadam *et al.* (2015) studied on the effect of seleniumdioxide, putrescine, and cadmium chloride treatments on a turnip. The experiment exhibited that seleniumdioxide and cadmium chloride treatment developed stress in turnip plants thereby inducing in maximized production of ROS, the increment of MDA and anthocyanin contents, and inhibited the biosynthesis of chlorophyll. Application of SeO_2 and putrescine enhanced the anti-oxidant activity and promoted better plant growth. Xiaopeng *et al.* (2015) reported that biosynthesis of polyamine took place due to the prevailing stress conditions. This biosynthesis pathway of polyamine conferred tolerance to stress. Polyamine pathway facilitated the coping mechanism and ameliorated abiotic stresses such as drought, salinity, heat. Chilling, heavy metal toxicity, etc. Yang *et al.* (2015) had reported that AMF was considered a biotechnological tool for enhancing the photostability efficiency. It also enhanced the tolerance capacity of the plant towards heavy metal. In an experiment conducted, it showed that the exposure of the leguminous plant to Lead (Pb) had a damaging effect on the plant while the inoculation of AMF counteracted the harmful effect of Pb on the plant. Pb induced stresses reduced the photosynthetic efficiency and increased the H_2O_2 and MDA content whereas the colonization of AMF lead to an increase in antioxidant enzymatic activity thereby coping with the Pb induced stresses. Zayneb *et al.* (2015) reported on the efficiency of Cadmium to get bioaccumulated. In the experiment conducted the fenugreek seedlings were grown in different $CdCl_2$ conc. The growth of the fenugreek seedling was affected even at a very low concentration. It had significantly decreased the amylase activity. Plants exposed to higher Cd concentration significantly decreased the chlorophyll content. It also caused oxidative stresses to plant therefore increasing the antioxidative activity. On contrary to shoot, the Cd accumulation was higher in roots thus reducing the root biomass. Zhang *et al.* (2015) reported that *Medicago truncatula* inoculated with arbuscular mycorrhizal fungi had a positive impact on plant biomass and increased the bioavailability of phosphorus by increasing the root surface area and decreased the arsenic concentration in roots and shoots of the plant. Arbuscularmycorrhizal fungi can methylate the inorganic AS into less toxic organic DMA. Malecka *et al.* (2014) reported on the production of ROS due to the presence of heavy metals which causes oxidative damages in plants. The metal when applied in combination of two or more elements together impacted the organisms in a more complex way. Exposure of plants to abiotic stresses restricted elongation of roots, decreased the biomass production and altered the morphological characters in plants. It also altered the production rate of ROS, increased the MDA content and also affected the gene expression of anti-oxidant. Pandey *et al.* (2012) According to the experiment conducted, it was reported that *Pisumsativum* treated with different concentration of Cd exhibited reduced growth of plant root and shoot. It also decreased the chlorophyll content thereby reducing the photosynthetic efficiency. The plant showed chlorosis, marginal yellowing and necrosis in young leaves. Cd-induced stress also enhanced the activity of SOD, APX, POD etc and evidently showed increment in concentration of H_2O_2 which reportedly decreased chlorophyll and carotenoid content.

CONCLUSION

Contamination with heavy metal is one of the major concern in agricultural soil as it possesses potential ecological threat and undesirable effect. Elements having a relative density greater than 5g cm^{-3} is termed as heavy metal. Elements like cadmium, arsenic, lead, chromium,etc are considered as heavy metals and these are very toxic in nature. These toxic elements are considered as soil pollutants which can cause both acute and chronic effect on plants grown in soil contaminated with these metals. These metals are very persistent and tend to remain in the soil for a very long period of time. Because of their toxic nature, non-biodegradability and lacking bio-disintegration, the bio-accumulate of heavy metals poses risk to the environment. In the past 150 years, the pollution level has increased more than 4000 times.

REFERENCES

Abeer H., Abd_Allah EF, Alqarawi AA, Al Huqail AA, Egamberdieva D and Wirth S. (2015). Alleviation of Cadmium Stress in Solanum Lycopersicum L.by Arbuscular Mycorrhizal Fungi via Induction of Acquired Systemic Tolerance, *Saudi Journal of Biological Sciences.*

Afridi MN, Lee WH, and Kim JO. (2019). Effect of Phosphate Concentration, Anions, Heavy Metals, and Organic Matter on Phosphate Adsorption from Wastewater using Anodized Iron Oxide Nanoflakes. *Environmental Research*, 171, 428-436.

Ahmad J, Ali AA, Baig MA, Iqbal M, Haq I, and Qureshi MI. (2019). Role of Phytochelatins in Cadmium Stress Tolerance in Plants. In *Cadmium Toxicity and Tolerance in Plants* (pp. 185-212). Academic Press.

Aldesuquy HS. (2016). Polyamines in Relation to Metal Concentration, Distribution, Relative Water Content and Abscisic Acid in Wheat Plants Irrigated with Waste Water Heavily Polluted with Heavy Metals. *International Journal of Bioassays*, 5(5), 4534-4546.

Alet AI, Sánchez DH, Cuevas JC, Marina M, Carrasco P, Altabella T, Tiburcio AF, and Ruiz OA (2012) New Insights into the Role of Spermine in *Arabidopsis thaliana* under Long-term Salt Stress. *Plant Sci* 182, 94-100.

Amir H, Jasper DA and Abbott LK (2008) Tolerance and Induction of Tolerance to Ni of Arbuscular Mycorrhizal Fungi from New Caledonian Ultramafic Soils. *Mycorrhiza* 19, 1-6.

Amir H, Lagrange A, Hassaine N, Cavaloc Y (2013) Arbuscular Mycorrhizal Fungi from New Caledonian Ultramafic Soils Improve Tolerance to Nickel of Endemic Plant Species. *Mycorrhiza* 23, 585-595.

Andrade SAL, Gratao PL, Silveira APD, Schiavinato MA, Azevedo RA, Mazzafera P (2009). Zn uptake, Physiological Response and Stress Attenuation in Mycorrhizal Jack Bean Growing in Soil with Increasing Zn Concentrations. *Chemosphere* 75, 1363-1370.

Asgher M, Khan MIR, Anjum NA, Verma S, Vyas D, Per TS and Khan NA. (2018). Ethylene and Polyamines in Counteracting Heavy Metal Phytotoxicity: A Crosstalk Perspective. *Journal of Plant Growth Regulation*, 37(4), 1050-1065.

Ashraf MW. (2012). Levels of Heavy Metals in Popular Cigarette Brands and Exposure to these Metals via Smoking. *The Scientific World Journal, 2012.* Article ID 729430, 5 pagesBal Ram Singh DKC and Asgeir RA (2017). Long-Term Effect of Phosphate Fertilization on Cadmium Uptake by Oat and its Accumulation in Soil. *Journal of Environmental Toxicology,* 7(6), 516.

Bali AS, Sidhu GPS, Kumar V, and Bhardwaj R. (2019). Mitigating Cadmium Toxicity in Plants by Phytohormones. In *Cadmium Toxicity and Tolerance in Plants* (pp. 375-396). Academic Press.

Basu S, Rabara R and Negi S (2017). AMF: The Future Prospect for Sustainable Agriculture, *Physiological and Molecular Plant Patholog.*

Benavides MP, Groppa MD, Recalde L, and Verstraeten SV. (2018). Effects of Polyamines on Cadmium-and Copper-mediated Alterations in Wheat (Triticumaestivum L) and Sunflower (Helianthus annuus L) Seedling Membrane Fluidity. *Archives of Biochemistry and Biophysics,* 654, 27-39.

Calzadilla PI, Gazquez A, Maiale SJ, Ruiz OA and Bernardina MA (2014). Polyamines as Indicators and Modulators of the Abiotic Stress in Plants. In: Plant Adaptation to Environmental Change: Significance of Amino Acids and their Derivatives. *CABI, Wallingford,* pp 109-128.

Chang Q, Diao FW, Wang QF, Pan L, Dang ZH, and Guo W. (2018). Effects of Arbuscular Mycorrhizal Symbiosis on Growth, Nutrient and Metal uptake by Maize Seedlings (Zea mays L.) Grown in Soils spiked with Lanthanum and Cadmium. *Environmental Pollution,* 241, 607-615.

Chen B, Roos P, Borgaard OK, Zhu YG and Jakobsen I (2005). Mycorrhiza and Root Hairs in Barley Enhance Acquisition of Phosphorus and Uranium from Phosphate Rock but Mycorrhiza Decreases Root to Shoot Uranium Transfer. *New Phytology* 165, 591-598.

Chen BD, Liu Y, Shen H, Li XL and Christie P (2004). Uptake of Cadmium from an Experimentally Contaminated Calcareous Soil by Arbuscular Mycorrhizal Maize (*Zea mays* L.). *Mycorrhiza,* 14, 347-354.

Chen BD, Yu M, Hao ZP, Xie W, and Zhang X. (2019). Research Progress in Arbuscular Mycorrhizal Technology. *The Journal of Applied Ecology,* 30(3), 1035.

Chen B, Nayuki K, Kuga Y, Zhang X, Wu S, and Ohtomo R. (2018). Uptake and Intraradical Immobilization of Cadmium by Arbuscular Mycorrhizal Fungi as Revealed by a Stable Isotope Tracer and Synchrotron Radiation µX-Ray Fluorescence Analysis. *Microbes and Environments,* 33(3): 257-263.

Chiao WT, Syu CH, Chen BC and Juang KW. (2019). Cadmium in Rice Grains from a Field Trial in Relation to Model Parameters of Cd-toxicity and-absorption in Rice Seedlings. *Ecotoxicology and Environmental Safety,* 169, 837-847.

Clemens S, Palmgreen MG and Kramer U., (2002). A Long way Ahead: Understanding and Engineering Plant Metal Accumulation. *Trends Plant Science.* 7, 309-315.

Cousin R. (1997). Peas (Pisumsativum L.). *Field Crops Research,* 53(1-3), 111-130.

D. Fern andez-Fuego A, Bertrand A. and Gonzalez (2017). Metal Accumulation and Detoxification Mechanisms in Mycorrhizal Betula pubescens. *Environmental Pollution.* 1-10.

Dias MC, Mariz-Ponte N and Santos C. (2019). Lead Induces Oxidative Stress in Pisumsativum Plants and Changes the Levels of Phytohormones with Antioxidant Role. *Plant Physiology and Biochemistry,* 137, 121-129.

Faten Dhawi RD and Wusirika R (2016). Mycorrhiza and Heavy Metal Resistant Bacteria Enhance Growth, Nutrient uptake and Alter Metabolic Profile of Sorghum Grown in Marginal Soil. *Chemosphere,* 157, 33-41.

Feng HY, Wang ZM, Kong FN, Zhang MJ and Zhou SL (2011). Roles of Carbohydrate Supply and Ethylene, Polyamines in Maize Kernel Set. *Journal of Integrated Plant Biology* 53, 388-398.

Fiala R, Repka V, Ciamporová M, Martinka M and Pavlovkin J. (2015). Early Cadmium-induced Effects on Reactive Oxygen Species Production, Cell Viability and Membrane Electrical Potential in Grapevine Roots. *VITIS-Journal of Grapevine Research,* 54(4), 175-182.

Franken P, and Bui VC. (2018). Acclimatisation of Rhizophagus irregularis Enhances Zn Tolerance of the Fungus and the Mycorrhizal Plant Partner. *Frontiers in Microbiology,* 9, 3156.

Gabriela Q, Gorka E, Lei D, François C, Ricardo A, Juan M and Ruiz L. (2019). The Arbuscular Mycorrhizal Symbiosis Regulates Aquaporins Activity and Improves Root Cell Water Permeability in Maize Plants Subjected to Water Stress. *Plant Cell Environ.*

Ghabriche R, Ghnaya T, Zaier H, Baioui R, Vromman D, Abdelly C and Lutts S (2017) Polyamine and Tyramine Involvement in NaCl induced Improvement of Cd Resistance in the Halophyte *Inulachrithmoides* L. *Journal of Plant Physiology,* 216, 136-144.

Goh DM, Cosme M, Kisiala AB, Mulholland S, Said ZM, Spíchal L, and Guinel FC. (2019). A Stimulatory Role for Cytokinin in the Arbuscular Mycorrhizal Symbiosis of Pea. *Frontiers in Plant Science,* 10.

Gong X, Liu Y, Huang D, Zeng G, Liu S, Tang H, and Tan X. (2016). Effects of Exogenous Calcium and Spermidine on Cadmium Stress Moderation and Metal Accumulation in Boehmerianivea (L.) Gaudich. *Environmental Science and Pollution Research,* 23(9), 8699-8708.

Grobelak A, Swiatek J, Murtaœ A, and Jaskulak M. (2019). Cadmium-Induced Oxidative Stress in Plants, Cadmium Toxicity, and Tolerance in Plants: From Physiology to Remediation. In *Cadmium Toxicity and Tolerance in Plants* (pp. 213-231). Academic Press.

Guan MY, Zhang HH, Pan W, Jin CW, and Lin XY. (2018). Sulfide Alleviates Cadmium Toxicity in Arabidopsis Plants by Altering the Chemical form and the Subcellular Distribution of Cadmium. *Science of the Total Environment,* 627, 663-670.

Guangjuan C, Shaoying A, Kang C and Xiurong W (2019). Arbuscular Mycorrhiza Augments Cadmium Tolerance in Soybean by Altering Accumulation and Partitioning of Nutrient Elements, and related Gene Expression. *Ecotoxicology and Environmental Safety.* 171, 231-239.

Gupta K, Dey A and Gupta B (2013) Plant Polyamines in Abiotic Stress Responses. *ActaPhysiol Plant* 35, 2015-2036.

Gupta K, Sengupta A, Chakraborty M and Gupta B (2016) Hydrogen Peroxide and Polyamines act as Double edged Swords in Plant Abiotic Stress Responses. *Front Plant Sci7.*

Gupta DK, Pena LB, Romero Puertas MC, Hernández A, Inouhe M, and Sandalio LM. (2017). NADPH Oxidases Differentially Regulate ROS Metabolism and Nutrient uptake under Cadmium Toxicity. *Plant, Cell & Environment,* 40(4), 509-526.

Ha HC, Sirosoma NS, Kuppusamy P, Zweiler JL, Woster PM and Casero RA (1998). The Natural Polyamine Spermine Functions Directly as a Free Radical Scavenger. *Proc Natl AcadSci USA* 95, 11140-11145.

Hartmann HT (1988). Plant Science: Growth Development, and Utilization of Cultivated Plants. 2nd ed. Prentice Hall Career and Technology, *Englewood Cliffs* (No. Libro 633 H37.).

Hasanuzzaman M, Nahar K and Fujita M. (Eds.). (2018). *Mechanisms of Arsenic Toxicity and Tolerance in Plants*. Springer.

Hediji H, Djebali W, Belkadhi A, Cabasson C, Moing A and Rolin D, *et al.* (2015). Impact of Long-term Cadmium Exposure on Mineral Content of Solanum Lycopersicum Plants: Consequences on Fruit Production. *South African Journal of Botany*. 97, 176-181.

Henson MC and Chedrese PJ. (2004). Endocrine Disruption by Cadmium, a Common Environmental Toxicant with Paradoxical Effects on Reproduction. *Experimental Biology and Medicine*, 229(5), 383-392.

Hsu YT and Kao CH (2007) Cadmium-induced Oxidative Damage in Rice Leaves is Reduced by Polyamines. *Plant Soil* 291, 27-37.

https://www.cadmium.org/cadmium-applications/cadmium-in-alloys

Huang H, Zhang S, Chen BD, Wu N, Shan XQ and Christy P (2006). Uptake of Atrazine and Cadmium from Soil by Maize (*Zea mays* L.) in Association with the arbuscular Mycorrhizal Fungus Glomus Etunicatum. *Journal of Agriculture & Food Chemistry*, 54, 9377-9382.

Hussain SS, Ali M, Ahmad M and Siddique KH (2011). Polyamines: Natural and Engineered Abiotic and Biotic Stress Tolerance in Plants. *Biotechnology Advancres*, 29, 300-311.

Pages: 107-126

Effect of Elements on Plants
Edited by: Dr. Prasann Kumar and Dr. Pawan Kumar 'Bharti'
ISBN: 978-93-88854-44-3
Edition: 2020
Published by: Discovery Publishing House Pvt. Ltd., New Delhi (India)

Aluminum Induced Oxidative Stress in Rice (*Oryza sativa* L.)

Prasann Kumar[1,2]*, Shipa Rani Dey[1]

GRAPHICAL ABSTRACT

Keywords: Aluminum, Basmati, Crop, Density

INTRODUCTION

Rice (*Oryza sativa* L) belongs to the grass family Poaceae. Genus Oryza consists of 22 wild species (Annual and Perennial) and two cultivated species i.e, sativa (Grown in Asia, America, and Europe) and glaberrima (grown

[1] Department of Agronomy, School of Agriculture, Lovely Professional University, Jalandhar - 144 411 (Punjab) (India)

[2] Divison of Research and Development, Lovely Professional University, Jalandhar - 144 411 Punjab, (India)

in Africa). In India, it has been mainly grown in the Gangetic plains and coastal areas (Bao, *et al.* 2018). Amongst the wild species, seven are tetraploid (2n=48) and rest are all diploids (2n=24). It is a semi-aquatic crop which is grown in standing water with very high water requirement. The word rice is derived from the French word is or the Italian word riso which came out to be a modification of the Sanskrit word vrihi. World paddy production was 759.6 million tonnes in 2017 where China leads India by producing 210.3 million tonnes as against 166.5 million tonnes by the latter (www.fao.org). Paddy yielded 3.85 tonnes per hectare and was harvested over 42.9 million hectares (ricestat.irri.org). Among the Indian states West Bengal bags first position (2015-2016) in rice production (15.10%) followed by Uttar Pradesh (11.99%), Punjab (11.33%), Tamil Nadu (7.65%), Andhra Pradesh (7.18%), Bihar (6.22%), Chattisgarh (5.84%), Orissa (5.64), Assam (4.93), Haryana (3.98) (www.apeda.com). Rice protein content differs from 6% to 14% based upon rice variety and culture environment (Lin, L. H., *et al.* 2019). It was thought that cultivated rice was originated in South India by De Candolle (1886) and Watt (1892). Vavilov, on the other hand, insisted on India and Burma to be the center of origin of cultivated rice. Pusa Basmati 1121 hasbeen widely celebrated for its grain quality especially the exceptional grain elongation upon cooking and its pleasant aroma, but it is clearly a modern variety with semi-dwarf plant type (Singh *et al.* 2018). The loci for extra-long grain came through transgressive segregation resulting from the inter-mating of the sister lines Basmati 370 and Type 3 (Singh *et al.* 2018). Research work done over this variety not only curtailed the total growing period from 160 to mere 140-145 days but also surged the yield two-fold from 2.5 t/ha to 5 t/ha, which further reduces the inputs and lessens the cost of production. It is a semi-dwarf variety of rice with plant height varying from (110-120) cm and yield potential reaching upto 5.5 tonnes per hectare. It could bear 350-400 panicles per m^2 with18-20 tillers per plant at the spacing of 20*15 cm^2.Its panicles could range between 26-28cm and the number of filled grains per panicle could vary between (105-110) and 1000 rain weight of fully matured grains are 27-28gm at 14% moisture (Singh et al 2018). Till now 29 varieties of basmati rice have been notified under the seeds act 1966, Pusa Basmati 1121 being one of them (www.apeda.com). Iran holds the highest share among Indian export of basmati rice of about 22% followed by Saudi Arab (20%), United Arab Emirates (10%) and Iraq (10%) (www.apeda.com). In India, it is cultivated in the states of J and K, Himachal Pradesh, Punjab, Haryana, Delhi, Uttarakhand, and western Uttar Pradesh. India has become the leading exporter of Basmati rice in the global market. The country has exported 4056758.62 MT of basmati rice to the world market worth of Rs 26870.17 crores (or 4169.48 US$ Mill) during the year 2017-2018 (www.apeda.com).

Soils having pH <5.5 are considered to be acidic or Ultisols or oxisols and are said to be generated from the parent material that is also acidic, where cation leaching has acted for a large span (Eimil-Fraga, Fernández-Sanjurjo, Rodríguez-Soalleiro, *et al.*, 2016). Acidic soils form a pool of available form of Al which further pose deficiency of both major and minor nutrients (P, Ca, Mg, K, Mn, Mo, and Zn) hence becomes the reason for the loss of large agriculture production (Choudhury and Sharma, 2017). They constitute almost 30% of the total area of the planet and also 50% of the total arable land in the world (Sade, *et al* 2016) Soil pH is normally not below 4, where hydrogen ions cannot pose toxic effect but on the contrary low pH allows for availability of free ions of Al and cause toxicity (Matsumoto *et al* 2013; Ivano, *et al.* 2013).

ALUMINUM AND ITS TOXIC ROLE IN PLANT

Aluminum is the most abundant element in the earth's crust after Oxygen and silicon (atomic number: 13; atomic mass: 26.982; melting point: 660.3°C).It was in the 19th century that a Danish physicist Christian Oersted first discovered Al by electrolytic reduction. Aluminum exposure on humans is said to have many deleterious effects. (1) Colon Inflammation and Inflammatory Bowel Disease (IBD) (Vignal, *et al.*, 2016). (2) Breast Cancer and Breast cyst Formation by the continuous usage of Aluminum-based antiperspirants (Darbre, 2016). (3) Dialysis encephalopathy and Osteomalacia (Chappard, *et al.*, 2016). (4) Exostosis (Benign Bone Tumor) Osteochondroma (Chappard, *et al* 2015). (5) Alzheimer Disease (Mirza, *et al.*, 2017). (6) Autism Spectrum Disorder (Mold, *et al.*, 2018). (7) Aluminum accumulation in patients suffering from Chronic Kidney Disease (CKD) and End Stage Renal Disease (ESRD) (Hsu, *et al* 2016).The ionic form of Al changes in accordance with the pH, so its toxicity. As the ph increases the Al ions show the following form; Al, Al $(OH)^{+2}$, Al (OH) $^{+2,}$ Al $(OH)^{-}_{4.}$ (Bojórquez-Quintal, *et al* 2017).

Genetic alterations were more eminent in Al-resistant cultivars. Glutathione Transferase Activity and Glycosyl Transferase Activity were responsible for the detoxification of Reactive Oxygen Species (ROS) and Cell wall modifications (Dmitriev, *et al* 2016). Tea plant is proved to be an Al hyperaccumulator crop (Ghanati,Morita and Yokota, 2005; Hajiboland, *et al.*, 2013; Karak *et al.*, 2015; Morita, *et al.*, 2004; Mukhopadyay *et al.*, 2012; Xu *et al.*, 2017). The Al has some beneficial roles also especially in tea where it enhances the leaf pigments,cell membrane stability and delaying the aging and death of plant cells (Bora, *et al.* 2018). Any interruption in photosynthesis exhibits generation of excess reactive oxygen species (ROS) such as Superoxide radicals (SOR;O_2^{-}) and hydrogen peroxide (H_2O_2) which moreover disrupts membrane integrity (Hasni *et al*, 2015; Kumar *et al.*, 2015; Silva *et al.*, 2018). Under such stress conditions organism (N fixing cyanobacteria) respond by activating enzymatic antioxidants like (SOD) superoxide dismutase, catalase (CAT), glutathione-S-transferase and also non-enzymatic antioxidants like (proline, cysteine and NP-SH,) to prevent damaging effects of ROS (Kumar *et al.*, 2015; Sun *et al.*, 2018). It disrupted the organization of microtubules and microfilaments in the root cells which further restrained longitudinal cell expansion and lateral cell swelling (Alessa and Oliveira, 2001; Singh *et al*, 2017a).

Aluminum reduced root biomass by 28.5% in ryegrass whereas no growth changes were found in shoots (Pontigo, *et al.*, 2017). Shoots exhibited enhanced (POD) Peroxidase Activity by 30% by exposure of Al whereas no such activity was visible in roots. Ascorbate Peroxidase (APX) was enhanced by 2.7 fold and 1.8 fold in shoots and roots by the addition of Aluminium in the growth media. Al enhanced the SOD activity in ryegrass by 37.2% in shoots and 27.5% in roots. Al toxicity also leads to ROS production (Kochian *et al.*, 2005) which further causes oxidative damage of biomolecules and the biological membranes (Yamamoto *et al.*, 2001, 2002, 2003; Singh *et al.*, 2017). Root lipid peroxidation was enhanced by 29% by the exposure of only 0.2 mM Al whereas no such change in the oxidative damage was visible in the shoots. The Al significantly increased Phenol content in the plant species (Pontigo, *et al.*, 2017). Its toxicity becomes the reason for several nutrient deficiencies such as Magnesium (Mg), Calcium (Ca), and Phosphorous, which further retard the growth of plants (Merino-Gergichecich *et al.* 2010). It reduced the content of photosynthetic pigments (Chl a, Chl b and total Chl (a+b) as compared to control treatment in wheat (Ahmad *et al* 2018) including eucalyptus (Yang *et al.* 2015) and barley (Shahnawaz *et al.* 201).Such a decrease in the chlorophyll content could be due to the hindrance of enzymes related to chlorophyll biosynthesis disrupted by oxidative stress or damaged protein-pigment complexes in the photosystems. Photosynthesis is heavily affected by the heavy metal stress due to the substitution of magnesium ions of the chlorophyll by the heavy metals (Cu, Zn, Cd, Hg) (Ahmad *et al* 2018). The Al is proved to reduce the number of Active reaction centers and disrupt the water-splitting complex (Li *et al.*, 2012, Singh *et al*, 2018). It also lowered the other photosynthetic aspects such as Fv/Fm and Total Performance Index (PIABS) (Yang *et al.* 2012). Further, photochemical events sluggishness in case of photosynthesis was accounted for inhibition of stomatal conductance in Citrus limonia (Silva *et al.* (2018). Aluminum on chelation with some flavonoids such as anthocyanin and flavonols was responsible for certain colour changes in flowers. It was found that flavonols on chelation with Al ions produces deep yellow color in some camellia species such as in Camellia chrysantha (Tanikawa *et al.*, 2008) whereas the same chelation with anthocyanin in Camellia japonica led to purple coloration (Tanikawa, *et al* 2016)

The Al induced Oxidative stress leads to splitting of membrane integrity and stability (Awasthi *et al.* 2017). Plants such as Vignita radiate (green gram), Oryza sativa (rice) and Lolium penne (ryegrass)(Singh *et al.* 2015; Pandey *et al.* 2016; Pontigo *et al.* 2017) exhibited enhanced Lipid peroxidation onto Al exposure.Even Brassia juices genotypes verified enhanced oxidative stress upon Al exposure. Al enhanced the content of (ASA), Ascorbate, dehydroascorbate (DHA) and total Ascorbate (ASA+DHA) in B.juncea species. (Ahmad *et al* 2018). When plants are brought under Al exposure they are seen to be involved in free radical scavenging activities such as DPPH and HRSA in two genotypes of mustard (Ahmad *et al* 2018). The same findings were shown by (Chutipaijit 2016) which exaggerates on better the DPPH activity, more shall the rice genotypes be adaptive to osmotic stress based on antioxidant activities. Aluminum at very low concentration induces growth in native crops which have developed adaptive mechanisms (Yoshii, 1937, Osaki *et al.*, 1997; Pilon-Smits *et al.*, 2009). Low level of Al-induced root biomass synthesis in Tabebuiachrysantha tree, whereas the effect was opposite when high levels of exposure were made. (Rehmus, *et al.*, 2014). An increased root growth Al can induce or even have no effect on the essential nutrient uptake especially in hyperaccumulator crops (Malta *et al* 2016). Al induces alkaline Phosphatase activity and organic phosphorus activity in the marine diatom *Thalassiosira weissflogii* (Zhou *et al.*, 2016) Aluminium induces color changes in some hyperaccumulator plants.

To cope with Aluminium toxicity plants have developed certain adaptive mechanisms to survive in even toxic conditions which are as follows. (1) Exclusion or Resistance to Aluminium to exclude the entry of metal into the cell by secreting certain Organic acids or phenolic compounds which further bind Al^{+3} and prevents its uptake into the cytosol. (2) Exhibiting of Internal tolerance by compartmentalizing Al in vacuoles, the formation of Al complexes with organic substances in the cytosol and improved scavenging via ROS, to avoid toxicity (Barcelo and Poschenrieder, 2002; Kochian *et al.*, 2005; Poschenrieder *et al.*, 2008; Bojórquez-Quintal, *et al* 2017). Ample of detoxification methodologies have been adopted by the plants in order to fight back with the metal toxicity and their accumulation such asa cellular antioxidant system which constitutes Superoxide dismutase (SOD), Ascorbate peroxidase (APX), Glutathione reductase (GR) and Catalase (CAT). They help in the detoxification of oxyradical which further inhibits the oxidation of biomolecules (Hossain *et al.*, 2015; Awasthi *et al.*, 2017).

Many plant species have developed certain plant species for alleviation of Al internally and/or externally such as secretion of various organic acids anions (citrate, malate, and oxalate)from roots which further chelate Al ions in the rhizosphere (Delhaize *et al.* 1993; Ma *et al.* 1997, 2004a; Zhao *et al.* 2003). Furthermore, a number of Al tolerance genes have been explored in plants especially rice (Huang *et al.* 2009; Yamaji *et al.* 2009; Delhaize *et al.* 2012; Ma *et al.* 2014). It was found that NH^+_4 ions reduced aluminum accumulations in the roots by altering the cell wall properties which took place due to a decrease in ph by the NH4 uptake (Wang, *et al* 2015).

NANOPARTICLES AND ITS ROLE FOR THE MITIGATION OF AL TOXICITY

Nanotechnology plays various roles in agricultural research namely, Agricultural diagnostics, Manipulation of agricultural crops, drug delivery, nanobiosensors, nanobiofarming, nano-pesticides, Nanoherbicides and controlled release of nano-fertilizers and nanocomplexes (Agrawal and Rathore, 2014).

Nanofertilizers possess certain specific features such as enhanced production, ultra-high absorption, enhanced photosynthesis and increased surface area in leaves (INIC, 2014). It was observed that wheat crop when treated with bulk material and chitosan NPK fertilizer where enhanced the polysaccharides content also lowered the total soluble sugars and protein content in the wheat grain of plants grown in clay, clay-sandy and sandy soils (Abdel-Aziz *et al* 2018) and increased the fat content in wheat crop (Liu *et al.*, 2008). Hence, harvested wheat grains were justified to be sensitive to nanoparticles and hence were affected by the same (Abdel-Aziz *et al* 2018). Foliar application of NPs at lower dosage was substantiated to significantly productive (Prasad *et al.*, 2012). Highest carbohydrate content was found in the wheat grain as well as the P and K content when applied with 10% nanoparticle solution as compared to higher concentration (100%) which on other hand decreased the foresaid parameters (Abdel-Aziz *et al* 2018). It was found that when 50% of urea was applied as a nanohybrid (Hydroxyapatite [Ca10(PO4)6(OH)2] nano particles) as against the 100% recommended urea dosage, the yield of rice came out to be 7.9 tonnes/acre as against 7.3 tonnes/acre, hence almost larger in value than the alone urea exposure. It concludes the usage of nanoparticles as fertilizers which could further reduce the toxic effects of harmful chemicals (Kottegoda *et al* 2017).

Zeolites are a sort of naturally wetting agents which go for the circulating the water all over the soil which further affects the conductance of water in the plants (Szerment *et al.* 2014; Ghazavi 2015). Both zeolites and nanozeolites provide for easy water penetration and water holding capacity for the soil due to their porous and capillary properties, for example, Si-NPs (Rastogi *et al* 2019). Both nanozeolite and zeolite were seen to affect the water-stable mean weight diameter (MWDw) which is an indicator of aggregation, strength, stability as well as aggregate size fraction of carbon.(Mirzaei *et al.* 2015) where aggregation plays an important role in enhancing the soil physical characteristics like water conduction, infiltration, and ventilation. (Rastogi, *et al* 2019)

Based on their composition, Engineered nanoparticles are classified into four categories (1) Carbon-based materials (2) Metal-based nanoparticles (3) Dendrimers (4) Bio-inorganic complexes having single (nanolayers), Double (Nanowires and nanotubes) or three dimensions (quantum dots, metal nanoparticles and fullness) on the nanoscale (US EPA 2007). The shape, surface composition, and size of the free nanoparticles define them with specific physicochemical characteristics which are further incorporated into different products and used in several applications such as biomedical imaging for diagnosis, Drug and gene delivery, pharmaceuticals, cosmetics, fuel additives,and electronics. (Nair, 2018).

Carbon-based nanomaterials give rise to almost 40% of the total engineered nanoparticles that are used in agriculture,which are used either as additives or as active components (Gogos *et al.* 2012). They find use in various environmental applications such as in solar cells for the generation of renewable energy, soil remediation, contaminant degradation and for the detection of several pollutants as a sensor (Mauter and Elimelech 2008; Rasool and Lee 2015). The absorption and translocation of various carbon nanomaterials arise serious concerns regarding their toxic effects on plants and environment due to their ultra-fine size and altered physical, chemical and structural properties since plants represent an association between environment and the biosphere (Nair, 2018).

Chitosan Nano particles (NP) are one of the engineered nanomaterials with brilliant physiochemical properties, moreover, they are bioactive (Agnihotri *et al.*, 2004). They are naturally occurring polysaccharide, derived by the N-deacetylation of chitin which is the main component of crustacean shells such as crabs, shrimps, and crawfish. (Orgaz *et al* 2011). Chitosan and its derivatives are nontoxic, biodegradable, and environmental friendly and find great opportunities in agriculture and in enhancing crop production (Chandrkrachang *et al* 2002, Sharathchandra *et al* 2004). These NPs may increase photosynthetic pigments and leaf area by increasing the endogenous amount of cytokinins, which further induced the synthesis of chlorophyll and growth. (Chibu andShibayama, 2001). Chitosan NPs are used these days to carry fertilizer ions to the plants. Their foliar application was seen to improve the growth and yield, especially at a lower concentration of 10% in wheat crop.(Abdel-Aziz *et al.*, 2016). They get easily absorbed into the epidermis of leaves and further transmitted to the stem which enabled the uptake of active molecules and increased the growth and productivity of various crops (Malerba and Cerana, 2016).

Nanosensors can be of many types but based on the food industry they are considered to be chemical or bio nanosensors. Both chemical sensor and biosensors are manufactured in a similar way by placing chemical or bacterial detectors (reagents) on the probe (Ileš *et al.* 2011). Nanoparticles or nanosensors are used in food and agricultural products such as food packaging, food additives, and also food preservation. Enhancing the food safety and also extending the product life is the major goal of nanosensors in the food industry where nanosensors are utilized for microorganisms and toxin material detection and nanomaterial for antibacterial properties for enhancing the product life (Ileš *et al.* 2011). Silica nanoparticles substantiate to be more beneficial than the other nanoparticles in terms of sensor stability, accuracy, and sensitivity due to their core-shell structure (Sun *et al.* 2016)

Nanosensors have many applications such as Detecting soil conditions (e.g. Moisture, soil pH); Monitoring food borne contaminants; Aptasensors for determining microbial toxins, antibiotics, drugs, and heavy metals, (4) Portable nanosensors for detecting chemicals, pathogens, and toxin in food items (5) nanosensors incorporated into packaging material to monitor chemicals released during food spoilage and serve as the electronic tongue. (6) To detect ethylene (7) As labels to add an intelligent function to food packaging for microbial safety. (8) Monitor environmental conditions during storage; Trace and monitor product conditions during transport and storage (10) Smart sensor technology for detecting the quality of the grain, dairy products, fruit, and vegetables in a storage environment. (11) As smart nanosensors for early warning of changing conditions (Jafarizadeh-Malmiri, *et al* 2019.

REVIEW ON THE AL TOXICITY WITH CONTEXT TO RICE AND OTHER

Bora *et al.* (2018) conducted field experiments on mature tea (*Camellia sinensis*L.) in Assam for a continuous four years of the time period. Organic and inorganic fertilizers were applied on to the soil to access the impact of long term exposure of aluminum on its dispersal in soil and in plant parts, plant yield, leaf pigment and many more. Municipal solid waste compost was utilized for organic treatments whereas Urea, Single Super Phosphate, Muriate of Potash were used for (N, P, K) inorganic treatments. Six fertilizer treatments were given in three splits per year, giving full nonsurprising results. It came out that organic material applied soil material retain a more considerable amount of alumina as compared to that of inorganics. In the case of the crop, it was seen that main roots accumulated more concentration of aluminum than the rest of the plant. The weight of the pluckable shoot also increases with the surging concentration of the alumina. Kodiango and Palapala (2016) worked on Leucaenaleucocephala (Leucaena) plants at two different places about 800 meters apart i.e University of Eldoret and Maseno (Kenya), in the greenhouse as well as in field conditions. Among these places, the macro was located at an altitude of 1500 meters, and both the places had almost same pH which was much lower than (6.8) the critical value for optimal growth and development of the crop. Maleno had still slightly more acidic soil (4.8) than that at university (<5). Three varieties were tested in three replications in both pots as well as field conditions. It became evident that aluminum concentration in seedlings increased at the maleno site, along with growth and nitrogen levels whereas in case of soil aluminum level dropped with an uplift in nitrogen content. Qian *et al.*(2018) revealed that biochar which is a solid residue from thermal decomposition can help alleviate heavy metal toxicity by curtailing the transport of heavy metals from soil to plants. He conducted a potted experiment on evergreen poplar plant grown in acidic red soils in China. Soils were mixed with biochar in 1,3,5 (%) equivalent of its weight. He concluded that biochar had increased the ph of the soil and reduced the absorption of alumina by plants and also changes the existing form of alumina in the soil. On the other hand, too much application of biochar can be highly toxic for the crop and its growth. Findings came out that biochar had reduced the exchanged state (Al $^{+3}$) of alumina in the soil which is the highly toxic state, seedlings with 3% biochar showed better growth than 1%. Pontigo *et al. (2017)* concluded that silicon acts as an aluminum toxicity ameliorator in ryegrass (*L.* perenne L. cultivar Nui). Nutrient solution was exposed to aluminium (0, 0s.2mM) and silicon (0, 0.5, 2.0 million M). The direct attack on root was seen by a reduction in its dry weight by 28.5% was a direct consequence of alumina whereas no such symptoms were visible in shoot growth. Silicon, on the other hand, showed opposing characters such as attenuation in the alumina concentration in the crop especially the root area, and a large improvement in the root yield by 51%.Whereas alumina silicon co-treatment was seen to give a mixed result. Hubova *et al.* (2018) explained how the herbs and green cover affected the different components in soil, especially Aluminium and its behavior. Fewer herb colonies experienced a downfall in low LMMOA (Low Molecule Mass Organic Acids) but high soil organic mass and even more cation exchange capacity. Aluminum pools were seen as limited to the organic regions due to its lack of mobility. doNascimento *et al.* (2018) explain how the crop price (Schizolubiumamazonicum Huber ex Ducke) responded to the different treatments of AlCl$_3$ in the naturally weathered soils of the Amazon region of Brazil? Many biochemical variations were seen in the crop after application of different dozes of Aluminium, which showed their reaction against sensitivity to Aluminium and the time they could survive against the artificial stress. Tammam *et al.* (2018) studied the response of an Aluminium tolerant wheat cultivar (Sakha 93) to different dozes of Aluminium (100, 200, 400, 500) micro. Seedlings were pretreated with boron and grown in hydroponic solution. The cultivar showed to have higher adaptive mechanism against the Al stress. Aluminum (200, 400) reduced the fresh weight of roots whereas the low concentration (100) did not have much significant effect. Ahmad *et al.* (2018) examined the damage as well as the response of Mustard

(Brassica juncea) to the Aluminiumstress.Eleven genotypes of mustard were studied for growth under Aluminium stress out of which two genotypes (PusaTarak and Pusa Vijay) were subjected to Aluminium stress for 24hour and 72 hours. Enzymatic activity was seen too much in PusaTarak in comparison to control and Pusa Vijay. Tiwari *et al.* (2019) have discussed the role of NO in ameliorating Aluminium toxicity in Cyanobacteria. Aluminum toxicity affects paddy productivity by reducing Nitrogen fixation as well as biomass. Jaiswal *et al.* (2018) discussed the legumes reaction on being exposed to Aluminium. When soil pH gets below5, the trivalent form of Aluminium becomes active and hence restricts their productivity by directly attacking the rhizobia Al+3 directly effects root elongation which can further reduce productivity. Furthermore, they insisted on selecting Al tolerant legumes can help enhance the yield in Aluminium abundant soils. The use of liming and Organic matter for ameliorating acidic soils Aluminium toxicity was also suggested. de Freitas *et al.* (2017) discussed the role of silicon in alleviating aluminum toxicity in upland rice plants (Oryza sativa L.) cultivar Maravilha by reducing the aluminum ion transport to the shoot without affecting the rate of uptake by roots. Where Silicon treatment enhanced the growth of shoot whereas aluminum reduced the plant growth and root growth which further reduced the Si (silicon) uptake capacity. Bera *et al.* (2017) discussed the effect of different concentrations of aluminum on the rice crop. There was significant linear growth in the root and the root hairs. Zhang *et al.* (2017) discussed the role of melatonin in the roots of soybean which acts as an ameliorator to aluminum toxicity.It was found that the exposure of less concentration of melatonin to aluminum effected plants showed an upsurge in the growth of roots and reduced the production of H_2O_2. Yu *et al.* (2016) discussed the role of putrescine in ameliorating aluminum (Al) toxicity in wheat seedlings. Al inhibited the root growth but putrescine exposure, on the other hand, mitigated the reduction in root growth. Here two wheat cultivars were tested i.e Al-tolerant and Al-sensitive varieties.Where Al-sensitive cultivar showed root inhibition and ethylene production at the root apices, all such symptoms were altered in the Al-tolerant cultivar by the presence of ethylene biosynthesis inhibitors. Tanik *et al.* (2017) have discussed the several aspects of Aluminium (Al) uptake and translocation within the plants. Myriad of industrialization in addition to fertilizer doze applications made the soil ph dip below 5, hence acidic soils lead to solubilization of trivalent form of Al that is the most toxic form of Al, which further causes inhibition of root growth and other metabolic functions. Rao *et al.* (2016) discussed the several adaptive phenomena adopted by the roots to survive in conditions of lower availability of water and mineral nutrients especially Nitrogen, Phosphorus and Potassium. Ample of Anatomical, Architectural, Morphological, and Metabolic phenes take the credit of roots being able to survive in even nonfertile and Al-rich soils. Prasad and Shivay (2017) discussed the role of Oxalates and oxalic acid in making the plants tolerant to Aluminium (Al) toxicity. Calcium oxalates are known for balancing the concentration of calcium which is needed by the guard cells. Hence both oxalic acid and calcium oxalates play a key role in protecting the plants against pests. Chen and Liao (2016) discussed in detail about the two major complications faced by the plants growing in acidic soils i.e, Al toxicity and Phosphorous (P) deficiency. To address such issues plants have developed certain adaptive mechanisms where they utilize Organic acid (OA) anions (Malate, Oxalate, and Citrate). This OA is secreted by the roots in the rhizosphere which further chelate the Al^{+3} and make P available to the plants via roots. Zhu *et al.* (2019) discussed the role of putrescine (PUT) in alleviating Al toxicity in two different cultivars of rice especially the roots. Where Al exposed rice roots exhibited inhibition in growth, application of PUT not only enhanced the growth but also decreased the Al concentration in the root apices and ethylene emission. Jaiswal *et al.* (2018) discussed in detail about the availability of Al in the soil at pH <5 and its toxic effects on the rhizobia and legumes which further has a strong impact on Nitrogen fixation in the soil. Ample of adaptive measures taken by the roots of legumes to survive in Al-rich soils have been discussed in detail. Vignal *et al.* (2016) discussed the heavy exposure of aluminum to humans via food and environment, because of the increasing industrialization and the use of aluminum cookwares. Al gets accumulated in the human gut and not only reduces its permeability but also poses severe bowel diseases. Though people have become tolerant of small amounts of Al in the food still people who are vulnerable to it are at the risk. Darbre (2016). Discussed the invasion of Al in the breast tissues by daily exposures of various cosmetics and daily use products especially the antiperspirants. Al was found to be in large concentrations in the breast tissues as compared to the blood stream and was assumed to be the reason of breast cyst formation, breast cancer and may other changes in the breast microenvironment. Mold *et al.* (2018) discussed the Autism Spectrum Disorder which occurs as a result of genetic or environmental toxicity of Aluminium. Five donors of different age groups brain tissues were analyzed to measure the aluminum content and its link with autism. Chappard *et al* (2016) discussed the major deleterious effects of Aluminium on bones especially osteomalacia which further becomes the reason for kidney failures in dialyzed patients. Aluminum was found in bones of patients suffering from high permeability in the intestines. Chappard *et al* (2015) discussed Exostosis which is the most prevalent benign bone tumor found in children as well as adults. It was found that Al^{+3} in combination with Fe+3 ion can substitute calcium in the hydroxyapatite crystals of bone matrix. Mirza *et al.* (2017) discussed the several environmental factors that may be responsible for causing Alzheimer disease. Examination of 12 patients suffering from familial Alzheimer's disease brought out that Aluminium concentration was much high in their brain tissues. Hsu *et al.* (2016) discussed the threats posed by Aluminium on kidney patients. Kidneys are the major organs responsible for flushing out Al from the body so the patients already suffering from renal disorders face problems of Al accumulation in the body especially those suffering from End Stage Renal Disease (ESRD). Krasnov *et al.* (2019) discussed the tolerance mechanism adopted in flax seeds (*Linumusitatissimum* L.) to Aluminium exposure. Here genes alterations were studied in four flax cultivars having different genotypic structure.They studied in detail the different genes that were in the process after Al exposure and also brought to light the difference in the gene expression alteration between Al-resistant and Al susceptible varieties. Dmitriev *et al.* (2016) discussed the adaptive mechanism prominent n flax to the aluminum toxicity.Here Al-resistant and Al vulnerable both types of cultivars were put to observation.Genetic expression of the same was analyzed and it came out that Reactive Oxygen Species (ROS) detoxification and cell wall modification were the results of Glutathione transferase and Glycosyl Transferase. Bojórquez-rao *et al.* (2017) discussed Aluminium and its abundance on earth inspite of its declared unessentiality.Though it is very abundant still its availability depends on the soil pH, where it becomes bio available only at acidic conditions. Here the adaptive mechanisms adopted by plants against Al toxicity have been discussed. Malta *et al.* (2016) discussed the soil fertility and its relation with the plant nutrients in the species Rudgeaviburnoides which is a natural Al hyperaccumulator. It was found that soil having low fertility still grew plants possessing enriched nutrients especially during the vegetative stage and even assembled a lot of Al (more than 10g Al kg^{-1}) on leaves. Al was seen deposited primarily on the cell walls (pectin) and secondarily on the chloroplasts and suberized cell wall. Moreno-Alvarado *et al.* (2017) discussed the effect of 200µM Al on the growth of four cultivars of rice crop. It was found that Al exposed plants indicated 30% more growth as compared with the control treatment, and also showed a significant increase of 140% in root dry biomass. Sugar concentration was found to increase tenfold in Al-treated plants as compared to the control treatment. Cooperative enhancement of P and K in the roots and Mg in the shoots were visible in the Al-treated plants. Moriyama *et al.* (2016) discussed the effect of Al on the sugars (Sucrose, Glucose, Fructose) and phytohormones in the roots of Quercusserrata Thumb seedlings. It was found that when the ten-week-old plant was hydroponically brought in contact with Al, the concentration of starch and sucrose was reduced but the concentration of glucose was enhanced in the roots. Even abscisic acid (ABA) was seen to increase at a gradual rate during the experiment. Al was seen to promote root growth by a signal pathway for which glucose served as an energy source.

Moustaka *et al.* (2016) found that Al on exposure to two different wheat cultivars having different Al resistance was found to reduce the Ca^{+2} and Mg^{+2} content of the leaves as well as a gradual increase in the lipid peroxidation. Further Al-resistant cultivar was seen to assemble more concentration of Ca^{+2} and Mg^{+2} in the leaves. Panda *et al.* (2013) discussed how Al stress on plants immediately suppresses the respiration process and produces Reactive Oxygen Species (ROS). Mitochondrial Alternative Oxidase (AOX) was found to suppress Al stress by inhibiting ROS accumulation thereby reducing mitochondrial oxidative stress and enhancement in the growth capability of tobacco cells. Schmitt *et al.* (2016) discussed the Al hyperaccumulator plants especially the Symplocaceae family which includes many tropical and evergreen plant species. These species (seedlings and saplings) were grown in a hydroponic system with and without Al. It was seen that these seedlings were able to absorb the Al from the solution if provided with so and they showed a comparatively less mortality rate as compared to control treatment. Sade *et al.* (2016) discussed Al as one of the major limiting factor affecting the plant productivity especially in the acidic soils and is said to pose around 25-80% of yield losses depending upon the plant's cultivar. Many Aluminium tolerance factors were discussed here such as the exclusion of Al from the roots and the tolerance ability of symplast for Al. Though no Al tolerant cultivar has been brought to light yet, still formation of transgenics has been discussed here. Safari *et al.* (2018) discussed the effect of Al on tea Camellia sinensis L. Al is seen to induce certain biochemical changes in the cell wall. It also reduced the amount of xyloglucan in the root apices thereby reducing the Al binding sites, initiated the activity of loosening agents and further enhanced the root length. Sharma *et al.* (2016) discussed the response of two species (Al-tolerant and Al-sensitive) of Cicer arietinum (Chickpea) upon exposure to Al. Al-tolerant plants were found to have less oxidative stress and reduced damage to root growth because of the accumulation of H2O2 and Lipid Peroxidation. Tanikawa *et al.* (2016) discussed the wild species and flowering species of Camellia japonica L. Wild species possess red colour whereas the flowering species possess purple colour which may revert back to red colour of the wild species the next year. This purple coloration in the plants was said to be the outcome of Al chelation with the anthocyanin. Wang *et al.* (2015) discussed the role of NO_3^- and NH_4^+ in Al binding capacity in the roots. It was found that on exposure to NH_4^+ rice roots Al binding capacity reduced as compared to NO_3^- exposure on roots. The reason being that NH_4^+ uptake by the roots led to ph changes which further gave rise to change in cell wall properties and reduction in not only the Al binding groups such as –OH and COO⁻ but also pectin and hemicellulose. Wang *et al.* (2019) discussed the Biological Nitrogen Fixation (BNF) in paddy soils and the composition of diazotrophs in paddy soils collected from different geographical locations cultivating rice from Northeastern to southwestern China. It was found that amorphous Al oxides posed a serious biotoxic effect on the BNF in paddy soils. Various techniques regarding the growing of the crop in acidic or ultisols were discussed here. Hence it was concluded that if amelioration of Al was to be practiced in acidic soils it could help in the enhancement of BNF in the near future. Xu *et al.* (2016) discussed the effect of Al in tea plant Camellia sinensis L. Tea is an Al hyperaccumulator crop so it can grow easily in acidic soils. Here two cultivars of tea were used JHC and YS, whose roots were exposed to different concentrations of Al. Accumulation of a huge amount of sugar alcohol was found in the roots of both the varieties, but YS leaves showed an extreme loss of sugar alcohols. It was concluded that any crop species adapting to the Al stress can be related by differential metabolism of amino acids, sugars, and shikimic acids. Yang *et al.* (2016) discussed the ability of Al alleviate fluoride (F) toxicity by forming Al-F complexes in Tea plant (Camellia sinensis L.).When tea plants were exposed to F alone root growth and shoot tips growth was greatly hampered whereas on exposure to Al in combination with F enhanced the root growth. Al also reduced F toxicity by enhancing the concentration of F in the roots and decreasing its concentration in the leaves. Zhou *et al.* (2016) discussed the effect of Al on the phytoplanktons in the sea water under Phosphorus limited conditions. Al enhanced the concentration of diatom cellular Alkaline Phosphatase Activity (APA) and their utilization efficiency of Dissolved Organic Phosphorus (DOP). Al enhanced the ocean carbon cycling by inducing the phytoplankton utilization of DOP. Tabuchi *et al.* (2004) discussed the effect of Aluminium on the osmotic solute concentration in both Al-resistant (Atlas 66) and Al susceptible (Scout 66) varieties of wheat (Triticum activism). It was found that sugar accumulation in the root cells of Al-resistant cultivar was more as compared to that of Al susceptible, which further reduced the osmotic potential in the former cultivar to help roots in the water uptake and to growth against the cell wall pressure under Al stress. Sharma and Dubey (2005) discussed the effect of both Aluminium and water stress on the Nitrate Reductase (NR) activity in rice seedlings. It was found that seedlings when grown in a high dose of Al (160 µM Al+3), showed a reduction in NR act and NR max. Hence Al stress and water stress in combination declined the functional NR for which osmolytes proline, glycine betaine, and sucrose proved to protect NR under such stress conditions. Kochian *et al.* (2004) discussed the various mechanisms adopted by the plants against Aluminium stress such as Al tolerance and Al exclusion. The literature on Al exclusion was discussed how the Al-activated carboxylates are released on exposure to Al from the root tips. Carboxylate ligands (deprotonated Organic acids) helped in the internal detoxification of the Al which further led to the sequestration of Al-carboxylate complexes in the vacuole. Jouili *et al.* (2011) discussed the peroxidase which is known for their variable structures and is present in plants, animals and even micro organisms. In plants, they not only function as plant growth regulators but also delineate biotic or abiotic stresses as biomarkers. The alterations in the quantitative and qualitative profiles of peroxidase indicate its role in the defense parameter. Horst *et al.* (2010) discussed the Aluminium pathway in inducing root growth inhibition by impairing apoplastic and symplastic cell functions. Root apoplast protection needs to be a major requirement for Al resistance. KuoandKao (2003) discussed the effect of Aluminium ($AlCl_3$) on lipid peroxidation in rice leaves. Application of Al on leaves uplifted the activities of catalase and Glutathione reductase but that of Superoxide dismutase was declined. It was found that after perpetuated Al treatment the activities of Peroxidase and Ascorbate peroxidase were enhanced. Al application was proved to induce oxidative stress which further led to Lipid Peroxidation.

EFFECT OF NANO PARTICLES ON CROPS

You *et al.* (2017) concluded that various soil enzymes, as well as microbial fauna, get influenced by the activity ofnano particles. Four different metal oxide engineered nano particles (Zinc oxide nanoparticles,Titanium dioxide nanoparticles, cerium dioxide nanoparticles, and magnetite nanoparticles) had experimented as amendments, three replicates each among two different soils i.e, black soil and alkaline soils in China. MO-engineered nanoparticles had been given under four concentration (0.5, 1.0 and 2.0 mg g -1) for 15 and 30 days). Soil enzymatic activities (invertase, catalase, urease, and phosphatase) under Zinc oxide nano particles visualized a greater significant effect in comparison to others and even that black soil was less vulnerable to nano particles as that in saline soils. Saline alkaline soils testing results showed a drop in its microbial community as a consequence of the treatments. Rajput *et al.* (2017) discussed on the threats that can be posed upon by the surging use of nano particles or nano-based products upon the various living and nonliving forms on earth. Mass research has been already performed on its construction and application but its contamination has still not been evaluated much. Agriculture and medicine have a lot of research going on upon nano products but they can be contaminative and can easily reach the soil or edible parts of the plant if applied in large quantities and could even be fatal in face of their ultra fine size. Kottegoda *et al.* (2016) discussed the loss of Nitrogen in the soil during the fertilization process. Nanotechnology plays a key role in increasing Nutrient Use Efficiency (NUE). Two nanocomposites based on Urea coated hydroxyapatite (UHA) displayed slow release behavior of Nitrogen in the soil. Kottegoda *et al.* (2017) discussed the slow delivery of fertilizers to plants by creating nanomaterial-based fertilizers. Here Hydroxyapatite [Ca10(PO4)6(OH)2] nano particles (NP) having a large surface area were bound with many molecules of urea to form a nanohybridsuspension.They could be used for providing nano fertilizers to the crops at less price and more efficiency. Chaudhry *et al.* (2018) discussed nanotechnology reaching heights in various sectors such as food and agriculture and their nano size ranging from 1-100 nm becomes the reason for their quick entry into the environment. There has been a green synthesis of nanomaterials (NM) which incorporate natural biomolecules such as plants, fungi, and bacteria. These green NMs not only are cost-effective but are also nonhazardous. They help in the synthesis of green fertilizers, pesticides,etc without any combination with toxic chemicals. Nair, P.M.G. (2018) discuss engineered nanoparticles (NP) and their large use in ample of fields leading to their easy entry into the environment. They'rea fine size and large surface area become the reason for their entry into the different environments especially the plants where NPs can be absorbed easily. Here phyto toxic effects of carbon nanomaterials were studied and found that they inhibit the growth of seedlings and also affect many biochemical and physiological aspects in plants. Jahan *et al.* (2018) have discussed the toxic effects and uptake of zinc oxide (ZnO) and Titanium dioxide (TiO2) nanomaterials in red bean (Vignaangularis) crop. It became evident from the biochemical analysis that ZnO got assimilated in the roots and further affected the physiological activities in the crop whereas TiO2 exposure, on the other hand, was seen to posit beneficial effects on the crop especially the surge in growth of the crop. Wan *et al.* (2019) studied the effects of Zinc oxide nanoparticles (ZnO) on sycamore maple (Acer pseudoplatanus). nZnO inhibited the growth of primary root whereas Zn^{2+} affected the meristem cells still the nZnO treated crops recuperated from the stress more quickly than the latter, after being Du, W., *et al* (2017) have discussed the effect of Metal Oxide nanoparticles (MONPs) on he terrestrial plants. However toxic effects of MONPs had soo far been visible only in seed plants. Dev *et al.* (2018) have discussed the interaction of nanomaterials with the plants. Nanomaterials, when entering the crops by any path, result in some changes in the growth of the crop.Plants, on the other hand, do possess several physical barriers to restrict their entry through plant parts and even after their entry plants exhibit certain adaptive mechanisms to fight against the toxic effects of nanomaterials. Verma *et al.* (2018) have discussed the advantages and disadvantages of (ENMs) Engineered Nanomaterials on various plant aspects such as quality and growth.The effects of ENM were different on different plant species and also showed a blend of effects on plants from yield to phytotoxicity.transferred to the normal conditions. Deng *et al.* (2014) discussed the Engineered nanomaterials (ENMs) and their uptake and translocation within the plants.The crops on being treated with ENM did express certain adaptive mechanism to the stress they were applied to such as the production of antioxidant enzymes.The toxicity imposed by ENM is still vivid and unclear hence food safety and trophic transfer of toxicity needs to be the subject of further research. Liu and Lal (2015) discussed the need fornano-fertilizers in the current era to have a significant upsurge in agricultural production.Four categories of nano-fertilizers have been described here i.e, macronutrient nano-fertilizers, micronutrient fertilizers, nutrient-loaded nano-fertilizers, plant growth enhancing nanomaterials. They thrust upon the N and P macronutrient nanofertilizer as a need for the sustainable agriculture. Sturikova *et al.* (2018) have discussed in detail about the zinc nanofertilizer. Conventional forms of zinc fertilizers were not found to give significant results owing to their fixation in the soil as an insoluble compound where arose the need for zinc nanofertilizer.They need to be applied at lower concentrations for the betterment of plant since the latter could cause damage to the plant. Venkatachalam *et al.* (2017) discussed the role of Zinc oxide nanoparticles in alleviating the oxidative stress imposed by the exposure of heavy metals, cadmium (Cd) and lead (pb) on Leucaenaleucocephala (Lam) de Wit. Abnormal band placement in the DNA was seen as an aftereffect of heavy metal exposure in the leaves. Reduced MDA-lipid peroxidation in the leaf tissues was observed as the ameliorating effect of NPs on the leaves. Prakash *et al.* (2018) discussed the nanotech growing at a fast pace which leads to the manufacturing of nano particle which different structures and properties in the vast sphere of field. Here the effects of carbon were studied either alone or in relation with other reactants.Result suggest that Carbon nano particle effect differently in different plant species and at different concentrations also.Further, it can constraint the growth of seedlings and many other biochemical characters. Jain *et al.* (2016) discussed the fine sized nano particles allowing quick transmission of nano particles in humans by various entry points which constraints its use in the therapeutics.The toxic effects of nano particles on different organs and also the management of such response was also discussed. Behboudi *et al.* (2018) experimented on chitosan nanoparticles under various concentrations, method of contact and irrigation scheduling in a barley crop.Thenano particles were exposed to barley crop at three stages which further appeared as symptoms in the form of colour and area of the leaf as compared to control.Where irregular irrigation leads to the decreased yield,the use of nano particles increased the relative water content compared to control. Abdel-Aziz *et al.* (2018) discussed the increase in the carbohydrate content of wheat grain on being exposed to nano chitosan NPK fertilizer via a foliar application on various soils. The saccharide content of the wheat grains on being exposed to the least concentration of nano particle (10%) was seen to increase as compared to control. The element content of grains such as potassium, phosphorous increased with the application of nano particles. Tamez *et al.* (2018) studied the consequences of applying copper nano particle such as Kocide 3000, CuO, CuCl, Cu metal nano particle under different concentration upon sugarcane crop. Large consumption of sugarcane in the formof sugar, or juice or others can easily find its way into the food chain.Coppernano particles showed the presence of stress indicators such as catalase as well as an increase in copper concentration in root tissues according to the treatment. Salehi *et al.* (2017) discussed the effect of CeO2 nano particles suspension upon bean (*Phaseolus Vulgaris* L.) crop. Nano particles exposure damaged the membrane, as shown by the increase in membrane lipids degradates. Nano particles were seen to pose toxic effects on plants at high concentrations, where aerial exposure resulted in more harm as compared to soil treatmentsince the results were quite insignificant in case of soil treatment. Rizwan *et al.*(2016) studied the influence of metal and metal oxide nanoparticles on various crops at several diagnostic levels.Where growth and yield of crops were seen to be highly constrained, the concentration of nano particle was seen to rise in different plant parts such as grains, which could lead an easy entry to the food and humans. The effects of nano particles were both positive and negative depending upon the crop cultivar,treatment, and several growth conditions. Rastogi *et al.* (2019) discussed the use of silicon as silicon nano particle in the field of agriculture.A metalloid and the second most abundant element in the earth crust after oxygen,Silicon gives many advantages in the form of nano particles if compared to the bulk material.They can easily enter plants because of their mesoporous nature, thus prove to be good transporters. A lot of literature regarding the impact of silicon nanoparticle as fertilizer, pesticide, weedicides has been discussed and also how it can protect the environment from the use of dangerous chemicals. Konate *et al.* (2017) discussed the role of magnetic (Fe3O4) nanoparticles in alleviating the toxic effects of heavy metals in wheat seedlings. The heavy metals in observation were lead, zinc, Cadmium, and Copper. The Petri dishes were sealed and shifted to a dark chamber for growth.After five days of germination, it came out that heavy metals affected the length of roots as well as shoot. Magnetic nano particles exposure, on the other hand, showed positive results in case of growth and also ensured that plant operates mechanisms to protect itself from oxidation stress. Sandhya *et al.* (2014) have discussed myriad applications of nanotechnology in the field of agriculture. Nano scale materials which range from (1-100 nm) possess specific physical-chemical and biological properties which account for their role in the plant systems. Their role as nano fertilizers, nanoweedicides,and their comparison has been discussed widely with the biopesticides where sustainability has been given core importance. Major Research institutes have been named and the granting of a patent to less number of Indian institutes was also discussed. Ali *et al.* (2019) discussed the effect of zinc oxide (ZnO) Nano particle (NP) alone and in combination biochar in alleviating cadmium toxicity in the cereals especially the rice (*Oryzasativa* L.) crop. The pot experiment was conducted where foliar applications of NPs and biochar were done and it came out that NP and biochar significantly enhanced the photosynthesis in the plant which further enhanced the income of farmers. It also increased the concentration of zinc in the crops hence can be useful for plants growing in zinc deficient soils. Dapkekar *et al.* (2018) discussed the role of zinc complexed chitosan nano particle (Zn-CNP) as a nano fertilizer in durum wheat crop. It was seen that nano fertilizer increased the zinc content of the grain unlike the micronutrients supplied individually. No harmful effect was visible on the overall yield of the grain which seemed quite satisfactory. Garcia-Gomez *et al.* (2018) discussed the role of zinc oxide nanoparticle (ZnONPs) on nine different crops in two types of soils i.e, calcareous and acidic soils. NPs were applied in the soil in four different concentrations. The nine crops taken under observation were wheat, maize, radish, bean, lettuce, tomato, pea, cucumber, and beet. It came out that the plant cultivar and soil pH play a key role in the availability of zinc. Pullagurala *et al.* (2018) discussed various advantages as well as the toxic effects of Zinc Oxide Nanoparticles (ZnO NPs) on terrestrial biota.nanoparticles these days are used on various items especially the cosmetics from where they can easily enter the environment and can be dangerous in large dozes.However, it came out to be an event that at low concentration (about 50 mg/kg) NP pose enhanced effects on plants whereas large concentrations (above 500 mg/kg) can cause havoc if grown in a zinc-deficient medium. Yanik *et al.* (2018) examined the after effect of different dose of Al2O3 Nano particle on wheat. Nano particles were 13 nm in dimension and were applied in three concentrations (5, 25, 30) mg mL. Oxidative stress was observed in the crop after 96 hours of exposure.Where H2O2 content surged as a result of Al2O3 nano particle,there was a decrease in the activity of catalase.

CONCLUSION

Aluminum is the most abundant element in the earth's crust after Oxygen and silicon (atomic number: 13; atomic mass: 26.982; melting point: 660.3°C).It was in the 19th century that a Danish physicist Christian Oersted first discovered Al by electrolytic reduction. Aluminum exposure on humans is said to have many deleterious effects. (1) Colon Inflammation and Inflammatory Bowel Disease (IBD). (2) Breast Cancer and Breast cyst Formation by the continuous usage of Aluminum-based antiperspirants. (3) Dialysis encephalopathy and Osteomalacia. (4)Exostosis (Benign Bone

Tumor) Osteochondroma. (5) Alzheimer Disease. (6) Autism Spectrum Disorder.(7) Aluminum accumulation in patients suffering from Chronic Kidney Disease (CKD) and End Stage Renal Disease (ESRD). The ionic form of Al changes in accordance with the pH, so its toxicity. As the ph increases the Al ions show the following form; Al, Al $(OH)^{+2}$, Al $(OH)^{+2,}$ Al $(OH)^-_4$.

REFERENCES

1. Abdel-Aziz H, Hasaneen MN and Omar A. (2018). Effect of Foliar Application of Nano Chitosan NPK Fertilizer on the Chemical Composition of Wheat Grains. *Egyptian Journal of Botany*, 58(1), 87-95.

2. Abdel-Aziz HMM, Hassaneen MNA, and Omer AM. (2016). Nano Chitosan-NPK Fertilizer Enhances the Growth and Productivity of Wheat Plants Grown in Sandy Soil. *Spanish Journal of Agricultural Research*, 14, 1-9.

3. Agnihotri SA, Mallikarjuna NN, and Aminabhavi TM. (2004). Recent Advances on Chitosan-based micro- and Nanoparticles in Drug Delivery. *Journal of Controlled Release*, 100, 5-28.

4. Agrawal S and Rathore P. (2014) Nanotechnology Pros and Cons to Agriculture: A Review. *International Journal of Current Microbiology and Applied Sciences*, 3, 43-55.

5. Ahmad J, Baig MA, Ali AA, Al-Huqail AA, Ibrahim MM, and Qureshi MI. (2018). Differential Antioxidative and Biochemical Responses to Aluminum Stress in Brassica juncea Cultivars. *Horticulture, Environment, and Biotechnology*, 59(5), 615-627.

6. Alessa L and Oliveira L. (2001). Aluminum Toxicity Studies in Vaucheria longicaulis var. macounii (Xanthophyta, Tribophyceae). II. Effects on the F-actin Array. *Environmental Experimental Botany*, 45, 223-237.

7. Ali S, Rizwan M, Noureen S, Anwar S, Ali B, Naveed M, and Ahmad P. (2019). The Combined use of Biochar and Zinc Oxide Nanoparticle Foliar Spray Improved the Plant Growth and Decreased the Cadmium Accumulation in Rice (Oryza sativa L.) Plant. *Environmental Science and Pollution Research*, 1-12.

8. Aluminum Toxicity is Associated with Mitochondrial Dysfunction and the Production of Reactive Oxygen Species in Plant Cells. *Plant Physiology*, 128, 63-72.

9. Awasthi JP, Saha B, Regon P, Sahoo S, Chowra U, Pradhan A, Roy A, and Panda SK. (2017). Morpho-physiological Analysis of the Tolerance to Aluminum Toxicity in Rice Varieties of North East India. PLoSONE 2, e0176357.

10. Bao J. (2018). Rice: Chemistry and Technology. *Elsevier.*

11. Barceló J. and Poschenrieder C. (2002). Fast Root Growth Responses, Root Exudates, and Internal Detoxification as Clues to the Mechanisms of Aluminium Toxicity and Resistance: A Review. *Environmental and Experimental Botany*, 48, 75-92.

12. Behboudi F, Tahmasebi Sarvestani Z, Kassaee MZ, Modares Sanavi SAM, Sorooshzadeh A., and Ahmadi SB. (2018). Evaluation of Chitosan Nanoparticles Effects on Yield and Yield Components of Barley (*Hordeumvulgare* L.) under Late Season Drought Stress. *Journal of Water and Environmental Nanotechnology*, 3(1), 22-39.

13. Bera S, De AK, and Adak MK. (2014). Modulation of Glycine Betaine Accumulation with Oxidative Stress Induced by Aluminium Toxicity in Rice. Proceedings of the National Academy of Sciences, India Section B: *Biological Sciences*, 1-11.

Pages: 127-152

Effect of Elements on Plants

Edited by: Dr. Prasann Kumar and Dr. Pawan Kumar 'Bharti'
ISBN: 978-93-88854-44-3
Edition: 2020
Published by: Discovery Publishing House Pvt. Ltd., New Delhi (India)

Cercospora Leaf Spot and its Impact on Biochemical Changes of Fenugreek

R.S. Mishra

Plants suffer from disease whose causes are similar to those affecting animals and humans (Agrios, 1998). Although we have no evidence that plants feel pain or discomfort. The development of disease in plants also fallows the same steps and is usually as complex as it is in animals. The mechanisms of plants which have produced disease vary with the causal agents. The reaction of a chemical nature is invisible, that soon becomes more widespread and starts histological changes which constitute the symptoms of the disease. The diseased cells and tissues do not preformed their normal physiological functions, as results of this plants growth is reduced and occurred considerable loss of yield. In India hardly any effort has been made to study the *Cercospora* leaf spot and its impact on biochemical changes of fenugreek. Hence, in this study, it has been reviewed under following sub headlines.

(i) Fenugreek and its importance.

(ii) Identification and characterization of *Cercospora* leaf spot of fenugreek.

(iii) Effect of *Cercospora* leaf spot disease on quality of fenugreek.

(iv) Management of *Cercospora* leaf spot of fenugreek with organic treatments.

(v) Effect of *Cercospora* leaf spot on growth and yield of fenugreek.

Department of Medicinal Plants, N.D. University of Agriculture and Technology, Kumarganj, Ayodhya - 224 229 (UP), (India)

FENUGREEK AND ITS IMPORTANCE

Fenugreek (*Trigonella foenum- graecum*. Linne) is on annual herb, origin of Indian sub continent and Easter Mediterranean region. The name fenugreek comes from *foenum- graecum*, meaning Greek hay, as the plants were used to scent inferior hay. The name of the genus *Trigonella* is derived from old Greek name three angled (little triangle) indicating the triangular shape of flowers (Rosengarten, 1969). Fenugreek is an erect, hardy annual plant, typically growing to a height of 30-60cm, it has a smooth hallow stem with alternate single trifoliate leaves borne on a short petiole with two small stipules at the base. Leaf lets are oval and slightly to the flower are yellow-white and developed in the leaf axils either single or in pairs. Pods are brown, slender and sickle-shaped with sharp beak at the end. They are 7-15cm long, each containing 10-20 seeds. The seeds are irregular rectangular 4-6mm long, 2-3mm wide and 18-22g/1000 seed weight (Slinkard, 2009). It is belong to sub family Papilionaceae under the family of Fabaceae.

Fenugreek is widely cultivated in warm temperature and tropical regions in the Mediterranean, Europe, Asia and Australia (Acharya *et. al.,* 2006). The major seed producing countries are India, China, Ethiopia, Egypt, Turkey and Argentina (Petropoulos, 2002). In India, it is grown Rabi season crop, considered to be one of the major seed spices (Lal *et. al.,* 2015). Major fenugreek growing states are Rajasthan, Gujarat, Madhya Pradesh, Uttar Pradesh, Maharashtra, Himanchal Pradesh and Punjab. It grows in about 93 thousands hectare area with annual production of about 113 thousand tonnes having average productivity 1215 kg per hectares (Tiwari *et. al.,* 2013). It is an important spice crop due to its multitudinous uses. Fenugreeks are extensively used as fresh leaves (green leafy vegetable), chopped leaves (flavouring agent), sprouts (salad), microgreens (salad), pots herbs (decoration), seed (spices, condiments or medicines) extract and powders (medicines). The seeds are also used to treat flatulence, dysentery, enlargement of lever span, gout, headache, deafness, baldness, vata disease, back pain, mouth ulcer, abdominal pain, kidney problem, diabetes, colic, heart disease and obesity (Rathore *et. al.,* 2013). Stem of fenugreek contain about 28% mucilage, 5% bitter fixed oil, 22% protein, volatile oil, two alkaloids (*Trigonella* and choline) and yellow colouring substance. Leaves contain moisture 86.1%, protein 4.4%, fat 0.9%, mineral 1.5%, fiber 1.1%, carbohydrate 6%, minerals, vitamins and 7 saponins is known as graecumin (Bukhari *et.al*, 2008). The seed of fenugreek contain lusine and L-tryptophan rich proteins, mucilaginous, fiber and other rare chemical constituents such as saponins, caumarine, fenugreekins, nicotinic acid, sapogenins, phyticacid, scopoletin and trigonelline, which are inhibit cholesterol absorption and thought to help lower down sugar levels (Billaud. 2001, Ribes *et. al.,* 1986, Sauvaire, *et. al.,*1991).

DISEASE OF FENUGREEK

Fenugreek appears very resistant to attacks by insects and animal enemies. The seeds of fenugreek can be stored for more than 10 years without any treatments due to peculiar smell of fenugreek plants. Apart from this, physiological disorder and biotic factors such as fungi, bacteria, virus, nematodes and insect are known to lower down foliage and seed yield of fenugreek (AAFRD, 1998, Fogg *et. al.,* 2000, Prakash and Sharma, 2000). Fenugreek seedlings are susceptible to *Pythium* (Damping off), *Rhizoctonia* and *Fusarium* (root rot disease), *Cercospora*, (Leaf spot), *Peronospora* (downy mildew), *Erysiphe* and *Laviellula* caused to Powdery mildew disease (Zimmer 1984, Gupta *et. al.,* 2015, Mishra and pandey 2015). Among the diseases *Cercospora* leaf spot is a common occurrence and is reported to the most destructive disease causing yield loss up to 80 percent under suitable environmental conditions (Khan *et. al.* 2014, Acharya *et. al.* 2014).

IDENTIFICATION AND CHARACTERIZATION OF CERCOSPORA LEAF SPOT OF FENUGREEK

Cercospora leaf lesions of fenug—reek initially produced as circular, sunken spots that were bleached in colour, with narrow1-2 mm chlorotic halos on the surface of the leaves. These lesions tended to elongate rapidly producing gray necrotic areas on the leaves. The necrotic areas were sharply defined with surrounded by a characteristics yellowish halo. The lesion size was bound increased on mature leaves, where the sporulations were significantly more. Several infected plants have found only few leaves toward the apex or no leaves without infection. Sunken and bleached lesions on stem, petioles and pod were also observed. In severe infections, stem were found yellowish and secondary branches become dry up. In case of disease symptoms on pods, it become discoloured shrunken and twisted (Sati 2015, Mishra and Pandey, 2016). Zimmer (1984) has been reported uniform distribution of *Cercospora* leaf spot disease in the field. Individual plants only upper few leaves remained olive and giving the appearance of tufts of green scattered in the field. On the older leaves, lesions size had increased where the sporulations were occurred higher and giving the white crashed lesions. He has also defined necrotic areas in the lesion surrounded by a yellowish halo. Stem and pod infected areas were found discoloured, shrunken and twisted. Acharya *et. al.,* (2014) described the *Cercospora* leaf spot of fenugreek as devastating in nature spreading quit uniformly in the growing areas. Only few terminal leaves survive in severally infected plants. The size of lesion increased due to rapid sporulations of *Cercospora* and necrotic areas were identified by the presence of encircling yellowish halo. Most severally infected leaves stem and pods were discoloured, deformed and sometimes wilted and dead.

Poornima and Hegde (2014). have characterized the symptoms of *Cercospora* leaf spot of palak with the production of small brown spot on leaves in the beginning which latter turned dark brown spots with circular or irregular margin, closely situated spots coalesced and formed large necrotic lesion and become papery thin and spots had straw coloured centre with brown margin. Elliott and Harmon (2001) characterized *Cercospora* leaf spot as narrow, dark brown, enlarge in to oblong to irregular shaped lesion with dark tan centre and dark brown to purple margin. Williams (1975) reported that symptoms of *Cercospora* leaf spot disease of cowpea are not seen until the time of flowering but after the flowering it may rapidly progress acropetally leading to premature defoliation. In case of severe infection, lesions developed on stem and pods which can reduce considerable yield of cowpea (Mulder and Holliday, 1975a, Hart 1977). Vakili (1977) noted that the shape of lesions was influenced by cultivar differences in leaf morphology and climatic conditions. Braun (1995) confirmed that *Cercospora* species cannot be identified reliably based on symptoms as lesion shape, size and colour because it can vary greatly depending on cultivars and environmental conditions. Hence correct identification may require microscopic examination of a representative sample of lesions (Braun, 1995).

CERCOSPORA A CAUSAL AGENT OF LEAF SPOT OF FENUGREEK

Sati (2015) have collected the leaf spot infected fenugreek seeds and evaluate the seed borne nature of the micro-organism in potato dextrose agar (PDA) media. The inoculated cultures were incubated at $25\pm2°$ C in darkness for 30 days to promote sporulations (Ryley 1989). The colonies of *Cercospora traversiana* were recorded from all contaminated seeds which conforming the seed borne nature of the pathogen. The mycelium were seen as cottony white and slightly raised on the upper side of the colony and the upper side of the colonies was olivaceous black to gray in colour. The colonies were circular 46 ± 4mm in diameter with irregular margins. Prasad *et. al.,* (2014) tested the *Cercospora traversiana* with the spraying of spore's concentration (1×10^4 spores/ml) on fenugreek accession and found most effective in developing disease symptoms, which confirmed disease symptoms produced by *Cercospora traversiana* with cultured on PDA media. Reley (1989), Zimmer (1984) and Lipik (1959) were also observed similar results. Prasad *et. al.,* (2014) described the conidiophores of *Cercospora traversiana* were dark paler towards the tip, unbranched and rarely geniculate or septate. He also found that these conidiophores developed in groups of 3 to 12 conidiophores per fascicle with a length ranging from 17.6 to 28.8µm and width 1.78 to 3.01µm. Acharya *et. al.,* (2014) reported that the conidiophores are dark, paler towards the tip, unbranched rarely geniculate and rarely septate. Conidiophores found in fascicle of 3-5 Conidiophores/ fascicle with the length of 420µm and width 3-5µm. Similar observation were reported by Sati (2015), Zimmer (1984), Relay (1989) and Bobev *et. al.,* (1999).

Zimmer (1984) measured 40 conidia, collected from leaf lesions in distilled water to which a small amount of lacto phenol containing cotton blue was added. He has reported varied conidial length of *Cercospora traversiana* from 48.1µm to 162.8µm. Conidia were acicular to cylendric, straight to curved, in distinctly multiseptate, base truncates tip sub acute to sub obtuse (Chupp 1953). Acharya *et. al.,* (2014) also reported that the conidia of *Cercospora traversiana* were similar to *Cercospora traversiana* sacc. (syns. *Cercospora trigonellae* maublance and *Cercospora traversiana* var. *trigonellae coruleae* savule Sanduville) and was acicular to cylindric, straight to curved, multiseptate, base truncate, tip subacuted subotuse. Baiyewu *et. al.,* (2005) worked on *Cercospora moricola* causing leaf spot disease on mulberry. The pathogen produced a compact mass of interwoven cushion like hyphae bearing conidia on the conidiophores. The conidia are 3-7 celled, hyaline and tapering at one end 70×30µm in size. Prasad *et al* (2014) reported the conidia of *Cercospora traversiana* were hyaline, acicular straight or slightly curved with a round apex, a tunicate base and multicellular with length 2.3 to 2.8µm and width 1.2 to 1.8µm. whereas, *Cercospora abelmosch* causing leaf spot of okra produces short unbranched conidiophores which was tabled, pale brown, septate and arise through disease lesions. The conidia were slender slightly curved, thin walled hyaline, multiseptate (3-6) and measuring 40-75×3-5µm in size (Farraq 2011).

GROWTH CULTURE

Zimmer (1984) successfully grown *Cercospora traversiana* on v-8 juice agar medium and tested pathogencity through artificial inoculation in fenugreek seedling. They lesions appeared 12 days after inoculation. A live pure culture of *Cercospora traversiana* was isolated from *Trigonella foenum-graecum* on potato dextrose agar media with repeated sub culture, which were inoculated 25±2°C in darkness for 30 days (Ryley 1989, Sati 2015). The *Cercospora species* was isolated from okra leaves showing typical leaf spot symptoms using glass needle and peated on tap water. The plates were inoculated at 25°C for 7 hrs. Then advanced hyphal tip of colony were transferred in to okra extract dextrose agar medium for culture purification (Hashem and Farraq 2005). Jenns *et. al.,*(1989) was developed method for the extraction and measurement of cercosporin in culture of *Cercospora* grown on six solid media, Malt and potato dextrose agar were generally favourable for growth of *Cercospora* and accumulation of cercosporin. The highest average mean colony diameter of 57.2 mm was recorded on PDA and lowest average mean mycelia growth diameter 53.11 mm was recorded on MEA. The effect of medium also influenced spore production by *Cercospora zea- maydis.* The good sporulations was observed on PDA and sparse sporulations on MEA. This could be due to faster growth of pathogen on PDA and attaining the average mean of 57.2 mm of colony growth followed by slower growth of pathogen on MEA.

DISEASE SEVERITY AND YIELD LOSS

Cercospora leaf spot disease severity was assessed using a 0 to 5 point scoring scale based on visual observation. Scoring scales based on visual observation of disease severity have been successfully used in many plants species including leguminous plants by many workers (Sati, 2015, Yadav *et. al.*, 2014, Elliott and Harmon, 2014, Iqbal *et. al.* 2011). The *Cercospora traversiana* infection is able to generate high levels of leaf infection on susceptible fenugreek plants, so it is relatively easy to see (Siuero *et. al.*, 2006). Prasad *et. al.*, (2014) used the percentage of leaves affected by *Cercospora* leaf spot and seen visually on a scale was 0=0% plant leaves affected (rated highly resistant), 1=1-15% plant leaves affected(moderate resistant), 3=41-65% plant leaves affected (moderate susceptible), 4=66-90% plant leaves affected (susceptible) and 5=91-100% plant leaves affected highly susceptible. The percentage of leaves affected by *Cercospora* was assessed visually on a 0 (highly resistant) to 5 (highly susceptible) scales (Iqbal *et. al.* 2011, Yadav *et. al.* 2014, Poornima and Heqde, 2014, Mishra and Pandey, 2015). The 0-5 scale used for evaluation of mungbean yellow mosaic virus (Khattak *et. al.* 2008), chickpea genotypes against *Ascochyta* blight (Reddy *et. al.* 1984), resistant of pea genotypes against powdery mildew and downy mildew (Fallon *et. al.* 1995).

Fenugreek accessions were evaluated against *Cercospora* leaf spot by Sati (2015) and found disease severity 2.08% to 41.66%. The effect of disease on plant height, pod number per plant, seed weight per plant and biomass per plant were found significant reduction up to 22.1 to 100% pod loss due to *Cercospora* leaf spot disease. Zimmer (1984) reported 20 per cent yield loss in Canada during 1983 in comparison to previous year. Rapid spread of *Cercospora* at the peak of rainy season could be due to humid condition prevailing which usually supports profuse growth of fungal mycelium (Baiyewu *et. al.* 2005), Yadav *et. al.* (2014) found 70.1 percent *Cercospora* leaf spot disease severity in mungbean crop at Gujarat. Prasad *et. al.* (2014) were tested 20 accessions of fenugreek against *Cercospora* leaf spot, two were found resistant (4.2 PDS), 7 were moderate resistant (14.6 PDS), 20 were moderate susceptible (37.5 PDS) and 18 were susceptible (41.7 PDS). Poornima and Hegde (2014) reported the favourable condition for leaf spot of palak was 28 days old plants because at this stage disease severity were found highest, where as the age of plants increased the disease severity decreased. It may be due to the presence of same nutrients in the plants which favour the development of the pathogen at seedling stage.

ORGANIC TREATMENTS

The organic farming is gaining impetus due to realization of inherent advantage because it increased the sustaining crop production and maintaining dynamic soil nutrient with safe environment (Lokanath and

Paramesh warappa, 2001). Cow urine has been applied as bio pesticide in organic farming along with cow dung, Cow milk and other herbal ingredient because cow urine is not only toxic material but it contain 95% water, 2.5% urea and remaining 2.5% is a mixture of minerals salts, hormones and enzymes (Bahadaunia 2002). Panchagavya is an organic product having potential source of nutrients to play the role for promoting growth and providing immunity in plant system (Pagar *et. al.* 2015). Panchagavya is being sought to improve crop establishment and health (Shakuntala *et. al.* 2012). It is an organic formulation, which in Sanskrit means the blend of five products obtained from cow i.e. milk, ghee, curd, dung and urine. All these products are individually called as "Gavy" and collectively named as Panchagavya. Panchagavya has got reference in the scripts of Vedas and Vrikshayurveda (Natarajan, 2002). Cow urine therapies in Indian system of medicine have a strong scientific base. Cow urine has been described in „Sushrita Samhita and Ashtanga Sangraha to be the most effective substance/secretion of animal origin with innumerable therapeutic values. Ancient books on ayurveda state that consumption of cow urine increase resistance to diseases by up to 104%. In India, drinking of cow urine has been practiced for thousands of years. Panchagavya is a term used in Ayurveda to describe five important substances obtained from cow namely Urine, Dung, Milk, Ghee and Curd. Many people use Panchagavya in some rituals (puja) and for medicinal purposes. It is also used in Yajur Veda for ark as a medicine. A work carried out on modern approaches has showed that cow urine has different activities like antioxidant, anti-diabetic, wound healing property, immune modulator, also act as bio enhancer to increase the efficacy of antibiotics, nutrients and anticancer drugs like taxol. Singla and Kaur (2016).

In India, use of Panchagavya in organic forming is gaining popularity in recent years especially in state like Tamil Nadu and Kerala (Shailaja *et. al.* 2014). It is also called cow pathway treatment based on products obtained from cows used in ayurvedic medicine and of religious significance for Hindu (Srimathi *et. al.* 2013). Panchagavya is an organic product recommended for crop improvement in organic agriculture (Sangeetha and Thevanathan, 2010). It is used as a foliar spray, soil application along with irrigation, as well as seed treatment (Natarajan, 2002). Panchagavya has played a significant role in providing resistance to pests and diseases, resulting in an increased over all yields (Tharmaraj *et. al.* 2011). Panchagavya possess the properties of fertilizers and bio pesticides and have been resulted in positive effect on growth and yield of crops as reported by Somasundaram *et. al.*, (2007). Effective microorganisms in panchagavya are a mixed culture of naturally occurring beneficial microbes mostly lactic acid bacteria (*Lactobacillus*), yeast (*Saccharomyces*), actinomycetes (*Streptomyces*), photosynthetic bacteria (*Rhodopsuedomonas*) and certain fungi (*Aspergillus*,

Penicillium etc.) reported by Xu, (2001) and Swaminathan *et. al.* (2007). Chemolethotrops and autotrophic nitrifies (Ammonifers and nitrifiers) are present in panchagavya, which colonize on the leaves and increased the ammonia uptake and enhance the total N supply (Papen *et al.* 2002). The P^H of panchagavya was lowered to 4.5 at 30 days of fermentation; it is might due to *Lactobacillus* bacteria in panchagavya, which produced more organic acid during fermentation (Mathivanan *et. al.,* 2006). Sakar *et. al.* (2016) reported that degree of efficiency of individual treatments varied but panchagavya +kunapajala was found to be best in better utilization of leaf nitrogen, efficient photosynthetic activity and improving yield. At the same time panchagavya can be used as prophylactic measures against the disease incidence of vegetable crops. Foliar spray of panchagavya provides the nutrient, IAA and GA to the plant which is present in the panchagavya (Somasundram 2002). Panchagavya created the stimuli in the plant system, which increased the growth and yield of groundnut plants (Mavarkar 2010).

Srimathi *et. al.* (2013) reported the *J. curces* and *P. pinnata* seeds fortification with panchagavya at 2 and 5% concentration for 16 and 8 hours, respectively. Panchagavya soaking had highest invigoration effect than water soaking and control. This study suggests that panchagavya application is one of the traditional, eco-friendly and low cost technique to enhance the better invigoration and promote the successful large scale afforestation in tree species. A field experiment was conducted during rabi season of the year 2010-11 at Agronomy Instructional Farm, Chimanbhai Patel College of Agriculture, Sardar krushi nagar Dantiwada Agricultural University, Sardar krushi Nagar to study the effect of Panchagavya on growth and yield of wheat under loamy sandy soils condition. The results showed that the treatment combination of T11 (RDF + Seed soaking in Panchagavya @ 3% + Foliar spray of Panchagavya @ 3% at tillering and jointing) significantly enhanced growth and yield parameters of wheat crop (Pagar, 2015). Jayachithra and Abirami (2016) was prepared the panchagavya with used of Cow dung (1kg) + cow urine (750ml) + cow milk (400ml) + cow curd (400ml) + ghee (200ml) and mixed thoroughly with ten litres of water, and thoroughly stirred the solution morning and evening daily, After ten days, He makes different concentrations of solutions viz. Control, 1, 3, 5, 7.5 and 10%. All the concentration of solution was sprayed on crops separately, which was effective for enhancing growth and yield of *Macrotyloma uniflorum*. Savaraj *et. al.* (2000) prepared panchagavya with the use of cow dung (7kg) + cow urine (10 L.)+ tender coconut water (3L.)+cow dung and ghee were mixed in 80 litre plastic container and stirred thoroughly both in morning and evening and kept air tide for 3 days. After 3 days cow urine and water added to the mixture and kept for 15 days with mixing twice every day. After 15 days rest of materials were added. The panchagavya was ready in 30 days after proper sieving through fine cloth. This mixture of panchagavya sprayed on seedling of tomato, chilli and cowpea increased the linear growth of both shoot and root system in all the vegetable seedling (Sakar *et. al.*, 2014) The have found induced defence mechanism acquired by the tomato, chilli and cowpea due to application of liquid organics, which was quantified in terms of polyphenol oxidase contained in panchagavya.

Maha panchagavya, a concoction made from five cow products was tested against *Pythium aphanidermatum* causing damping-off in tomato and results showed 48.2 per cent control of disease in nursery beds (Kumar *et. al.* 2010). Investigated the effect of panchagavya (3%), cow urine (10%), butter milk (2%), cow milk (10%) and vermiwash (50%) against soybean rust. Cow urine has resulted reduced disease index (36.0%) followed by butter milk (39.5%), cow milk (40.8%), panchagavya (41.5%) and vermiwash (43.1%). Soil application of compost tea has resulted decreased incidence of *Fusarium* wilt. Amin *et. al.* (2016) reported that plant extract and cow urine at specific concentration significantly inhibit the mycelial growth of *S. rolfsii* over control. It was due to addition of 30% cow urine concentration. Prabhu (2009) have prepared panchagavya by using the ingredients viz. cow dung (5kg),cow urine (3litre), cow milk (2 litre), cow curd (2 litre), cow ghee (1 litre), sugarcane juice (3 litre), tender coconut water (3 litre) and ripened banana (12 NO_3). Umaharan (2007) reported that *Cercospora* leaf spot (CLS) disease is an important constraint to cowpea (*Vigna unguiculata*) production, particularly in the humid tropics (Schneider *et. al.* (1976). Yield loss attributed to CLS in susceptible cowpea varieties varies between 36% and 42% (Schneider *et al.* 1976; Fery *et. al.* 1977). CLS disease symptoms are not apparent until the time of flowering (Williams 1975), but can rapidly progress acropetally leading to premature defoliation. Severe infections can results in lesions developing on pods and stems (Mulder and Holliday 1975; Williams 1975; Hart 1977; Vakili 1977).

Kekuda *et. al.* (2014) performed the study using Poisoned food technique to determine the antifungal effect of cow urine extracts of selected plants. PDA media amended with cow urine extracts (5%) were sterilized by autoclaving, poured into sterile petriplates and allowed to solidify. Fungal discs of 5mm diameter were cut using a sterile cork borer from the periphery of 5 days old culture of *C. capsici*, the discs were transferred aseptically at the centre of poisoned plates and the plates were incubated for 5 days at 28°C. The diameter of colonies in mutual perpendicular directions was measured after incubation (Rakesh *et. al.*, 2013). Antifungal activity of cow urine extracts was recorded in terms of inhibition of mycelial growth (%).

The beneficial microorganisms of panchagavya and their establishment in the soil hove improved the sustainability of agriculture as the microorganisms present in the rhizospheric environment i.e. around the roots, which influence the plant growth and crop yield was might due to presence of growth accelerating enzyme in panchagavya which favoured rapid cell division and multiplication (Vasumathi 2001, Sanjutha *et. al.* 2008).

Naik and Sreenivasa (2009) reported that panchagavya contains bacteria producing plant growth promoting substances. The microbes viz. *Rhizobium, Azotobactor, Azospirillum, Trichoderma* and *Pseudomonas* present in panchagavya act as liquid bio fertilizers and bio pesticides (Ali 2011). Sometimes seed germination and seedling quality have reduced with increasing concentration of organic fortification which might be due to optimal dose of the organic product, which is normally specific for crops to crops. Panchagavya enhance the growth and vigour of crops, including resistance to pest and diseases with increasing the keeping quality of vegetables and fruits (Natarajan 2002). Mishra *et. al.* (2015) was reported that the maximum reduction of mycelium growth was found in cow urine based botanical formulation 50.83 to 56.05% followed by acetone based botanical formulation 49.92 to 54.31% and distilled water based botanical formulation 44.51 to 52.35%. The highest effectiveness of cow urine based onion extract was 51.58% at 20% concentration after 72 h incubation.

Sugha (2005) evaluated the antifungal potentiality of panchagavya against *R. solani, S. rolfsii, F. solani, S. sclerotiorum* and *Phytophthora colocasiae,* which resulted complete suppression of mycelial growth of *R. solani* and other pathogens, the growth inhibition was ranged between 88.1-92.3%. The antifungal activity of panchagavya against major soil borne pathogens viz. *F. solani* f. sp. *pisi, F. oxysporum* f. sp. *pisi, R. solani, S. Solfsii* and *S. Sclerotiorum* were studied, and found 90 per cent inhibition in *F. oxysporum* f. sp. *pisi* and *F. solani* f. sp. *pisi* and 100 per cent inhibition in *S. rolfsii, S. sclerotiorum* and *R. solani.* Dogra (2006). Basak and Lee (2005) conducted the experiment on the efficacy of cow urine and cow dung *in vitro* for controlling wilt caused by *F. oxysporum* f. sp. *Cucumerinum* and *F. solani* f. sp. *cucurbitae* in cucumber. Cow dung solution showed 80-84 per cent and cow urine showed 100 per cent inhibition of wilt pathogens. Plotnikova (1977) observed the presence of mycolytic bacteria in cow manure. The extract of cow dung compost has showed the presence of bacterial isolates, which inhibited the mycelial growth of *Fusarium oxysporum* f.sp. *cucumerinum* and *Helminthosporium sigmoideum* (Kai *et. al.* 1990). Czaczyk *et. al.* (2000) isolated four strains of *Bacillus* from cow dung which has possessed strong inhibition properties 56.2-71.0 per cent against the mycelial growth of *R. solani, Bipolaris sorokiniaria, S. sclerotiorum, Trichothecium roseum, F. solani* and *F. oxysporum.* Chung *et. al.* (2000) isolated *Paenibacillus koreensis* from compost that have antifungal activity against *Fusarium oxysporum, Colletotrichum lagenarium, Sclerotinia sclerotiorum, Botrytis cinerea* and *Rhizoctonia solani.*

Muhammad and Amusa (2003) were found major microbes *Aspergillus niger,* *Trichoderma harzianum, Bacillus cereus* and *Bacillus subtilis* in cow dung compost. The microbes *Bacillus subtilis* and *B. cereus* were sprayed on seedling blight inducing pathogens such as *Sclerotium rolfsii, F. oxysporum, Pythium aphanidermatum, H. Maydis* and *R. solani,* the mycelial growth of all tested pathogenic fungi were inhibited to the tune of 40.0-57.8 and 35.5-53.3 per cent, respectively. Charest *et. al.* (2005) observed the presence of two bacteria *Pseudomonas aeruginosa* and *Rhizobium radiobacter* in cow dung manure. Both bacterial isolates were evaluated against *Pythium ultimum* and was resulted 2-3 per cent mycelia growth inhibition by *R. radiobacter* and *P. aeruginosa.*

Khaing *et. al.* (2008) were reported the presence of ten species of beneficial microbes such as *Serrati amarcescens, Bacillus megatarium, Azotobacter chroococcum, Pseudomonas medocina* and *Flavobacterium* spp. in vermiwash. Species of *Bacillus, Serratia, Pseudomonas* and Actinomycetes were obtained from panchagavya and evaluated for their antifungal potentiality against soil borne pathogens *viz. S. rolfsii, F. oxysporum, F. Solani* and *R. solani.* The maximum inhibition was possessed by *Serratia* (99.0%) followed by *Bacillus* (72.7-99.0%) and Actinomycetes (48.6-99.0%) against all the test pathogens (Ashlesha and Sugha 2008). Actinomycetes present in cow dung compost possessed antimicrobial activity against fifty three pathogens (Pinto *et. al.* 2010). Sinha *et. al.* (2010) documented the presence of nitrogen fixing bacteria, phosphate solubilising bacteria, Actinomycetes and mycorrhizal fungi in vermicompost and vermiwash, which showed antifungal activity against soil borne pathogens. Sreenivasa and Naik (2011) exhibited the presence of beneficial microorganisms in panchagavya and beejamrutha, which has been reported to improve the seed germination, seedling length and vigour in wheat and soybean. There are numerous reports on the effectiveness of cow milk, cow urine and cow dung in the management of viral diseases of ornamental and other plants (Joseph and Sankarganesh 2011). Nakasone *et. al.* (1999) advocated the use of cow dung paint for the control of smoky blight canker of apple and obtained 86.7 per cent healing of wounds. Sinha *et. al.* (2010) Studied the antifungal properties of vermicompost and vermiwash against soil borne pathogens (*Pythium ultimum, R. Solani* and *Fusarium* sp.) and recorded 51-72 per cent inhibition in mycelial growth of pathogens. Sang *et al.* (2010) reported the reduction in mycelial growth of *Phytophthora capsici* and *Colletotrichum coccodes* in pepper and *C. orbiculare* in cucumber by water extracts of compost. Joseph and Sankarganesh (2011) studied the antifungal activity of panchagavya and cow urine against soil borne pathogens. Sreenivasa and Naik (2011) observed 92.1 and 57.3 per cent inhibition in mycelial growth of *Fusarium* sp. at 15 and 20 per cent concentrations of cow urine *in vitro. Bacillus thermocloacae* found in compost and showed antifungal activity against *Fusarium*. Observed the appearance of beneficial bacteria, fungi and actinomycetous population in vermicompost. Six bacterial strains were isolated from compost which showed antifungal properties against soil borne pathogens (Abdel *et. al.* 2010). Gopal *et. al.* (2010) reported that *Pseudomonas fluorescens* was predominantly present in coconut leaf vermiwash. The use of cow dung paint in the control of smoky blight canker of apple and obtained 86.7 per cent healing of wounds. Application of clay with cow dung to stems and branches of apple trees gave good control of canker disease and increased the yield (Kamchatyi and Prikhod 1989).

Raja and Kurucheve (1999) studied the fungi toxicity of animal dung and urine against *Fusarium oxysporum* f. sp. *lycopersici*, the causal agent of tomato wilt. The highest (96.6%) germination percentage was found when seeds of jamun were treated with cow dung and urine for 24 h. Soils amended with composts provided 20-60 per cent reduction in *Pythium ultimum, Rhizoctonia solani, Phytophthora, Fusarium oxysporum, Verticillium dahlia* and *Sclerotinia* (Noble and Coventry 2005).

Sharma and Deshpande (2006) soaked pigeon pea seeds in 10 per cent cow urine, vermin wash, neem leaf extract, biogas slurry, cow dung slurry, homa farming ash and cow dung slurry (10%) + homa farming ash (10%) for 6 h. All the treatments significantly enhanced seed germination, shoot length, root length and vigour index. Fruit yield of guava was found maximum (38.8 kg/tree) when homa forming ash sprayed followed by 29.2 kg with homa + Rishi Krishi and homa + panchagavya (Ram and Pathak 2007). Amendment of soil with cow dung compost caused more than 50 per cent reduction in *Fusarium, Sclerotinia* and *Phytophthora* and 26 per cent reduction in *Rhizoctonia solani* (Bonanomi *et. al.* 2007). Sahni *et. al.* (2008) showed 25 per cent reduction in disease incidence while studying the effect of vermin compost amendment in soil along with seed bacterization with *Pseudomonas syringae*a gainst *Sclerotium rolfsii*. Manandhar and Yami (2008) observed 25.6 per cent control of foot rot disease of rice caused by *F. moniliforme* with the application of vermicompost tea. showed the neem based formulations among the treatments were found to be superior over control not only shoot height, number of leaves, number of buds, number of flowers, number of fruits of brinjal but also in respects disease control such as wilt and leaf spot. They have suggested, the use of neem extracts are a good alternative to synthetic pesticides because they are easily available, safe to environment, cost effective, non hazardous, natural enemies have low to moderate mammalian toxicity.

BIOCHEMICAL CHANGES

Plants produce a myriad of secondary metabolites, many of which can inhibit the growth of microbes. These inhibitory compounds may be synthesized during normal growth and development (Schonbeck and Schlosser 1976). Many of compounds may be absent in healthy plants and accumulating only in response to pathogen attack or stress called phytoalexins (Muller and Borger, 1940, Paxton 1981). The antimicrobial compounds of plant origin encompass a diverse array of different classes of compounds including saponins, Phenolics, cyclic hydroxanic acids, is flavonoids, sesqusterpenes, sulphur containing indole derivatives and many others (Papodopoulou *et. al.* 1999). The contribution of antimicrobial compounds to plant defence have tended to focus on phytoalexins, because these molecules are actively synthesized as part of the battery of induced defence responses associated with disease resistance.

TOTAL PHENOL CONTENT

It has been reported that fenugreek husk is a remarkable source of dietary fiber and phenolic acids which could be an effective source of natural antioxidants and natural ingredients in functional food (Naidu *et. al.* 2011). Pathak *et. al.* (2014) reported the total phenolics content from 1.51±0.03 to 1.92±0.06 mg/g in fenugreek. The total phenolics content in fenugreek genotypes has also been reported Singh *et. al.* (2013). They reported polyphenolic content in fenugreek genotypes ranging from 0.9947mg/g to 1.12mg/g. The presence of phenolics in appreciable amount makes the substance suitable as a neutraceutical. Muller (1990) reported that phenolics and flavonoids compounds are widely distributed in fenugreek that have been exert multiple biological effects including antioxidant, free radical scavenging anti-inflammatory and anti carcinogenic. Kaur and Kapoor (2002) found very high phenolics contents with high antioxidant activity. Ammar *et. al.* (2014) found high phenolics compound in methanolic extract of cotyledons of fenugreek (412.08mg/g) followed by 211.19mg/l in methanolic extract of hypocotyls and 124.84 mg/l in methanolic extract of seeds. He has calculated phenolic content as mg/l gallic acid equivalent of phenols. Payal (2007) was recorded higher amount of total phenols in diseased plants and lower amount of o-dihydroxy phenol, peroxidase and polyphenol in *Romularia* blight infected plants of *Foeniculum Vulgare* in comparison to healthy plants. Kuvalekar *et. al.* (2011) have reported no significant alteration in the activity of polyphenol oxidase and peroxidase in *Uromyces habsoni* infected and healthy stem tissues. Leaf tissue showed a significant increase in the activity of these enzymes at advanced disease stages. A significant increase in amount of phenolics was observed at early advanced stages of disease in leaves and stem. They concluded the correlation with susceptibility of the host and concentration of performed antimicrobial compounds and temporal activity of defence enzyme during progress of disease. Phenolic substances have various important roles in defence mechanisms of the host plants against fungal invasion. Phenolic compounds may confirm resistance to disease by limiting the growth of the pathogen (Isaac 1992). The certain common phenolic compounds that are toxic to pathogens are produced and accumulate at a faster rate at the site of infection (Agrios, 1997). Seasotiya *et. al.,* (2014) reported high value of phenolics contents 186mg gallic acid/g dry weight in methanolic extract of *T. foenum- graecum* seeds.

Bukhari *et. al.* (2008) was determined total phenolics contents by modified folin Ciocalteu reagents methods and expressed Gallic acid equivalent. The total amount of phenolics compounds in seed of fenugreek was highest in ethanol extract 6.85mg/g while lowest in hexane 1.33mg/g. Anjum *et. al.,* (2012) have showed different orientation of phenolics content for changing in various parts of crops plants. In roots early stage of infection, the total phenolics content was found 97.8% higher in healthy plants in contrast to the diseased ones. However, with the development of disease, root had a higher amount of phenolics when compared to leaves and stem. The diseased roots showed 161.8% increased over healthy roots checked at 140 DAS. Stem had about 50% increase in phenolics content in infected plants in comparison to healthy. In case of leaves at early stage of disease, there was insignificant difference in phenolics content of healthy and diseased leaves. But in latter stage the diseased leaves have 31.76% lower phenolics content in comparison to healthy leaves. Although, infection appears on aerial parts of the plants, the roots were found to be the most sensitive plants parts for production and accumulation of phenolics compound because plant defence responses can be activated at site or distantly from the point of pathogen attack (Dean and Kuc 1985). A gradual increase in phenolics and advancement of infection provides intimation for the activation of pentose pathways in infected plants. De Armas *et. al.,* (2007) reported a significant enhancement in hydrocinnamnic and hydrobenzoic acid in sugarcane infected with smut. Similarly, Sahoo *et. al.,* (2009) studied the biochemical changes in *Colocasia esculenta* attacked by *phytophthora colocasiae*. They reported 68-115% increase of phenolics compound after infection of pathogen.

Gupta *et. al.* (1990) studied the reduction of total phenol content in the leaves of mustard cultivars infected with *Alternaria brassicae* and *A. brassicola*. The reduction was found higher in infected susceptible cultivars as compared to infected tolerant cultivars. Plant flavonoids are an important part of human nutrition because of their anti-pathogenic effects (Frankel, 1995). These phytochemical can modulate lipid peroxidation involve in antherosenensis, thrombosis and carcinogenesis. Scapari *et. al.,* (2005) reported that healthy and infected plants have similar amount of flavonoids contents up to 14 days after infection, but significantly lower in infected tissues at 21 and 60 days after infection in witches broom disease of cocoa plants. Singh and Bedi (1976) estimated the phenolic and sugar constituents in resistant and susceptible gram cultivars against *Operculella padwickii*. They were found high amount of total phenols, flavonoids and tannin content in resistant cultivar as compared to susceptible ones. As a result of fungal infection, total phenols, flavonoids and tannins increased in both the cultivars but increase in phenolics was more in resistant cultivar G-543 than in susceptible cultivar K-4. Sugars contents were higher in the healthy tissues of the susceptible cultivar than the resistant ones. Lily and Ramadasan (1979) determined the changes in phenolic content of coconut leaf in relation to the development of leaf rot caused by *Bipolaris halodes*. Observations exhibited a significant increase in the total phenol content in the inoculated leaves as compared to healthy leaves. Anjum (2012) Total phenolics content expressed as milligram per gram of sample was determined according to Yang *et. al.*,(1997). One gram plant material (roots, stem and leaves) per replication per treatment was extracted in 50 mL of 95% ethanol. The samples were stored at 0°C for 48 h. After filtration, the supernatant was used for assaying total phenolics. Supernatant (1 mL) was mixed with 1 mL 95% ethanol and 5 mL of distilled water. Folin-Ciocalteu reagent (50%, 0.5 mL) was added to each sample. After 5 min, 1 mL of 5% Na_2CO_3 was added and mixed with vortex mixer and the reaction mixture was allowed to stand for 60 min in dark. The absorbance was measured at 725 nm in ultra violet visible spectrophotometer. A standard curve was built with different concentrations of catechol, used to quantify the phenolics, which was expressed as milligram catechol produced per gram fresh leaf weight (mg D g FW).

Tambe, and Bhambar. (2014) was reported the concentration of phenolics in plant extracts using spectrophotometric method. Folin-Ciocalteu assay method was used for the determination of the total phenol content. The reaction mixture was taken 1 ml of extract and 9 ml of distilled water in a volumetric flask (25 ml). One millilitre of Folin-Ciocalteu phenol reagent was treated to the mixture and shaken well. After 5 minutes, 10 ml of 7% Sodium carbonate (Na_2CO_3) solution was treated to the mixture. The volume was made up to 25 ml. A set of standard solutions of gallic acid (20, 40, 40, 60, 80 and 100 ìg/ml) were prepared in the same manner as described earlier. Incubated for 90 min at room temperature and the absorbance of standards solution were determined against the reagent blank at 550 nm with an Ultraviolet (UV)/visible spectrophotometer. Total phenol content was expressed as mg of GAE/gm of extract.

Gogoi *et. al.,* (2001) established the phenols as the biochemical basis of resistance against karnal bunt disease of wheat. They observed an immediate accumulation of phenolic following pathogenic attack in resistant varieties whereas susceptible varieties did not accumulate significantly higher amount of phenolics. The formation of phenols in response to pathogen may also lead to the modification of the cell walls surrounding the tissues (Lorena *et. al.*, 2001) and increased phenolic contents might be attributed to defence mechanism. The suppression of phenolic compounds synthesis leads to disease susceptibility in transgenic tobacco (Chong *et. al.*, 2002). The increase amount of phenols in severely infected plant parts could be attributed to the induced resistance for further invasion of pathogen (Kuvalekal *et. al.*, 2011).

Epstein (1972) studied the effect of *Longidorus africanus* on phenol content in roots of *Bidens tripartite* and *Vitis vinifera.* He concluded that the phenols of the infected root tips differ from those of the healthy tips both quantitatively and qualitatively. The amount of phenols in infected roots was more than double as compared to healthy roots.

FLAVONOIDS CONTENT

Fenugreek contains different alkaloids flavonoids and saponins (Kumar *et. al.*, 2012). The highest concentration flavonoids were found in fenugreek (Singh and Garg, 2006). Alkaloid and volatile constituents of fenugreek seeds are two major components which cause bitter taste and bad odour (Faeste 2009). The level of flavonoids in fenugreek is more than 100mg/g of seeds (Naidu *et. al.*, 2011). Benayad *et. al.*, (2014) investigated the phenolics compounds of fenugreek crude seeds from morocco by 1+PLC-DAD-ESI/MS. Analysis of most of the identified compounds were acylated and non acylated flavonoids with apigenin, luteolin and Kaempferol as aglycons. It is reported that significant antioxidant activity in germinated fenugreek seeds may be related to the presence of flavonoids and Saponins (Altuntas *et. al.*, 2005). Ammar *et., al.* (2014) were detected highest level of flavonoid contents in methanolic extract of seeds (217.28mg/l) and found total flavonoid content in fenugreek seeds (4.99q/100g dry weight). This variation in phenolics and flavonoid contents may be due to the variety of fenugreek and the difference in environmental conditions. Bukhari *et. al,.* (2008) was estimated flavonoids using the $Alcl_3$ reagent and quercetin as standard (R2 = 0.9990), the total flavonoids was in the range of 208-653µg/g of quercetin equivalent. The highest value for ethanol was 653µg/g and lowest was 208µg/g of the fenugreek seeds. Tambe and Bhambar (2014) were estimated the concentration of flavonoids in various plant extracts *Hibiscus tiliaceus* wood using spectrophotometric method with aluminium chloride: The contents of flavonoids were expressed in term of quercetin equivalent (The standard curve equation: y = 0.009×-0.006 R^2=0.999) mg of QE/g of extract. Ethyl acetate of wood contains the highest concentration of flavonoids: The concentration of flavonoids in plant extracts depends on the polarity of solvents used in the extract preparation (Zhuang 1992). Plant flavonoids are an important part of human nutrition because of their anti-pathogenic effects (Frankel, 1995). These phytochemical can modulate lipid peroxidation involve in antherosenensis, thrombosis and cavcinogenesis. Scapari *et. al.*, (2005) reported that healthy and infected plants have similar amount of flavonoid contents up to 14 days after infection, but it was significantly lower in infected tissues at 21 and 60 days after infection in witches broom disease of cocoa plants. Parihar (2012) concluded that high content of flavonoids and other metabolites impart resistant development in Ec-399299, Ec-399296 and PHR-2 against *Alternaria brassicae.* Whereas, lower amount of secondary metabolites were accumulated in susceptible genotypes (varuna and Ec-3999302) in response to pathogen.

TOTAL SAPONIN ESTIMATION

Fenugreek seeds are rich source of soluble dietary fibre Sharma *et. al.*,(1990). The 100g of seeds provides more than 65% of dietary and contains saponins, hemicelluloses, mucilage, tannins and protein, which help to decrease the level of low density lipoprotein cholesterol (LPL) in blood by decreasing bile salts reabsorption in the colon. It has been reported that fenugreek fibre bound to taxins in the blood and helped to protect the colon mucus membrane for cancer toxins as well as lowering the rate of blood sugar levels. (Mohammadi and Martazavin 2011). Dande *et. al.*, (2012) reported saponin extract of *Trigonella foenum- graecum* 8g i.e.13.33%w/w on dried weight basis and indicated the major chemical constituent was steroidal saponin in the crude saponin extract of *Trigonella foenum- graecum.* Diosgenin is an important precursor for synthesis of steroidal hormone like testosterone and progesterone (Norton, 1998). This steroidal saponins are present in fenugreek seeds. The esterogenic effect shown by the saponin extract of fenugreek may be due to the presence of diosgenin, yamogenin and trigogenin (WHO, 2008). Mahak and Sahu (2014) reported that neem leaves have phenols, flavonoids, tannins, alkaloids and saponins. These compounds are active ingredient of insecticide and fungicidal properties for effective control of wilt and leaf spot disease of brinjal. (Gajalakshmi and Abbasi, 2004). Saponins are an important group of preformed plant secondary metabolites in protecting plants against fungal attack (Price *et. al.*, 1987). They are glycosylated triterpenoid, steroid or steroidal alkaloid molecules that occur constitutively in many plant species (Osbourn 1996, Schonbeok and Schlosser 1976). It have potent antifungal activity and are often present at high levels in healthy plants, saponons have been implicated as antimicrobial phytoprotectants (Osbourn 1996). It has been reported in a common variety of higher plants and usually found in roots, tuber, leaves, blooms and seeds (Sparg *et. al.*, 2004). The saponins present in these species were most likely to be the triterpane. The triterpane are found mostly in dicotyledonous plant species, while many other saponins are found in monocotyledonous plant species (Osbourne, 2003). The high level of saponins in the root might be due to result of the need to protect plants against soil pathogen attacks. It has been noted that many saponins are present in healthy plants in higher concentration because of their antifungal properties (Papadopoulou *et. al.*, 1999)

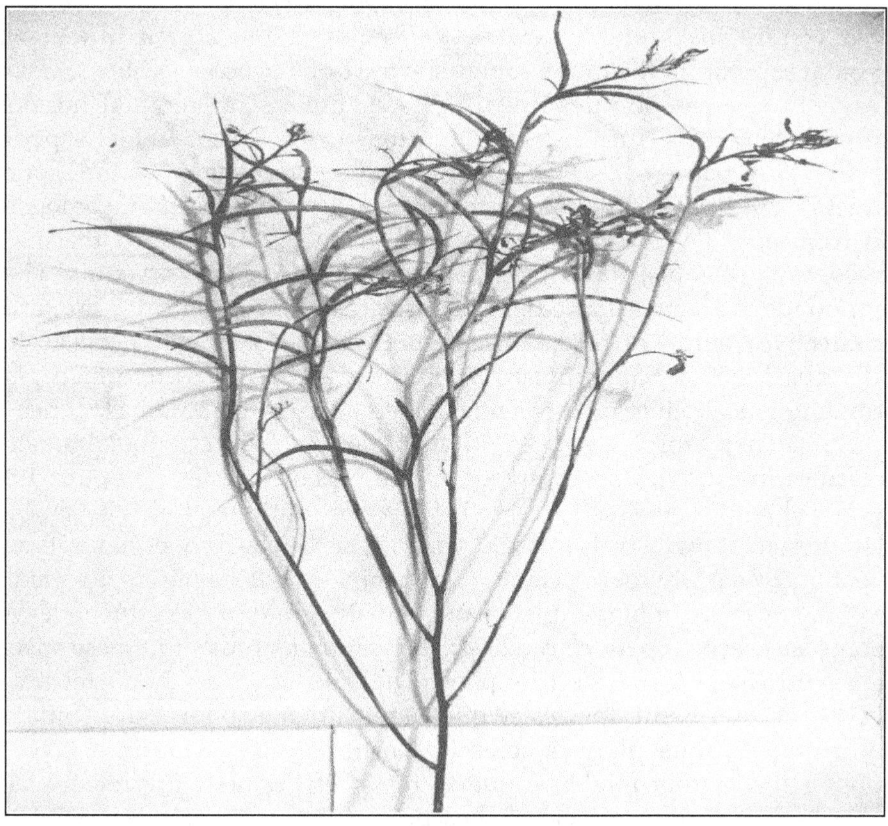

Leaf spot infected plant

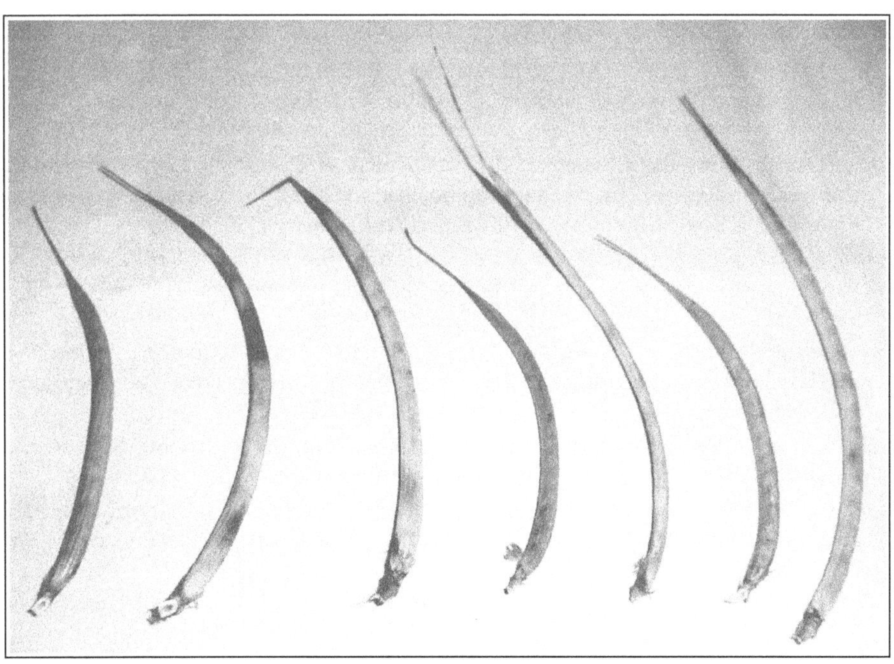

Leaf spot infected pods

<u>REFERENCES</u>

AAFRD. (1998). Fenugreek. Agrifax Agdex.147/20-25. Alberta Agriculture, Food and Rural Development, Alberta.

Abdel, M.H. Yamamoto, N.Otawa K., Tada C. and Nakai Y. (2010). Isolation of Bacterium like Substances producing Bacteria from Finished Cattle Manure Compost and Activity Evaluation against some Food Borne Pathogenic and Spoilage Bacteria. *Journal of General and Applied Microbiology.* 56(2): 151-161.

Acharya, K. Chakraborty, N. Chatterjee, S. and Basu S.K. (206). Fungal Diseases of Fenugreek. *American Journal of Social Issues and Humanities.* Special Issue: 2276-6928.

Acharya, S., Rajib, P. Scott Erickson and James Thomas. (2014). Identification of Cercospora Leaf Spot Resistance Among Fenugreek Accessions and Characterization of the Pathogen. *AJCS*8(6): 822-830.

Agrios, G.N. (1997). Plant Pathology, 4th Edition, *Elsevier Academic Press.*

Agrios, G.N. (1998). Plant Pathology. 4th Edition, *Academic Press.*, London, (UK).

Ali M.N., (2011). Sustainable Agriculture with Low Cost Technologies (SALoCT). School of Agriculture and Rural Development, Ramakrishna Mission Vivekananda University, Belur Math, West Bengal pp. 47.

Altuntas, E. Engin, Zgo, O. and Faruk Taser. (2005). Some Physical Properties of Fenugreek (*Trigonella foenum-graceum* L.) Seeds. *Journal of Food Engineering* 71: 37-43.

Amin, A., Alkaabi, A., Al-Falasi, S. and Daoud, S.A. (2005). Chemopreventive Activities of *Trigonellafoenum-graecum* (Fenugreek) against Breast Cancer. Cell Biol. Int. 29: 687-694.

Acharya, S.N. Thomas J.E. and Basu S.K. (2006). Fenugreek: an "Old World" Crop for the "New World". *Biodiversity Tropical Conservancy.*7(3&4): 27-30.

Ammar, M.A. Ali, Mawahib E.M. and El Nour. (2012). Antioxidant Activity, Total Phenolic, Flavonoid and Tannin Contents of Callus and Seeds Extracts of Fenugreek (*Trigonella foenum-graecum* L.). *International Journal of Science and Research.* 3: 2319-7064.

Armas, De. R., Santiago R., Legaz M.E. and Vicente C. (2007). Levels of Phenolic Compounds and Enzyme Activity can be used to Screen for Resistance of Sugarcane to Smut (*Ustilago scitaminea*). *Australasian Plant Pathology.* 36: 32-38.

Ashlesha and Sugha S.K. (2008). *In vitro* Antifungal Bio Efficacy of Microbes Present Panchagavya against Major Soil Borne Pathogens. *Plant Disease Research.* 23 (1): 68-74.

Baiyewu, R.A., Amusa, M.A. and Idowu, J.B. (2005), Leaf Spot in Mulberry *Morus alba* in the Lowland Humid Tropics of Southernwestern Nigeria. *Plant Patnology Journal* 4(2): 103-106.

Basak, A.B. and Lee, M.W. (2005). Efficacy of Cow Dung in Controlling Root Rot and *Fusarium* Wilt of Cucumber. *Indian Journal of Plant Pathology,* 23(1&2): 81-84.

Basak, A.B. Min Woong Lee and Tae Soo Lee. (2002). Inhibitive Activity of Cow Urine and Cow Dung against *Sclerotinia sclerotiorum* of Cucumber. *Mycobiology* 30(3): 175-179.

Bhadauria, H. (2002). Vishwa Ayurveda Parishad Cow Urine- A Magical Therapy. *Int J Cow Sci.*1: 32-6.

Billaud, de. (2001). Biochemical Parameters and Flag Smut Resistance in Wheat. *Indian Sciences-des-ailments.*, 21-23.

Bobey, S.G. Margina, A.F. and Gruytor, de J. (1999). First Report of *Cercospora traversiana* on *Trigonellacaerulea* in Bulgaria. *Plant Dis.* 83: 783.

Braun, U. Mouchacca, J. and McKenzie, E.H.C. (1995). Cercosporoid Hyphomycetes from New Caledonia and some other South Pacific Islands. *New Zealand Journal of Botany.* 37: 297-327.

Bukhari, S.B. Muhammad, Iqbal, Bhanger and Shahabuddin Memon. (2008). Antioxidative Activity of Extracts from Fenugreek Seeds (*Trigonella Foenum-Graecum*). *Pak. J. Anal. Environ. Chem.* 9(2): 78-83.

Charest, M.H. Beauchamp, C.J. and Antoun H. (2005). Effects of the Humic Substances of Deinking Paper Sludge on the Antagonism between Two Compost Bacteria and *Pythium ultimum. FEMS Microbiology Ecology* 52(3): 219-227.

Chong, J. Baltz R., Schmitt C. Beffa R. and Saindrenan P.(2002). Down Regulation of Pathogen-responsive Tobacco UDP-Glc: Phenyl Propanoids Glucosyltransferase Reduces Scopoletinglucoside Accumulation, Enhances Oxidative Stress, and Weakness Virus Resistance. *Plant Cell,* 14: 1093-1107.

Chung, Y.R. Kim, C.H. Hwang, I. and Chun J.(2000). *Paenibacillus koreensissp. nov.,* a New Species that Produces an itur in like Antifungal Compound. *International Journal of Systematic and Evolutionary Microbiology.* 50(3): 1495-1500.

Chupp, C.A. (1953). Monograph of the Fungus Genus *Cercospora.* Ithaca, New York.: 667.

Czaczyk, K. Trojanowska, K. and Stachowiak B. (2000). Antifungal Activity of *Bacillus* sp. Isolated from Compost. *Folia Microbiology.* 45(3): 552.

Dande, P.and Suraj Patil. (2012). Evaluation of Saponins From *Trigonella Foenum Graecum Seeds* for Its antifertility Activity. *Asian J Pharm Clin Res.* 5(3): *154-157.*

Dean R.A., and Kuc J. (1985). Induced Systemic Protection in Plants. *Trends in Biotechnology* 3: 125-129.

Dogra S., (2006). Anti-fungal Potential of Panchagavya against some Soil Borne Pathogens. M.Sc. Thesis, Department of Plant Pathology, CSK Himachal Pradesh Krishi Vishvavidyalaya, Palampur, India. p. 76.

Elliott, M.L. Professor, Plant Pathology, Fort Lauderdale Research and Education Centre; and P.F. Harmon, Associate Professor, Plant Pathology Department, UF/IFAS Extension, Gainesville, FL 32611.

Epstein E., (1972). Biochemical Changes in Terminal Root Galls Caused by *Protomyces macrospores..* Australian J. Biol. Sci. 25: 1-8.

Faeste, CK Namork E and Lindvik H. (2009). Allergenicity and Antigenicity of Fenugreek (*Trigonella foenum-graecum*) Proteins in Foods. J Allergy Clin Immun. 123(1): 187-194.

Falloon, R.E., Viljanen-Rollinson, S.L.H., Coles,G.D. and Poff, J.D. (1995). Disease Severity Keys for Powdery and Downy Mildews of Peas and Powdery scab of Potatoes. *New Zea. J. Crop Hort. Sci.* 23: 31-37.

Fery, R.L. and Dukes, P.D. (1977). An Assessment of Two Genes for Cercospora Leaf Spot Resistance in the Southernpea (Vigna unguiculata (L.) Walp.). *Journal of the American Society for Horticultural Sciences,* 12(5), 454-456.

Fogg, M.L. D.Y, Kobayashi, S.A. Johnston and W.L., Kline. (2000). Bacterial Leaf Spot of Fenugreek: A New Disease in New Jersey caused by *Pseudomonas syringae* pv. *syringae.* Publication No. P-2001-0012-NEA. *In* Northeastern Division Meeting Abstracts, 1-3 Nov. 2000. Cape Cod, North Falmouth, MA.

Frankel, E. (1995). Nutritional Benefits of Flavonoids. *International Conference on Food Factors: Chemistry and Cancer Prevention*, Hamamatsu, *Japan Abstracts*, C 62.

Gogoi, R. Singh, D.V. and Srivastava, K.D. (2001). Phenols as a Biochemical basis of Resistance in Wheat against Kernel Bunt. *Plant Pathology*, 50: 470-476.

Gopal, M. Gupta, A. Palaniswami, C. Dhanapal, R. and Thomas, G.V. (2010). Coconut Leaf Vermin Wash: A Bio-liquid from Coconut Leaf Vermin Compost for Improving the Crop Production Capacities of Soil. *Current Science*. 98(9): 120-121.

Gupta, S.K. Gupta, P.P. Yadava, T.P. and Kaushik C.D. (1990). Metabolic Changes in Mustard due to *Altemaria* Leaf Blight. *Indian Phytopath*. 43: 64-69.

Hart, R.O. (1977). Etiology of Cercospora Cruenta Sacc. On *Vigna unguiculata* (L.) Walp. M.Sc. Dissertation The University of Guyana, Turkeyen, E.C.D. Guyana.

Iqbal, U. Iqbal, S.M. Afzal, R. Jamal, A. Farooq, M.A. and Zahid, A. (2011). Screening of Mungbean Germplasm against Mungbean Yellow Mosaic Virus (MYMV) under Field Conditions. *Pak J Phytopathol.*; 23(1): 48-51.

Kai, H. Ueda, T. and Sakaguchi, M. (1990). Antimicrobial Activity of Bark-compost Extracts. *Soil Biology and Biochemistry*. 22(7): 983-986.

Kaur, C. And Kapoor, H.C. (2002). Anti-oxidant Activity and Total Phenolic Content of some Asian Vegetables. *Int. J. of Food Sci & Tech*. 37(2): 153-161.

Kekuda, P.T.R. Vivek, M.N. Manasa M., Yashoda Kambar, Noor Nawaz A.S, and Raghavendra H.L. (2014). Antifungal Effect Of Cow Urine Extracts of Selected Plants Against *Colletotrichum Capsici* Isolated from Anthracnose of Chilli. *IJACS.*7(3) 142-146.

Khaing, N.S. Khai, A.A. Aye, K.S. and Khaing, O.Z. (2008). Maintenance of Beneficial Microbes in Vermin Wash Carrier System and its Application in Crop. *GMSARN International*, 14(3): 12-16.

Khan, M.B., M.A. Khan and M. Sheikh. (2005). Effect of Phosphorus Levels on Growth and Yield of Fenugreek (*Trigonella foenum graceum* L.) Grown under Different Spatial Arrangements. *Int. J. Agric. Biol*. 7: 504-507.

Khattak, G.S.S. Iqbal, M. and Shaw A.S. (2008). Breeding High yielding and Disease Resistant Mungbean (*Vigna radiata* (l.) wilczek) Genotypes. *Pak. J. Bot.*, 40(4): 1411-1417.

Krishnaveni, V.T. Padmalatha, S.S.V. Padma and A.L.N. Prasad. (2016). Influence of Pinching and Plant Growth Regulators on Flowering, Yield and Economics of Fenugreek (*Trigonella Foenum-Graecum* L.). *Journal of Spices and Aromatic Crops*. 25 (1): 41-48.

Kumar, M. Parsad, M. Arya, R.K. (2013). Grain yield and Quality Improvement in Fenugreek: A Review. Forage Res; 39 (1): 1-9.

Kumar, P. Kale, R. McLean, P.and Baquer N. (2012). Antidiabetic and Neuroprotective Effects of *Trigonella foenum-graecum* Seed Powder in Diabetic Rat Brain. *Prague Med Rep*. 11(1): 39:484.

Kurucheve, V. Echilan, J.G. Jayaraj, J. (1997). Screening of Higher Plants for Fungitoxicity against *Rhizoctonia solani* in vitro. Indian Phytopathol 50(2): 235-241.

Kuvalekara, A. Redkara, A. Gandheb, K. and Harsulkara, A. (2011). Peroxidase and Polyphenol Oxidase Activities in Compatible Host-pathogen Interaction in *Jasminum officinale* and *Uromyce shobsoni*: Insights into Susceptibility of Host. *New Zealand Journal of Botany*, 49(3): 351-359.

Leppik, E.E. (1959). World Distribution of *Cercospora traversiana*. F.A.O. PI. *Prot. Bull.* 8: 19-21.

Lily, V.G. and Ramadasan, A. (1979). Changes in Phenolic Content of Coconut Leafin Relation to the Development of Leaf rot. *Indian Phytopath,* 32: 112-113.

Lokanath, H.M. and Parameshwarappa, K.G. (2006). Effect of Organics on the Productivity of Spanish Bunchgroundnut under Rainfed Farming Situation. *In Proceeding of 18th World Congress of Soil Science.* pp. 62-63 Philadelphia, Pannsylvania, USA.

Lorena, T., Calamassi, R., Mori, B., Mugnai, L. and Surico G. (2001). *Phaeomoniella chlamydospora*_grape vine Interaction: Histochemical Reactions to Fungal Infection. *Phytopathologia Mediterrranea,* 40: 400-406.

Mathivanan, R. Edwin, S. Viswanathan, K. and Chandrasekaran, D. (2006). Chemical Microbial Composition and Antibacterial Activity of modified Panchagavya. *International Journal of Cow Science,* 2(2): 105-109.

Mavarkar, N.S., Basavaraj Naik T., Suresh Naik, K.P., and H.G., *Sharanappa.* (2016). Effect of Organic Source of Nutrients on Groundnut (*Arachis Hypogaea* L.) Under Southern Transitional Zone of Karnataka. *International Journal of Tropical Agriculture.* 34: 567-571.

Mishra R.S., Ramveer and Pandey V.P., (2015). Antifungal Effect of Cow Urine Extracts against *Colletotrichum capsici* Causing Leaf Spot Disease of Turmeric, *African Journal of Biotechnology,* 14(20): XXX.

Mishra, R.S. and Pandey, V.P. (2013). Effect of Bio Agents and Fungicides on the Management of Stem Gall of Coriander. Presented in National Symposium on "Emerging Pollutant and Pathogen due to Climate Change Challenges and Risk Reduction", pp. 82.

Mishra, S.P. Asthana, A.N.& Yadav, L. (1988). Inheritance of Cercospora Leaf Spot Resistance in Mung bean, *Vigna radiata* (L.) Wilczek. *Plant Breeding,* 100: 228-229.

Mohammad, M.A., Nasim, K., Mojtaba Y.A., Masoumeh, A, Abolfazl A.M. and Amir (2016). Fenugreek: Potential Applications as a Functional Food and Nutraceutical. *Nutrition and Food Sciences Research.*3(1): 5-16.

Mohammadi M, Kazemi H (2008) Changes in Peroxidase and Polyphenol Oxidase Activities in Susceptible and Resistant Wheat Heads Inoculated with *Fusarium graminearum* and Induced Resistance. *Plant Science* 162: 491-498.

Mohammed, E.and Nuha. Sati. (2015). Screening Resistant Fenugreek Genotypes against *Cercospora* Leaf Spot Disease. *J Am Sci.;* 11(12): 202-215.

Muhammad, S. and Amusa, N.A. (2003). *In vitro* Inhibition of Growth of some Seedling Blight inducing Pathogens by Compost Inhibiting Microbes. *African Journal of Biotechnology.* 2(6): 161-164.

Mulder, J.L., and Holliday, P. (1975). Cercospora canescens. CMI Descriptions of Pathogenic Fungi and Bacteria No. 462. Kew, Surrey, UK: *The Common Wealth Mycological Institute.*

Müller, K.O. and Börger, H. (1940). Experiment Elleuntersuch Ungenuber Die *Phytophthora* resistenzder Kart Offel. *Arb. Biol. Reichsasn Stalt Landw Forstw Berlin.* 23: 189-231.

Naidu, (2012). Effect of Drying Methods on the Quality Characteristics of Fenugreek (*Trigonella foenum-graecum*) DryTechnol. 30: 808-816.

Naik, N. Sreenivasa, M.N. (2009). Influence of Bacteria Isolated from Panchagavya on Seed Germination and Seed Vigour in Wheat. Karnataka J. Agric. Sci. 22(1): 231-232.

Noble, R.I. (1990).The Discovery of Vinca Alkaloids Chemothera-peutic Agents against Cancer. Biochem. Cell. Biol., 68(12): 1544-1551.

Nwosu, J.N. (2011). The Effect of Processing the Anti-nutritional Properties of Oze (*Bosqueiaangolensis*) Seed. *J. America Science.* 7 (1). 1-7.

Osbourn, A.E. (2003). Saponins in Cereals. *Phytochemistry.* 62: 1-4.

Osbourn, A.E. (1996). Preformed Antimicrobial Compounds and Plant Defence against Fungal Attack. *Plant Cel*, 8: 1821-1831.

Pagar, R.D. M.M. Patel and S.D. Munde. (2015). Influenced of Panchagavya on Growth and Yield of Wheat (*Triticum aestivum* L.). Agriculture for Sustainable Development 3(1): 57-59.

Papadopoulou, K. Melton, R.E. Leggett, M. Daniels, M.J. and Osbourn, A.E. (1999). Compromised Disease Resistance in Saponin-deficient Plants. *P. Natl. Acad. Sci. USA.* 96 22): 12923-12928.

Papen, H. Gables, A. Zumbusch, E. and Rennenberg, H.(2002). Chemolitho Autotrophic Nitrifies in the Phyllosphere of a Spruce Ecosystem Receiving High Nitrogen Input. *Curr. Microbial.* 44: 56-60.

Parihar, P.S. (2012). Changes in Metabolites of *Brassica juncea* (Indian mustard) during Progressive Infection of *Alternaria brassicae. Nature and Science*, 10(3): 39-42.

Paxton, J.D. (1981). Phytoalexins-a Working Redefinition. *Phytopathol Z*, 101: 106-109.

Petropoulos, G.A. (2002). Fenugreek –The Genus *Trigonella*. Taylor and Francis, London and New York. pp. 1-127.

Pinto, S.S., Mann, M.B., Campos, F.S. Franco, A.C. Germani, J.C. and Van Der S.S.T. (2010). Preliminary Characterization of some *Streptomyces* Species Isolated from a Composting Process and their Antimicrobial Potential. *World Journal of Microbiology and Biotechnology.* 26 (10): 1847-1856.

Plotnikova L.Z. (1977). Dung Infusion as a means for Controlling Powderymildew of Rose. *Zashchita Rastenii*, 2: 28.

Poornima and Hegde. Y.R. (2014). Study on Host Range and Susceptible Stage of the Leaf Spot of Palak Caused by *Cercospora Beticola* Sacc. *Internat. J. Plant Protec.*, 7(2): 489-491.

Prakash, S. and Sharma, G.S. (2000). Conidial Germination of *Erysiphe polygoni* causing Powdery Mildew of Fenugreek. *Indian Phytopathol.* 53(3): 318-320.

Price, K.R. Johnson, I.T. and Fenwick, G.R. (1987). *CRC Crit. Rev. Food Sci. Nutr.*, 26: 27-133.

Raja, J. and Kurucheve, V. (1999). Fungicidal Activity of Buffalo (*Babulus bubalis*) Urine: a New Record. *Madras Agricultural Journal* 86(10/12): 614-616.

Raju, J. Gupta, D. Rao, A.R. Yadava, P.K. Baquer, N.Z. (2001). TSP *Foenum graecum* (fenugreek) Seed Powder Improves Glucose Homeostasis in Alloxan Diabetic Rat Tissues by Reversing the Altered Glycolytic, Gluconeogenic and Lipogenic Enzymes. *Mol Cell Biochem.* 224: 45-51.

Rakesh, K.N. Dileep, N. Junaid, S. Kekuda, P.T.R. Vinayaka, K.S. and Nawaz, A.S.N. (2013). Inhibitory Effect of Cow Urine Extracts of Selected Plants against Pathogens Causing Rhizome Rot of Ginger. Science Technology and Arts Research Journal 2(2): 92-96.

Reddy, M.S. and Kramer, C.L. (1975) A Taxonomic Revision of the Protomycetales. *Mycotaxon*, 3: 1-50.

Ribes, G.Y., Sauvaire and C.D. Costa. (1986) *Proc SocExp Biol Med.*, 18: 159.

Rosengarten F. (1969). The Book of Spices. *Livingstone*, Wynnewood, Pennsylvania.

Ryley, M.J. (1989) *Cercospora traversiana* on Fenugreek (*Trigonella foenum-graecum*) in Queensland. *Austra. Plant Pathol.*18(3): 60-63.

Sahoo, M.R. Kole, P.H. Dasgupta, M. Mukherjee, A. (2009). Changes in Phenolics, Polyphenol Oxidase and its Isoenzyme Pattern in Relation to Resistance in Taro against *Phytophthora colocasiae. Journal of Phytopathology* 157: 145-153.

Sangeetha, V. Thevanathan, R. (2010). Effect of TMV Strains in a Local Lesion Host. Journal of Panchagavya on Nitrate Assimilation by Experimental Ecobiol. Plants, *The Journal of American Science,* 6: 80-86.

Sankar, P., Garim, S., Muddasarul Hoda, Varalakshmi Durairaj and Rukkumani Rajagopalan. (2014). GC-MS Analysis, *In Vitro* Antioxidant and Cytotoxic Studies of Wheatgrass Extract. *AJPCT*2(7): 877-893.

Sakar, S.S. Kundu and D. Ghorai. (2014). Validation of Ancient Liquids Organics-Panchagvya and Kunapajala as Plant Growth Promoters. *Indian Journal of Traditional Knowledge* 13(2) 398-403.

Sati, N.M.E. (2015). Screening Resistant Fenugreek Genotypes against *Cercospora* Leaf Spot Disease. *Journal of American Sci.* 11(12): 202-205.

Sauvaire, Y. Ribes G. and Baccou, J.C. (1991) Implication of Steroid Saponins and Sapogenins in the Hypocholesterolemic Effect of Fenugreek. Lipids; 26: 191-197.

Sauvaire, Y.G. Ribes, J. C. Baccou and M.M. Loubatieres-Mariani, (1991). *Lipids*; 4: 54-56.

Scarpari, L.M. Meinhardt, L.W. Mazzafera, Pomella P.A. Schiavinato, A.M, Cascardo, J.C.M. and Pereira G.A.G. (2005). Biochemical changes during the Development of Witches' Broom: the most Important Disease of Cocoa in Brazil caused by *Crinipellis perniciosa. Journal of Experimental Botany,* 56(413): 865-877.

Schlösser, E. Schönbeck, F. and (1976). Preformed Substances as Potential Protectants. In: Heitefuss R., Williams P.H., Editors. *Physiological Plant Pathology.* Berlin, Germany: *Springer Verlag* K.G, 653-678.

Seasotiya, L. Siwach, P. Bai, S. Malik, A. Bharti P (2014). Free Radical Scavenging Activity and Phytochemical Analysis of Seeds of *Trigonella foenum-graecum. AsianPac. J. Health Sci.* 1(3): 219-226.

Shah, M.H. Khan, S.N. Tahira, J.J. Nasrullah, RSWAS and Moazzam, Z. (2010). Impact of Pathogenic Fungi and Bacteria on Fenugreek (*Trigonellafoenum-graecum*L) Plant Stand Quality under Natural Condition. *Pak.J. Phytopathol.* 22(2): 130-134.

Shailaja, B. Ipsita Mishra, Srihima Gampala, Vikram Jeet Singh and Swathi. K. (2014). Panchagavya- An Ecofriendly Insecticide and Organic Growth Promoter of Plants. *International Journal of Advanced Research* 2(11): 22-26.

Shailaja, B. Mishra, Ipsita. Gampala Srihima, Singh Vikram Jeet and Swathi K (2014). Panchagavya- an Eco-friendly Insecticide and Organic Growth Promoter of Plants. *International Journal of Advanced Research,* 2:(11) 22-26.

Sharma, R.D. Raghuram, T.C. and Rao, N.S. (1990). Effect of Fenugreek Seeds on Blood Glucose and Serum Lipids in Type I diabetes. *Eur J. Clin Nutr,*44: 301-306.

Singh, G and Bedi D.S., (1976) Phenolic and Sugar Constituents of Gram Cultivars Resistant and Susceptible to *Operculella padwickii.Indian Phytopath.,* 29: 191-192.

Singla, S. and Satwinder Kaur. (2016). Biological Activities of Cow Urine: An Ayurvedic Elixir. *Ejpmr.* 3(4): 118-124.

Sinha, R.K. Valani, D. Chauhan, K. and Agarwal, S. (2010). Embarking on a Second Green Revolution for Sustainable Agriculture by vermin Culture Biotechnology using Earthworms: Reviving the dreams of Sir Charles Darwin. *Journal of Agricultural Biotechnology and Sustainable Development,* 2: 113-128.

Somasundaram E., Mohamed M., Manullah A., Thirukkumaran K., Chandrasekaran R., Vaiyapuri K. and Sathyamoorthi K. (2007). Biochemical Changes, Nitrogen Flux and Yield of Crops due to Organic Sources of Nutrients under Maize Based Cropping System. *J. Appl. Sci. Res.* 3(12): 1724-1729.

Somasundaram, E. and Amanullah, M.M. (2007). Panchagavya on Growth and Productivity of Crops: *A review. Green Farming,* 1: 22-26.

Sparg, S.G. Light, M.E. and Student, J. (2004). Biological Activities and Distribution of Plant Saponins. *J. Ethno pharmacol,* 94: 219-243.

Srimathi, P. Mariappan, N. Sundara Moorthy, L. and Paramathma M. (2013). Efficacy of Panchagavya on Seed Invigoration of Biofuel Crops. Academic *Journals.* 8 (41): 2031-2037.

Srimathi, P.N. Mariappan, L. Sundaramoorthy and M. Paramathma. (2013). Efficacy of Panchagavya on Seed Invigoration of Biofuel Crops. Scientific Research and Essays. Vol. 8(41), pp. 2031-2037.

Sugha, S.K. (2005). Antifungal Potential of Panchagavya. *Plant Disease Research* 20: 156-158.

Swaminathan, C. Swaminathan, V. and Vijay, Lakshmi K. (2007). Panchagavya Boon to Organic Farming. *International Book Distributing Co. Lucknow,* p. 332.

Tambe V.D, Bhambar R.S (2014) "Estimation of Total Phenol, Tannin, Alkaloid and Flavonoid in *Hibiscus Tiliaceus* Linn. Wood Extracts" *RRJPP,* 2(4): 41-47.

Tharmaraj, K. Ganesh, P. Suresh, Kumar. R. Anandan, A. and Kolanjinathan K. (2011). "A Critical Review on Panchagavya Boon Plant Growth," *International Journal of Pharmaceutical and Biological Archive,* 2(6): 1611-1614.

Tiwari, R.K.S. Das, K. (2013). Inhibitory Effect of Cow Urine based Plant Extracts against *Rhizoctonia solani* causing Sheath Blight of Rice. *Indian Phytopathology* 64(3): 265-268.

Umaharan, P. Helen, M. Booker (2007). Identification of Resistance to *Cercospora* Leaf Spot of Cowpea. *Eur J Plant Pathol.* 118: 401-410.

Vakili, N.G. (1977). Field Screening of Cowpeas for Cercospora Leaf Spot Resistance. *Tropical Agriculture* (Trinidad), 54(1), 70-76.

W.H.O. (2008). Monographs on selected Medicinal Plants. Vol 3. Geneva, Switzerland: *World Health Organization.*

Williams, R.J. (1975). Diseases of Cowpea (*Vigna unguiculata* L.Walp.) in Nigeria. *PANS.* 21: 253-267.

Xu, H.L. (2001). Effects of a Microbial Inoculant and Organic Fertilizers on the Growth, Photosynthesis and yield of Sweet Corn. *J. Crop Prod.* 3: 183-214.

Yadav, B. K. and Chistopher Lourduraj, C.A. (2006). Effect of Organic Manures and *Panchagavya* Spray on yield Attributes, yield and Economics of Rice (*Oryza sativa* L.) Quality. *Crop Res.,* 32(1): 1-5.

Yang, R. Potter, T.P. Curtis, O.F. Shetty, K. (1997). Tissue Cultured based Selection of High Rosmarinic acid Producing Clones of Rosemary (*Rosmarinus officinalis*) using *Pseudomonas* strain. Food Biotechnology. 11: 73-88.

Yazdani, D. Tan, Y.H. Abidin, Z.M.A. Jaganath, I.B. (2011). A Review on Bioactive Compounds isolated from Plants against Plant Pathogenic Fungi. Journal of Medicinal Plants Research 5(30): 6584-6589.

Zhang, M.J. Liu, P.R. Zhao, J. Z. (1993). Study on the Comprehensive Utilization of *Sapindus mukorssi. Natural Product Research and Development,* 5: 76-78.

Zimmer, R.C. (1984). Cercospora Leaf Spot and Powdery Mildew of Fenugreek, a Potential New crop in Canada. *Canadian Plant Disease Survey.* 64(2): 33-35.

Index

CPSIA information can be obtained
at www.ICGtesting.com
Printed in the USA
BVHW021956060623
665501BV00004B/128